The Great Kentucky Tragedy

&

My Old Kentucky Plays, II

RICHARD CAVENDISH

authorHOUSE®

AuthorHouse™
1663 Liberty Drive
Bloomington, IN 47403
www.authorhouse.com
Phone: 833-262-8899

Published by AuthorHouse 08/29/2024

ISBN: 979-8-8230-2176-0 (sc)
ISBN: 979-8-8230-2175-3 (e)

Library of Congress Control Number: 2024902909

Print information available on the last page.

Frontispiece: Solomon Porcious Sharp (1780-1825) painted by Matthew Harris Jouett c. 1820. Permission granted by private Kentucky collector.

Back cover: Madison Conyers Johnson (1806-1886) painted by Matthew Harris Jouett. Andrew A. Tribble (1879-1935) photograph.

This book is printed on acid-free paper.

Contents

List of Illustrations

Dedication

To my parents.

Russell Richard Rechenbach, Sr. and Myrtle Vest. Loving and encouraging to me every day of my life. I was extremely blessed. Dad worked almost fifty years as head of the Dry House at what would become known as Buffalo Trace Distillery. My mom toured us around the historic sites of Kentucky every summer throughout our childhood.

The Rev. Dr. John Claude Cavendish, who was sent from Heaven into my life in the spring of 1979. For forty-two years he walked beside me. My teacher, my mentor, my best friend. My greatest cheerleader. Where there is great grief, there was great love.

Preface

I was born a II. Richard Cavendish is my pen name. If Russell Richard Rechenbach was not enough to spell in the First Grade, there was a II added to the end; when everyone else had put down their big red pencils, I was still working at it. And confusing to me that I was not a "Jr." But to have a "II" at the end of my name meant that I was the second in the family using it: my Dad was Russell Richard Rechenbach. I was the II, although the Rechenbachs in Bright, Indiana cursed him with "Big Russ" and me "Little Russ," to distinguish us from each other. His marriage to my mother was a second marriage; I was his second family, his second son. There is no little about II. It indicates that more has been and more is to come. This is my second book of Kentucky historical plays. My Old Kentucky Plays.

A second is the base unit of time, sixty of them make a minute. Second may mean that you are runner up to the first, as in second place. "Give me a second," refers less to time than to an immeasurable moment. In baseball, it means you are stationed near second base. It may be a transfer to a different assignment. To give one's support to a motion in Roberts Rules of Order. The attendant to a contestant in a duel. Imperfect clothing item. Another helping of food. It is two for tea. As this is my second book of plays, this is also a collection of plays about seconds.

The Great Kentucky Tragedy A play of two rivals. It follows second behind numerous versions of the Sharp/Beauchamp love tragedy than one can remember. I have fashioned mine from the attempted version of Edgar Allen Poe. A friend of Emma Watts, my heroine in *Emma of Elmwood,* even left his attempt at the story in her library. Jereboam Beauchamp was a second to his father trying to live up to his father's reputation and a second lover to Anne Cooke. A play first and world known as The Kentucky Tragedy.

Botherum A play of two men, one white and privileged, the other black and enslaved. They are two worlds apart at first. They are two gentlemen from the old school. This is the story of the first men who inhabited the home my father and I bought so many years ago. A play about Madison Conyers Johnson and historic Botherum hall.

Beating the Dark Home A play of two brothers. Amos and Andy. And two noble professions, the farm and the stage. Both brothers attempting to build lives for themselves that were as honorable as their father's life. A father who went before the judge to right the wrong another child had played on his son, a father who later ended up being murdered for a matter of justice that newspapers did not find important enough to explain. Andy Tribble finds himself in a vaudeville lineup of acts like everyone else. He wants to make a mark on the world and ends up making the world laugh and heal itself during a time of political turmoil. A play about the first comic African American female impersonator of the Broadway stage.

Day of Releasement A play of two star crossed lovers, separated by time and race. Two centuries connected by the magic of music. A play about Shaker Village of Pleasant Hill. Mother Ann Lee understood God in a duality, as male and female.

Pioneer Christmas in Kentucky A play about two county seats. One built upon the old order of its previous state and government, and the other branching out into a new state and identity. Kentucky was carved out of Virginia. When Black Bob Morgan's Gang came riding into Milford that winter of 1786, every second counted. And the people of the new town were ready in a minute to defend their territory. A play about Milford, the first county seat of Madison County.

Moon Above Benson Valley A play about two taverns. One in the Crawfish Bottom near the Kentucky River, and the other looking down on it from atop Bald Knob. It is the true story of my grandmother and grandfather, and the secret that haunted our family until their deaths. John Fallis was "King of Craw." A handsome bootlegger during Prohibition, as violent as he could be charming, but the Robin Hood hero of the poor and African Americans in the impoverished Crawfish Bottom of Frankfort. Charlie, a regular at the bars in the bottom and atop the Knob, he is found dead and his wife too eagerly takes the blame for the murder. A play about John Fallis and Bald Knob.

There is a "II" in world religions and in philosophy. There are two creation stories in the Bible, the first in Genesis finishes with two human beings making the garden of God's creation complete; the second, their fall from Paradise. There are two genealogies of Jesus of Nazareth. In Taoism, there is the Jin and the Jang, the balance of opposite forces. Dark-light, negative-positive. In music, two notes will create harmony.

Carl Jung saw a duality in the human person. He identified the "Shadow side" as a living part of the personality that cannot be repressed out of existence. The aspects of its traits need to be embraced, understood, accepted, and brought into the light and allowed to express themselves in positive, healthy ways.

We were probably all meant to be "too" of something. Danielle Laporte is credited for writing, "You will always be too much of something for someone: too big, too loud, too soft, too edgy. If you round out your edges, you lose your edge. Apologize for mistakes. Apologize for unintentionally hurting someone — profusely. But don't apologize for being who you are." Maybe you are too tall, too fat, too slow, too fast. Too old, too young. Too poor, too rich. Be proud of being "too." That is your mission. That is your ministry on this earth at this time given to you.

"People don't read plays." I never expected the prejudice shown me because my first collection was a book about plays. Doors closed in my face. Every time I have a book signing and reading, the first question I ask is, "How many of you have read a play lately?" No one raises their hands. Oh, novels, yes, and newspapers, but never plays. I'm on a crusade to get people to read plays again . . . too.

After the death of my Father John Cavendish in 2021, I took his name to mine. Russell Richard Reichenbach Cavendish. My second legal name on this earth. He was my mentor, my best friend, my teacher—everything in the world to me. And in the last years of his life, he became my whole world. When he left, my world was gone, and worse, it was as if the presence of God in my life went with him. I experienced a grief that no one warned me about in seminary, although I had heard of people grieving themselves to death. This was my ration. In almost forty years of active ministry in the Church, I had come across maybe four examples of this killing grief, and to all of them I had no means of understanding. It came from a foreign planet that I had never traveled. I was not empathetic, because I could not be. Now I have met a few broken souls who understand this grief of mine because they have been crushed by it. The challenge, of course, is to see it not as a curse but to embrace it as a blessing. Somehow. Someday. But now, it is a matter of learning to live again each morning. "I'll Begin Again," by Leslie Bricusse has been my daily mantra for two years. And so, I seek to begin a new life. My second life.

Richard Cavendish

The Great Kentucky Tragedy

Adapted from Edgar Allan Poe's
"Scenes from Politian an Unfinished Drama"
With completed scenes by Richard Cavendish

Introduction

There is a radical error, I think, in the usual mode of constructing a story. Either history affords a thesis, or one is suggested by an incident of the day; or, at best, the author sets himself to work in the combination of striking events to form merely the basis of his narrative, designing, generally, to fill in with description, dialogue, or authorial comment, whatever crevices of fact, or action, may, from page to page, render themselves apparent.

I prefer commencing with the consideration of an *effect*. Keeping originality *always* in view — for he is false to himself who ventures to dispense with so obvious and so easily attainable a source of interest. I say to myself, in the first place, "Of the innumerable effects, or impressions, of which the heart, the intellect, or (more generally) the soul is susceptible, what one shall I, on the present occasion, select?" Having chosen a novel, first, and secondly a vivid effect, I consider whether it can best be wrought by incident or tone, whether by ordinary incidents and peculiar tone, or the converse, or by peculiarity both of incident and tone, afterward looking about me (or rather within) for such combinations of event, or tone, as shall best aid me in the construction of the effect.[1]

Mr. Charles Fenno Hoffman's work *Greyslaer* is a romance based on the well-known murder of Solomon Sharp, the Solicitor-General of Kentucky, by Jereboam Beauchamp. W. Gilmore Simms has far more power, more passion, more movement, more skill than Mr. Hoffman and has treated the same subject more effectively in his novel *Beauchamp*. *Beauchamp* was issued anonymously, the author wishing to ascertain whether the success of his books (which was great) had anything to do with his mere name as the writer of previous works. The result proved that popularity, in Mr. Simms' case, arose solely from intrinsic merit, for *Beauchamp* was among the most popular of his fictions, and excited very general attention and curiosity.[2]

But the fact is that both gentlemen have positively failed, as might have been expected. That both books are interesting is no merit either of Mr.

---

[1] Edgar Allan Poe, *Edgar Allan Poe Essays and Reviews*, "The Philosophy of Composition (April 1846)," Literary Classics of the United States, Inc., New York, N.Y. copyright, The Library of America, 1984, pp. 13-14. Edited by R. Cavendish.
[2] Ibid, "William Gilmore Simms," from *Godey's Lady's Book*, January 1846, p.903, edited by R. Cavendish.

Hoffman or of Mr. Simms. The real events were more impressive than are the fictitious ones. The facts of this remarkable tragedy, as arranged by actual circumstance, would put to shame the skill of the most consummate artists. Nothing was left to the novelist but the amplification of *character*, and at this point neither the author of *Greyslaer* nor of *Beauchamp* is especially well informed, *au fait*. The incidents might be better woven into a tragedy.[3]

Edgar Allan Poe

---

[3] Ibid, "The Literati of New York City," pp. 1208-1209, edited by R. Cavendish.

The Great Kentucky Tragedy

CHARACTERS

Edgar Allan POE	Writer of *Scenes from an Unpublished Drama*
ANNA Cooke	Owner of the farm Retirement in Glasgow
ELIZA Scott	Wife of Solomon Sharp
HYACINTH	Servant girl to Anna Cooke
SOLOMON Sharp	Colonel from War of 1812, attorney in law
LEANDER Sharp	Brother to Solomon, medical doctor
Jereboam BEAUCHAMP	Young attorney, later husband to Anna
Captain John F. LOWE	Law officer
PREACHER	Anna's minister
HUGO	Servant to Leander Sharp
BEN	Servant to Solomon Sharp
RUPERT	House servant to Solomon Sharp
John MCINTOSH	The jailer
THOMAS Beauchamp	Father of Jereboam

This play has thirteen scenes, and apart from Poe, thirteen characters.
The trial of Jereboam Beauchamp took thirteen days.

Act One
Scene One

A cold autumn night. Early morning hours of November 7, 1825. Madison Street in downtown Frankfort, the home of Colonel Solomon Sharp. Only the heavens light the streets. All is quiet. Dressed in a dark cape and hat with a black mask on his face, scarf over his forehead, Jereboam BEAUCHAMP, a man in his early twenties, walks down the street. BEAUCHAMP walks up to the front door of the Sharp House. He knocks three times. From inside the house, we hear the voice of SOLOMON Sharp:

SOLOMON

Who's there?

BEAUCHAMP

"Covington." I've come to town late—all the taverns are full. I was looking for a place to stay for the night. Can you help me?

ELIZA
[As we hear the sound of SOLOMON fumbling with the lock, his wife's voice is heard over the metallic clatter:]
Don't open it.

[BEAUCHAMP removes his mask. The lock is released. SOLOMON opens the door, a man in his late thirties, he is dressed in night clothes and dressing gown.]

SOLOMON

What Covington is this?

BEAUCHAMP

I am John A. Covington; don't you know me?

SOLOMON

I don't think I do.
[ELIZA, his wife, approaches in nightgown and with a candle]

BEAUCHAMP

Then, damn you, you soon shall know me!
[BEAUCHAMP pulls off his hat and scarf.]

7

SOLOMON

Great God! It's him!

BEAUCHAMP

Die, you villain!

>*[He plunges the dagger into SOLOMON's heart. ELIZA*
>*screams. BEAUCHAMP runs away down the street past*
>*Edgar Allan POE who appears from the mist.]*

POE

Murder on a moonless night. No sound but the dry autumn leaves dragging
across the brick pavement in the wind. The house of Solomon Sharp,
Madison Street, downtown Frankfort. The night before the Legislature
convened November 7, 1825. Just days after All Hallow's Eve and All
Souls, the nights of the dead. It would be forever remembered as The
Kentucky Tragedy.

>*[POE looks to the Left.]*

The only witness silent just there across the street: the ashes of the state Capital
building. On a cold November night just a year before, that splendid edifice
stood to compare great things to small. But like a vast lighted lamp, its cupola
caught fire and shot a blazing flame high into the air. What once stood in
Romanesque grandeur quickly fell to this graveyard of gloom and glory.

>*Lone amphitheater! Grey Coliseum!*
>*Type of the antique Rome! Rich reliquary*
>*Of lofty contemplation left to Time*
>*By buried centuries of pomp and power!*
>*I feel ye now- I feel ye in your strength-*
>*O charms more potent than the rapt Chaldee*
>*Ever drew down from out the quiet stars!*

Now, re-erect its columns and portico . . . five years earlier, when the State
House stood tall and new. The Sharp House overlooking its grandeur, left
to his sons by father Thomas Sharp, Captain from the Revolutionary War.
Solomon Sharp, the elder son, had enlisted in the Kentucky militia during
the War of 1812, and had been promoted in only twelve days to major, later
elected to the House of Representatives. But there is a phantom shadow in
the background of Solomon Sharp, one that is slowly rising from its grave.

>*[POE disappears as BEN and an intoxicated JUGO, the*
>*gardener and lackey arrive, both African enslaved persons.*
>*Cards, bottles, a lady's slipper, and the mask used by*

8

BEAUCHAMP in the previous scene are strewn around the street displaying traces of a protracted revel in celebration of Solomon Sharp's first-born child. Outside the Sharp House, Frankfort, Kentucky. Early morning June 1820]

HUGO

Oh! Is that you, Ben? Are they gone?

BEN

Now, that there is the question, Hugo, and hard to answer: are the bottles empty?
[Picking up a bottle.]

Then they're gone. As for the brother Leander who almost knocked me down the stairs, I am quite sure of him. He's gone, I'm sure of that — pretty *far* gone!

HUGO

Is my villain gone?
[He picks up a slipper]
Did you say his Excellency had departed? Are all the fiddlers off? To hell with 'em! I'm positively stupid for want of sleep!

BEN

Oh, you are right, quite right, being as you say, Hugo, most positively a stupid man.

HUGO

Sir! I said no such thing. I lied.

BEN

I don't have no doubt, good Hugo, that you lied, being, as you observe, a most notorious liar —
[HUGO sits, and helps himself to a drink of liquor. Enter RUPERT, a house butler, very proper.]
Well, Rupert, what have you done with Colonel Sharp?

RUPERT

Colonel Solomon Sharp, the proud father? What *should* I do with such a respectable one as he? I pulled him from under the table where he lay and tumbled him into bed.

9

BEN

Good job, Rupert! You think the old Captain would approve of these wild parties of his son? What a shame for such a proper young man. And of so gentle blood?

RUPERT

The birth of one's first child is cause to celebrate.

BEN

He looks for any cause to celebrate. He's changed. Sadly, changed like I thought I'd never see.

RUPERT

His brother Leander has sure changed. He's never been an uncle before.

HUGO

He was drunk, Ben! You said it so yourself, Rupert. Most men are *changed* when they're drunk. Oh, I am sadly changed when I'm drunk--you should see me sometime!

BEN

That baby has brought something to mind that bothers him.

RUPERT
[To BEN, picking up a card]
You think Colonel Sharp altered? It may well be. Before his father died, he was a very noble man in heart . . . barring a few trivial improprieties.

BEN
[Picking up a card]
I don't trust him anymore. Not after the way he treat poor Miss Anna Cooke!

RUPERT

Truly, Benjamin, his conduct there has haunted him. I think he led her on to imagine he would marry her and raise a family with her.
[HUGO picks up a card, but it is paper money! Quickly, he sneaks it into his pocket.]
It all seemed to start after his father died. And it led to that most base seduction of Miss Anna Cooke out there in the western part of the state. I've noticed we can date his ruin—that's what I call it, a "ruin"--his low

10

debaucheries, his gambling habits, and all his numerous vices, we can date it to that time last year when he moved here to get away from her.

BEN

Oh, villain! The sin sits heavy on his soul and causes him to do these things. It's a good thing the old Captain aint living, for it would break his heart. His son is just pain cruel when he speaks of Miss Cooke; his words would humble her to the dust.

RUPERT

They tell me that she sits alone at her farm there with clasped hands.

BEN

Poor Miss Cooke. She sobs upon her knees and murmurs the name of Colonel Sharp. She still loves him.

RUPERT

He chose instead to marry Miss Eliza Scott, daughter of a physician and high in the ranks of society and move here to the capital to further his political career.

BEN

It is just too bad.

HUGO

Bad?! No, it aint! This whiskey's *good*! Fellas, why do you blame Colonel Sharp in this matter? Who the hell is this Anna Cooke? God only knows! I don't raise my eyebrows at nobody who play'd the guitar like he does, and serves most excellent bourbon! Pride should have such a fall. Colonel Sharp's a womanizer or he was, that is very sure, but he's reforming: he don't drink no *cheap* bourbon no more. He drinks the very *best* of bourbon.

RUPERT
[To BEN of HUGO]
Let's go to bed! The man is steeped in liquor.
        [BEN throws his arm around RUPERT]
To your own bed!
        [RUPERT exits comically fighting BEN off]

HUGO
[Arousing.]

11

What did they say? To bed! Is it so late? Is it all gone?
[Seeing HYACINTH approach. Seductively:]
Very well! I'll go to bed shortly.
[Enter HYACINTH decked out in jewelry around her neck, on her shawl, and at her wrists.]
Ah! Bless my eyes. Hyacinth! Come to town again. Is that you?!

HYACINTH
Why, yes, it is and no it aint, Mr. Hugo, there's a riddle! She was Hyacinth last night, but now she is *Madam* Hyacinth, if you please, Mr. Hugo!

HUGO
Sweetheart, I'm afraid you've been hittin' the bottle. Pretty "*Madam Hyacinth*!"

HYACINTH
You may say that Mr. Hugo. *Very pretty*! Colonel Sharp says Hyacinth is pretty.
[She extends her hand showing a ring.]
Drunken fool, look at this!

HUGO
Where?

HYACINTH
Here! Look here!

HUGO
Hyacinth! Why, Hyacinth! You don't mean to tell me that my master Colonel Sharp done give that there ring to you?!

HYACINTH
What if he did Mr. Hugo? What if he did?

HUGO
Look here! I'll swear I saw that there ring upon the finger--the middle-- the fore--no on the little pinkie of Colonel Sharp. I'm done with you, Hyacinth! Oh, you, vile bitch! I'll not marry you, Hyacinth! Oh, I'm in despair! I'll do some desperate deed! I'm desperate!

12

HYACINTH

You're drunk!

HUGO

I'm gunna cut . . . gunna cut . . . .

HYACINTH

--"Your throat!" O Heaven!

HUGO

. . . Cut you out of my life altogether! I'm gonna, Hyacinth!
[He starts to go]

HYACINTH

*[Pulling him back, she would have him see that she is now
a rich woman]*
Stop! You sniveling fool! Will you not see the jewels? Look you here! This
broach, these pearls, these rubies? Don't you see?

HUGO

[Sulkily]
I see.

HYACINTH

These emeralds and this topaz! *Won't* you see?
*[HYACINTH stops at the threshold of the Sharp House.
She sees POE, but the others cannot see him. POE and
HYACINTH look at each other for a moment. She picks up
the mask and senses something evil.]*

HUGO

I see.
*[POE is gone and so in the premonition. HYACINTH awakes
from what she saw.]*
I see!

HYACINTH

You see! You see!
[She throws the mask at him.]
Can I get nothing more out of your ugly mouth but "I see, I see"? I'm not
sure you see or if you *see*. You certainly see double.

13

[She shows him a cross]

Here's a cross, a cross of rubies, you dumb ass! A cross of rubies! Don't you hear: a cross which never cost a penny less than five hundred dollars!

HUGO

I see. Oh, I see it all.

HYACINTH

"You see it all!" You don't see it *at all*. Heaven, give me patience! You don't see it at all!

[Mocking him]

You don't see that Hyacinth's the richest lady's maid in Kentucky. The richest farmer's daughter owning these jewels! You don't see. Her mistress Anna Cooke gave them to her, don't you hear? Miss Anna Cooke done give them to her as a gift: for a wedding present. She gave Hyacinth her jewels. Every one of them. She is certainly gone mad.

HUGO

Anna Cooke *gave* you them jewels!? How'd you come by that there <u>ring</u>?

HYACINTH

Colonel Solomon Sharp, your sweet master, he done give it to Miss Anna Cook my sweet mistress, as a token of his love. And then she gave it to Hyacinth. Don't you see?

HUGO

[With a sneer]

Hyacinth!

HYACINTH

[Returning the sneer.]

Hugo!

HUGO

What dear, Hyacinth?

HYACINTH

Don't you see?

[As a last resort she opens her shawl revealing necklaces of jewels on a very immodest bosom.]

14

HUGO

Oh, nonsense, sweet Hyacinth, let me look again at them jewels!

HYACINTH

Don't you see?

HUGO

Damn! Let me look!

HYACINTH

Don't you see?
>[She holds up the jewels. HUGO moves in to admire, not her necklaces but her bosom!]

HUGO

Sweet, dear, Hyacinth! Madame Hyacinth--

HYACINTH.

Oh, I see!
>[She whacks him with her shawl, turns and leaves, followed by HUGO staggering.]

Act One
Scene Two

Inside the Sharp House on Madison Street, later that morning. SOLOMON and LEANDER Sharp, brothers in their thirties, shirtless, wearing their trousers, getting dressed in their dressing-room. There is a table set with two wash bowls, combs, and a mirror; RUPERT carries towels and BEN carries a pitcher. BEN pours the water into the bowls.

LEANDER
>[Splashing his own face from the bowl:]

That's a funny joke, Solomon! That's great!
>[He laughs]

— the best I've heard! You kill me, brother! I shall die! Oh, I shall die of laughing!
>[He splashes his brother to make him laugh but is unsuccessful.]

15

SOLOMON

[Warding off the splashing; sullenly, washing under his arms, etc.]

Stop it! Leander, I didn't mean it as a joke.

LEANDER

Oh, no! oh no! You don't mean it as a joke. Not you!

[Laughing]

I'll die, I'll die! It's a very serious business. You must be drunk! A very serious business.

[RUPERT gives him a towel and he dries himself, his face and then his underarms.]

So, you've turned penitent at last. Bravo! I tell you what: I've got a rosary at home-- I'll send it to you. Every bible and cross I can find. You shall have them all. A robe of sackcloth, too, that I used at a masquerade, you shall have it. You shall have it! And I'll go home and send you a tub of excellent ashes!

[Playfully, he wraps the towel over his brother's head like a monk and combs his own hair. BEN holds the mirror.]

SOLOMON

Oh, brother! I'm done for——

[He retrieves the towel and uses it. RUPERT helps LEANDER into his shirt]

LEANDER

Oh! I am, too. I am done for. Completely done for. I'll die: I shall die of laughing. Yes! I'm done for!

SOLOMON

[Sternly]

Leander!

LEANDER

[Buttoning his shirt.]

Yes, brother Solomon?

SOLOMON

I'm serious.

[BEN holds the mirror while SOLOMON combs his hair.]

LEANDER.

I know it. Very!

SOLOMON

Then why do you make fun of me? I've got a headache; and besides, I'm not well in body or soul. When did you last see Anna?

[RUPERT helps him into his shirt.]

LEANDER.

Anna? Anna Cooke? Not for months. What could have put that Fury in your head?

SOLOMON

Leander!

LEANDER

Yes, my brother?

SOLOMON

[After a pause. He buttons his shirt.]

When did you say you spoke to Anna?

LEANDER

I didn't. Brother, dear, I haven't seen her for months. Our father would not want me to go near her. And he would be right in it. Neither of us for that matter.

[Laughing]

You understand?

[He is fastening his tie, BEN holding the mirror.]

SOLOMON

No, Leander, I don't understand.

LEANDER.

Well! Well! Never mind.

[Sings:]

> *Birds of so fine a feather*
> *And of so wanton eye*
> *Should be caged — should be caged*
> *Should be caged in all weather*
> *Lest they fly!*

17

[RUPERT helps him into his waistcoat.]
No, I have not seen nor spoken to that toothless, stooped-shouldered woman.

SOLOMON

Leander! You do her wrong—unmanly wrong. She has a pure heart. If ever there was a fallen woman with an excuse for falling, it's Anna Cooke! If ever there were plighted vows sacredly sworn and deceitfully broken that would damn a man, I am that damned villain!
[He begins fastening his tie, BEN holding the mirror now for him.]
Young, ardent, beautiful, and loving well and pure as beautiful, how could she think — how could she dream, being herself all truth, of my black disloyalty? I wish I weren't Solomon Sharp but some farmer behind his plow tending to his field to make me honest.

[RUPERT helps LEANDER into his coat. BEN mistakenly holds the mirror for RUPERT who gruffly shoos him away to bring the brush. RUPERT brushes the coat.]

LEANDER

Exceeding fine! I never heard a better speech in my life. I think you must marry every lonely creature you meet. All of them, honestly! Heaven forbid any should be without a husband! Honesty, poverty, and true content, with the unutterable ecstasies of butternuts, gingerbread, and milk and water!

[BEN holds the mirror as LEANDER admires himself. RUPERT helps SOLOMON into his waistcoat. BEN holds the mirror to RUPERT who fumbling wards him off.]

SOLOMON
[Trying to suppress a smile.]
Leander, you're a fool!

LEANDER.

You're right again, big brother. Now, I'm going home, before I become tainted with your wisdomship. And before you pass the scullery maid and propose marriage to her. Good day! I crave your patronage when you become a cardinal! In the meantime, I'll take the opportunity of sending the sackcloth and the ashes.

[He grabs the towel and snaps it at SOLOMON who quickly arms himself and retaliates. The two frolic with the towels before LEANDER exits in great fun and laughter, having lifted the spirits of his younger brother. RUPERT helps SOLOMON into his coat. BEN hands him a brush.]

SOLOMON.

Be gone, you crazy devil!
[He laughs]
He makes me laugh in spite of myself, Rupert. For the life of me. After all, I don't see why I should so grieve about this little matter. This everyday occurrence. Should I have married her? No! Solomon Sharp marry a wanton woman! Never!

RUPERT

Never, sir.
[He brushes the coat.]

SOLOMON

Oh, never! What would they say at the club? What would Leander, think? What would my father think? Ha! What would my wife think! I have no right had I the will, to bring such foul disgrace upon my family. My father's family line. My father's haughty and time-honored line!

RUPERT

No, sir.

SOLOMON

No right at all to do it. It's water over the dam. After all, I am now married to my cousin Elizabeth and God has blessed us with a little daughter. A daughter. Honor is important! I cannot pawn my honor. My honor. And poor Anna . . .
[He remembers something and his countenance changes back into gloom. He sighs. More to himself.]
I can't get her out of my mind. Here I am with every blessing, and she . . . . It doesn't seem fair. If only I could save her.

RUPERT

Yes, sir. I mean, no, sir.

19

SOLOMON

It is but the hangover, the consequence of last night's drunkenness that gives me these qualms of conscience. Be a man! A man, Solomon Sharp, be a man! Is there nothing better than a glass of bourbon to set everything right? Call Hugo.

RUPERT

No, sir. I mean, yes, sir!
[Taking BEN to one side]
Ben, did you hear? Call for Hugo.

BEN

Hugo! Bourbon!
[HUGO is already on his way loaded down with a bundle and a basket full of bottles.]
That was fast.
[Of the bundle]
What the devil's that?

HUGO

[Hesitantly]
It's for the master!

BEN

[Of the basket]
What's that? He asked for bourbon!

HUGO.

Bourbon. Here it is. A dozen of the best bottles. From his reverence the good doctor.

BEN

[To RUPERT]
A dozen bottles of the best bourbon from his brother, the doctor.

RUPERT

A dozen fools!

SOLOMON

Rupert?

RUPERT

Yes, sir. It seems we have a delivery of the best Kentucky bourbon sent as a present by your brother, Dr. Sharp.

BEN

From "his reverence."

RUPERT

From *"his reverence."*

SOLOMON.
[Smiling]

Really? I'm much obliged to his *reverence* — Did you not say his "reverence?" Uncork a bottle, Rupert, and let me see what it is made of.

RUPERT

Uncork a bottle, Ben.

HUGO
[To BEN]

No, he can't have any.

BEN

How, Sir! Not have it? What do you mean by that?

HUGO

Not a drop.

BEN

And why?

HUGO

Why? Why, you see, I've been told to tell him that he's not to have the bourbon, only his choice.

BEN
[To RUPERT]

He's not to have the bourbon, only his choice.

RUPERT

What do you mean, "his choice?"

21

HUGO
[To BEN]
There's another present down in the hall, Sir. He's to have his choice of the
bourbon or of that.

RUPERT
[Pushing BEN aside.]
Blockhead! Why don't you bring the other present in?

HUGO
Eh? Sir?

RUPERT
Dolt! Dunderhead! Why don't you bring me up the other present and let
him see it?

HUGO
I can't.

RUPERT
You can't! You villain? Ben!

BEN
[BEN turns him and attempts to push him off.]
Scoundrel, bring it up!

RUPERT
Hugo, stay! What's that you have on your shoulder?

HUGO
Sir? It's the sackcloth, and that down below . . .
[He whispers in BEN's ear. BEN whispers in RUPERT's ear.]

SOLOMON
Rupert?

RUPERT
It appears that your brother wants you to make a choice. Between the
bourbon here or . . . a *monstrous* tub of ashes down below.

HUGO

I can't lift it.

SOLOMON

A monstrous tub of ashes? Leander's a comedian!
[He cannot help but laugh]
Too bad upon my soul! A tub of ashes! Too bad! I can't be angry if I should
die for it — To have my choice: the bourbon or the ashes!
[He laughs loudly]
Rupert, send word to my brother that I'll keep the bourbon, and he may
have the ashes!
[RUPERT waves HUGO away with the message.]
Rupert! Go tell my brother that I've been thinking. I've been thinking of
what he said. He knows. And that I'll meet him at the masquerade, and
afterwards crack a bottle.
[RUPERT exits. BEN follows.]
A tub of ashes! I *can't* be angry with him! He's a fine fellow after all, my
little brother Leander!
[He exits laughing.]

Act One
Scene Three

*[Glasgow, Kentucky. The Library of the Cooke plantation house
"Retirement," with a window open that looks out over the garden. ANNA,
in deep mourning, is reading at a table on which lies a large stack of books
and a hand mirror. HYACINTH, her maid, is looking out the window,
angry and examining the light that reflects on her ring].*

ANNA

Hyacinth! Is that you?

HYACINTH

Yes, Ma'am, Hyacinth is here.

ANNA

I didn't know, Hyacinth, that you were waiting. Sit down!
[HYACINTH rolls her eyes and sits.]
I think I shall send you back to the Capitol tomorrow.

23

HYACINTH

Again? It's such a long ride—

ANNA

I like to keep abreast of the politics going on. You are so good to bring me back the news from there. And it will give you a chance to see your Hugo.

HYACINTH
[To herself]
'Give you a chance to hear all about Colonel Sharp's goings on, you mean. There's too much smokin' and spittin' in the Capitol. Besides, whenever Hyacinth look up that dome she feels like she's gunna fall. 'Can't stand to look up! It scares her. Hyacinth don't like it.

ANNA
[Not having heard her.]
Don't let my presence bother you. Sit down!
[HYACINTH gawks at her. Stands up. Sits back down. But ANNA is oblivious.]
I am feeling depressed, most depressed.

HYACINTH
[To herself:]
It's about time.
[Hyacinth puts her feet up on a table and folds her arms, regarding her mistress with a contemptuous look. ANNA continues to read her book:]

ANNA
"It in another climate, so he said,
"Bore a bright golden flower, but not I' this soil!"
[She pauses -- turns over some leaves, and resumes]
"No lingering winters there, nor snow, nor shower --
"But Ocean ever to refresh mankind
"Breathes the shrill spirit of the western wind."
O, beautiful! Most beautiful. That is how my fevered soul dreams of Heaven! O happy land . . .
[She pauses, surprised by her reading.]
She died! -- the maiden *died*!
[Desperate for something positive:]
There could not have been a *happier* maiden to die! Hyacinth!

[HYACINTH returns no answer, and ANNA presently resumes to another book]

Again! A similar tale told of a beauteous dame beyond the sea! Spoken by Ferdinand in the words of the play:

"She died full young"

One Bossola answers him:

"I think not so -- her infelicity
"Seemed to have years too many"

Ah, luckless lady! Hyacinth!

[Still no answer. She opens yet another book.]

Here's a far sterner story, but like -- oh, very much like it in its despair --of that Egyptian queen, winning so easily a thousand hearts -- losing at length her own. She died. Thus ends the history. And her maids lean over and weep. Two gentle maids with gentle names: Eiros and Charmion! Rainbow and Dove! Hyacinth!

HYACINTH

[Pettishly.]

Madam, what is it?

ANNA

Would you be so kind, dear Hyacinth, as to go down to the library and bring me something a little cheerier, a little more redeeming?

[With sarcasm]

The Holy Evangelists, perhaps?

HYACINTH

God's nightgown!

[She laughs and exits.]

ANNA

[She gathers another book]

If there is a balm in Gilead for the wounded spirit it is there! Will there be found dew in the night time of my bitter trouble?

[She opens and reads:]

"Dew sweeter far than that
Which hangs like chains of pearl on Hermon hill?"

My father, my brothers, my friends have died by the most strange succession of calamities. Now my heart is lost by one who cannot be trusted—who is so unworthy of my affections. But whom yet I still love!

25

HYACINTH
[Re-enters and throws a volume on the table.]
There, madam's the book.
[To herself:]
Indeed, she is very troublesome.

ANNA
[Astonished.]
What did you say, Hyacinth? Have I done something to grieve you or anger you? I am sorry. You have served me long and ever been trust-worthy and respectful.
[She resumes her reading.]

HYACINTH
[To herself:]
Hyacinth can't believe my lady has any more jewels -- no -- no -- she gave Hyacinth all of them.

ANNA
What did you say, Hyacinth? Now, I think you have not spoken lately of your wedding. How is Hugo, and when is it to be?
[But ANNA is more attentive to her reading.]

HYACINTH
[To herself]
How' Hyacinth going to marry a man way off at the Capitol? Miles away? She only likes me seeing him sos I can tell her about Colonel Sharp. She'd do better to move us next door to him and his wife. But no, she'll string Hyacinth along as her spy and what is Hyacinth to do? Hyacinth will never get married this way—doomed to wait on this pig hand and foot. No wonder Hugo drinks so. 'Maybe it'd be better for Hyacinth'd to join him!--

ANNA
Did you say something? Can I do anything? Is there anything at all that you need, Hyacinth?

HYACINTH
[To herself:]
"Is there anything at all that you need!" That's meant for Hyacinth. When Hyacinth thought she could pay for her freedom with those jewels. Be free and get Hugo to get free from his drinking. She had such plans. But now—

[To ANNA]

I'm sure, Madam, you don't need to be always throwing those jewels in Hyacinth's face.

ANNA

Jewels! Hyacinth. Now, indeed, Hyacinth, I wasn't thinking of jewels.

HYACINTH

Oh, Hyacinth is sure you weren't! Well, let Hyacinth tell you, that Hugo says the ring you gave her is a fake, and he's sure that Colonel Solomon Sharp never would have given a real diamond to such as you; and at the best Hyacinth's certain, Madam, you have no use for those jewels now, she swears! Hyacinth'll send up the Holy Evangelist himself!

[She exits triumphantly to bring the PREACHER. ANNA bursts into tears and leans her head upon the table.]

ANNA

Poor Anna! And is it come to this? Thy servant maid! But courage! She is a viper whom you have cherished, and she stings you to the soul!

[Taking up the mirror. Of the mirror:]

Ha! Here at least is a friend. Much more a friend when I was younger. Fair mirror and true! Now tell me, for you can, a tale -- a pretty tale -- and do not stop even if it is full of woe. It answers me. It speaks of sunken eyes, and wasted cheeks, and beauty long deceased. It remembers me of Joy departed--Hope, the Seraph Hope, inurned and entombed. For now, in a tone low, sad, and solemn, but most audible, it whispers of this ruined maid's early grave. Fair mirror and true, you do not lie! You have nothing in the end to gain -- no heart to break --Solomon lied who said he loved you. You were true and he was false. False! False! There is no refuge for me anywhere on this earth!

[While she speaks, a PREACHER approaches.)

PREACHER

There is refuge for you in Heaven, sweet daughter. Think of eternal things! Give up your soul to penitence. Pray with me.

ANNA

[Arising hurriedly.]

I cannot pray! My soul is at war with God! The frightful sounds of merriment below disturb my senses. Go! I cannot pray. The sweet airs from the garden worry me! Your presence grieves me. Go! Your reverend raiment fills me with dread; your ebony cross with horror and awe!

PREACHER

Think of your precious soul!

ANNA

Think of my early days! Think of my father and mother in Heaven, think of our quiet home, and the stream that ran before the door! Think of my little brothers! Think of them! And think of me! Think of my trusting love and confidence: his vows, my ruin. Think. Think of my unspeakable misery! Get out of here! No, stay! No, stay! What was it you said of prayer and penitence? Did you mean faith and vows?

PREACHER

I did.

ANNA

Then all is well. I must make a vow that is fitting. A sacred vow, imperative, and urgent, A solemn vow!

PREACHER

Daughter, this zeal is good!

ANNA

Father, this zeal is anything but good! Do you have a cross fit for this thing? A cross where I may register this sacred vow?
[The PREACHER hands her a cross]
Not that. Oh! No, no, no!
[Shuddering]
Not that! Not that! I tell you, holy man, your raiments and your ebony cross scare me! Stand back! I have a cross myself. I have a cross that I think is fitting the deed. The vow. The symbol of the deed, and the deed's register should count it, Father!
[She draws a cross-handled dagger, and raises it on high]
Behold the cross wherewith a vow like mine is written in Heaven!

PREACHER

Your words are madness, daughter! They speak an unholy purpose. Your lips are livid. Your eyes are wild. Tempt not God's divine wrath! Pause before it is too late! Oh, be not, be not rash! Do not swear the oath, oh, do not swear it!

ANNA

It is sworn!

28

Act Two
Scene One

[The Sharp House in Frankfort, Kentucky. ELIZA and SOLOMON stand over the crib of their new born daughter who is peacefully sleeping. But SOLOMON sighs and turns away to pace the room]

ELIZA

You are sad, Solomon.

SOLOMON.

Sad? No, I'm not. Oh, I'm the happiest, happiest man in Kentucky. I have a beautiful wife and daughter. Oh, I am very happy!
[He sighs]

ELIZA

I think you have a strange way of showing your happiness. Something is bothering you; I can tell. That was a heavy sigh.

SOLOMON

Did I sigh? I was not conscious of it. It is a habit, a silly--a most silly habit I have when I am very happy. Did I sigh?
[Without knowing it, he sighs again.]

ELIZA

There you go again. You are not well. You are working too hard. I hate to see it. And you are drinking too much; it will be the ruin of you. I'll not have my husband looking so very old! Nothing wears away the constitution more than late hours and too much drink.

SOLOMON

Nothing, fair cousin, nothing--not even deep sorrow--wears it away like evil hours and drink.

ELIZA

Sorrow? A newborn child should bring happiness. What is it, dear? What is it about a baby that makes you sad?

29

SOLOMON
[Taking her hands]
I will do better for you.

ELIZA
Do it for yourself. Drop this riotous company you are keeping. They are too low born. They do not suit the likes of you as your father's heir and my husband. Do it to honor his memory. Do it for our daughter. You can't be all things to all people. If you lose their votes, so be it: they weren't worth having.

SOLOMON
I will drop them.

ELIZA
You need to——and you must. You are a man who serves in the House of Representatives, a public figure. Appearances are very important for a State Senator.

SOLOMON
I'll see to it.

ELIZA
Please, my love. See to it. Pay more attention, sir, to becoming a dignified gentleman and father.

SOLOMON
Oh! I want very much to be dignified!

ELIZA
You are making fun of me!

SOLOMON
*[Abstractedly, he puts his arms around her in a wrestling
embrace but from his lips too quickly comes:]*
Sweet, gentle Anna!

ELIZA
[Did she hear him correctly?]
Anna?

30

[She places her hand on his shoulder. There is something strange about his behavior.]
Are you asleep? Are you dreaming? What ails you, Solomon?

SOLOMON
[Startled at himself]
Cousin! Fair cousin! Madam--

ELIZA
While I was speaking you called me *Anna*.

SOLOMON
Did I? I beg your pardon--

ELIZA
Anna Cooke? From Glasgow? Stop worrying about her, my love.

SOLOMON
Indeed, I am not well.
[He moves away and falls into a chair. ELIZA goes to him and sits on the floor beside him.]

ELIZA
You have no feelings for her. She's entertained some ridiculous romantic notions of you that do not exist. Who could blame her? For I have the most handsome of husbands.

SOLOMON
You do not find her pursuits most oppressive?

ELIZA
Why should I, and neither should you. What of it? So, you were flattered by the attention she gave you. But that was before you met me . . . and I stole your heart. If I worried about every woman who noticed you, where would I be? I wouldn't want you to worry if I were noticed by another gentleman--

SOLOMON
What?

ELIZA
[She is teasing him and wraps his arm around her.]

31

Oh! Did I say that?! Forgive me, my sweet. I meant gentle*men* . . .

SOLOMON
[Laughing he squeezes her]
As there no doubt are *many* . . .

ELIZA
Let her find another attorney. It's too far now for you to ride, anyway.
I would not trust her as far as I could throw her. There is something
very strange about a woman who has passed thirty years and never been
married. And not for lack of suitors with her property and position.

SOLOMON
I probably should tell you something.

ELIZA
About Anna Cooke of Glasgow?

SOLOMON
You've no doubt heard the rumors?

ELIZA
I try not to listen to rumors.

SOLOMON
But I know something—

ELIZA
Then she must tell me. For you must not share it without her permission.

SOLOMON
[Her sensibleness refreshes him.]
You are my delight!

ELIZA
Sometimes you worry too much for others. It's because you have a good
heart. I wouldn't want you any other way. That's what makes you a good
leader: you generally care about others. You want to save the world. But
just don't let it destroy you, because then you won't be of use to any of us.
[SOLOMON starts to speak but she stops him.]
You can't save her. You aren't expected to. We have but one Savior.

32

[Enter LEANDER.]

LEANDER
My brother, I have news for you! Hey? What's the matter?
[Observing ELIZA]
You are upset. Is this a quarrel I've walked in on? Kiss her, Solomon! Kiss her, you dog, and make it up, I say, this minute!
[SOLOMON eagerly kisses ELIZA]
See, it's a good thing your brother lives in the same house with you. I really must take some credit for the happiness in this marriage!
[But they are still embraced]
Now, that's enough. Enough I say! There is a young attorney who has come to town. From Glasgow-

SOLOMON and ELIZA
[With laughter]
Glasgow?!

LEANDER
I wonder if we should invite him to your party?

ELIZA
I had hoped it would be a small affair. With just close friends and family--

LEANDER
Yes, but his father and our youngest brother were in the same company together during the War. He has spoken so highly of you, Solomon. His name is Jereboam Beauchamp.

ELIZA
Ah, Mr. Beauchamp.

SOLOMON
Not that young boy who keeps hanging around?

ELIZA
Yes. The very same.

LEANDER
Be honored that he's chosen you for his role model. He is a prodigy pre-eminent in arts and arms, and wealth, and highly descent. Good, that's

settled: we'll have him at the party! I knew it. That's why I invited him for you.

ELIZA

[To SOLOMON]
He has put you high upon a pedestal!

SOLOMON
The higher they place you, the farther the fall.

ELIZA
I have heard that Jeroboam Beauchamp is volatile and giddy. Isn't he? And little given to thinking? I was just discussing with my husband the importance of proper company--

LEANDER
Oh, he is quite proper, I assure you. They tell me that there is no branch of philosophy he has not mastered. Not even the most complex; he is highly learned as few are learned. But so very melancholy. He's liable to kill the party. You probably should not have agreed to invite him.

ELIZA
Isn't that strange! I know that men seek out his company and speak of him as though he entered madly into life, drinking the cup of pleasure to the dregs.

LEANDER
He's melancholy.

ELIZA
He's wild.

LEANDER
Melancholy!

ELIZA
Wild!

SOLOMON
Stop it, you two! He's not a melancholy scholar and he's not a wild merry soul. He's probably just a dreamer and has shut out the common passions

34

that would distract a man of his age. Maybe he'd do better to enjoy his young years, for they pass too quickly.

ELIZA
[Teasing her husband, fingering his graying hair]
Spoken by one so old!

LEANDER
Children, we disagree. Let's get out of here and as Father would have said, taste the fragrant air of the garden.
[ELIZA checks on her daughter as the men depart.]
I thought I heard that Jereboam Beauchamp was a melancholy man. With a strain like the low moaning of the distant sea. He will douse the flame of your party, I know it. You really must consult with me before you invite these people!

Act Two
Scene Two

[The Sharp House a few days later, the night of the party to celebrate the birth of their child. LEANDER and SOLOMON stand by the door greeting guests as they arrive. RUPERT takes their coats, BEN assists him.]

POE
Here, where a hero fell, a column falls;
Here, where the mimic eagle glared in gold,
A midnight vigil holds the swarthy bat:
Here, where the dames of Rome their yellow hair
Wav'd to the wind, now wave the reed and thistle:

LEANDER
[To his brother]
Have you seen Mr. Beauchamp yet? I'm quite curious to meet him. His father came from Delaware and was one of the first settlers in the southern part of our State. A good honest man. A farmer. And he served in the War with our little brother. If he is anything like his father, he is brilliant. And you thought him melancholy!

SOLOMON

I'm sure I did not, brother.
            [He laughs at his brother's silliness.]

LEANDER

You did! You did! Why do you laugh?

SOLOMON.

Indeed. I hardly know myself.
            [He laughs to himself]
It was a few days ago, I remember it well, we were speaking of Jereboam
Beauchamp--

LEANDER

Perfectly. I do remember it. What of it? What then?

SOLOMON

            [There is no winning with his wit. He laughs.]
Oh, nothing. Nothing at all.

LEANDER

Nothing at all! It is remarkable that you should laugh at nothing at all!

SOLOMON

Most singular. Singular!

LEANDER

Look you, brother dear, be so kind as tell me, sir, at once: what are you
talking about?

SOLOMON

Wasn't it so? We differed in our opinions about him.

LEANDER

Him! Whom?

SOLOMON

Beauchamp!

LEANDER

Beauchamp! The young lawyer? Yes! The one that hangs in your shadow?
Is that who you mean? We differed, indeed. If I now recollect the words you
used were that the Beauchamp you knew was neither learned nor mirthful,
but melancholy!

SOLOMON

[Laughing]

Now, did I?

LEANDER

That you did sir, and well I knew at the time that you were wrong, it being
not the character of that young man--whom all the world allows to be a
most *hilarious* man. Don't be so sure of yourself, brother. And you insisted
he was Melancholy Jaques!

SOLOMON

How extraordinary. Remarkable! I can't believe that so little time could so
much alter someone! To be honest with you, earlier today, as I was walking,
I met the very man Jereboam Beauchamp, with his friend, John Lowe,
having just arrived in Frankfort. He is changed! Such an account he gave
me of his journey! It would have made you die with laughter. Such tales he
told of his caprices and his merry freaks along the road. Such oddity. Such
humor. Such wit, such whim. Such flashes of wild merriment set off too in
such full relief by the grave demeanor of his friend, Lowe, --who, to speak
the truth, was gravity itself . . .

LEANDER

Didn't I tell you?

SOLOMON

Did you? I thought it was my Eliza. And yet it is strange! How much I must
have been mistaken! I always thought Jereboam Beauchamp was neither
melancholy nor marvelous. I invited him to join us tonight.

LEANDER

[He notices someone eating and drinking]

Good God! Don't look now, but there is the monstrous Mr. Patrick Darby.

SOLOMON

Darby? Here?

37

LEANDER

Did you invite him?

SOLOMON

Why would he be here? The man professes to be my archenemy.

LEANDER

He is your newest best friend, at least while the food and drink hold out!

SOLOMON

I suppose that's just the man's way. We do him an injustice to think he will ever change.

LEANDER

Yes, the only horror greater than having to deal with the Patrick Darbies in this world, is to wake up one morning and find that you are one!

SOLOMON

But by the grace of God go we . . .
            [BEAUCHAMP enters and his face is ignited at the sight of
            SOLOMON whom he had entertained just hours ago. LOWE
            enters with him.]

LEANDER

Whom have we here? It cannot be the young attorney himself? Your student!

SOLOMON

My student?

LEANDER

Of course. He studies your every move, he does.

SOLOMON

Beauchamp? He came. And with his very grave friend John Lowe. Welcome, sir!
            [To BEAUCHAMP and LOWE with great anticipation.
            BEAUCHAMP meets SOLOMON with hand outstretched
            and shakes his hand ferociously!]

Mr. Beauchamp and Mr. Lowe, welcome! Allow me to introduce you to my brother, Dr. Leander Sharp. Leander, this is the young lawyer Jereboam Beauchamp, nephew of Colonel Beauchamp, Senator from Washington.

> *[BEAUCHAMP finally stops shaking SOLOMON's hand to bow haughtily to LEANDER, but his eyes stay fixed on SOLOMON and his face is ecstatic.]*

That, his friend, Mr. Lowe. We were just discussing your fine reputation: it precedes you.

LOWE
[Immediately warm and friendly.]
And we had hoped our letters would do that! Don't believe everything you hear!

SOLOMON
But it was all good.

LOWE
Good? Dear, sir, when it could be *better*!
> *[They laugh with him.]*

Mr. Beauchamp has letters of our introduction.

LEANDER
[Laughing]
Letters of introduction. Of course. As only he would! Welcome to our fair town and to this home. We remember your father, Jereboam; he and our little brother Absalom were enlisted in the same company during the War: the Kentucky Mounted Volunteer Militia. Solomon, get your cousin's attention for a minute, and let me make these men acquainted with your lovely wife.

> *[SOLOMON excuses himself to bring his wife to meet BEAUCHAMP and LOWE. BEAUCHAMP's spirits suddenly descend at his absence. His eyes follow after SOLOMON. LOWE is excited to search out the room.]*

You come, sir, at a time most seasonable. The birth of my niece.

BEAUCHAMP.
I have here our letters, sir; I dare touch them now, sir, but I will not present them. If it has to be done, my friend Lowe here--Lowe! Ah! My friend Lowe here will hand them to Your Grace.

[He hands the letters to LOWE and trails after SOLOMON]
I would retire.

LEANDER

Retire? So soon?
[Dumbfoundedly LOWE receives the letters.]
Come, what ho! Rupert! Ben! Show our guest to his chamber. He is unwell.
[The servants go after BEAUCHAMP]
Retire? Unwell?

LOWE

So please you, sir. I'm afraid it is as you say—Mr. Beauchamp is unwell.
The damp air of the river--the fatigue of a long journey--the--indeed I had
better follow him. He must be unwell. I will return shortly.
[LOWE hands the letters to LEANDER and exits.]

LEANDER

Now this is very strange! If I didn't know better, I would say . . . Solomon!
Elizabeth! This way, I wish to speak with you.

SOLOMON

*[Arriving with ELIZA who holds the newborn in her arms.
Eagerly they look to address BEAUCHAMP.]*
Here is my lovely bride, Mr. Beauchamp, and our daughter Kate.

ELIZA

The best little baby in the world--

SOLOMON

[He kisses the child and then his wife]
My dear, may I present Mr. Beauchamp and—
*[But there is no BEAUCHAMP and no LOWE. They look to
each other bewildered. They look to LEANDER. The brothers
look to each other and are speechless.]*

ELIZA

I told you Beauchamp was a melancholy man!

Act Two
Scene Three

[In Glasgow, Kentucky we hear the horses of BEAUCHAMP and LOWE as they ride on the Beauchamp farm. They dismount their horses and walk.]

LOWE

Don't worry about it, Jerry. You mustn't. Indeed, indeed, don't give away to these depressions. Come to yourself. Shake off the idle fancies that trouble you and enjoy life. For now, you look half dead!

BEAUCHAMP.

That's not true, John! I enjoy my life.
[But he is anything but convincing]

LOWE

I hate to see you like this.

BEAUCHAMP

John, it bothers me that I am causing you grief, my honored friend. Command me, sir! What would you have me do? At your bequest I will shake off that nature which I inherited from my forefathers; from the time I was a baby in my mother's arms. And I will no longer be Jereboam Beauchamp, but some other man. I know! Solomon Sharp, perhaps. Yes. If there were a man I would rather be, it would be he. Such a man of grace and dignity. Integrity. Command me, sir!

LOWE

Keep your mind on the fields around you. To the Senate and your campaign or to the work here on your farm.

BEAUCHAMP

His shadow would follow me even there. It has followed me even here! There is––What voice was that?

LOWE

I heard nothing. I heard no voice except your own, and the echo of your own.

BEAUCHAMP

Then I must have dreamed it.

LOWE

Don't give in to dreams. You have nothing but success awaiting you in life. And you won't hear its trumpet if you give heed to imaginary sounds and phantom voices.

BEAUCHAMP

It is a phantom voice! Didn't you hear it then?

LOWE

I heard nothing.

BEAUCHAMP

You heard nothing? John, speak no more to me of my successes. Oh! I am sick, sick, sick to death of the hollow and high-sounding vanities of the populous Earth! Bear with me awhile! We have been boys together -- schoolfellows – and although our politics have sent us different directions, we remain the rarest of friends. But not for so long, for in Heaven, you will do me a kind and gentle office, and a power. A Power great, benignant and supreme –which shall then absolve you of all further duties to me.

LOWE

You speak in riddles that I don't understand.

BEAUCHAMP

Yet now as Fate approaches, and the Hours are breathing low, the sands of Time are changed to golden grains, and dazzle me, John. Oh, God! I cannot die, for in my heart there is a flame that burns for the beautiful. I think the air is balmier now than it was meant to be. Rich melodies are floating in the winds. A rarer loveliness bedecks the earth. And with a holier luster the quiet moon sits in Heaven. Listen! Listen! You cannot say that you heard nothing just now?

LOWE

Indeed, I hear nothing.

BEAUCHAMP

Not hear it? Listen now! Listen. The faintest sound and yet the sweetest that the ear ever heard!
A lady's voice! And sorrow in the tone! John, it oppresses me like a spell! Again! Again! How solemnly it falls into my heart of hearts! A more

eloquent voice surely, I never heard. I wish that I had heard it's thrilling tones years ago!

LOWE

I hear it now. Be still! The voice, if I'm not greatly mistaken, comes from the farm over there--which you can see very plainly from here. "Retirement," that's the name of the plantation, belonging to the Cooke family.
[Hesitating]
The voice is undoubtedly that of the eldest sister, Anna.

BEAUCHAMP

I must meet her. Do you know her?

LOWE

I know of her. And her brothers.

BEAUCHAMP

And what do you know of her?

LOWE

After their parent's death they came here from Virginia to build back their fortunes. They have been hit hard by the collapse of the banks. Her family is Old Court through and through. Unlike you, they demand that the creditors be paid what was borrowed. Most of her family died not long ago. During The War that took the prominent men of Kentucky at the Battle of the River Raisin.

BEAUCHAMP

Is she beautiful?

LOWE

She has a demeanor that goes beyond looks. Her heart was broken by Solomon Sharp. Have you not heard the rumors?

BEAUCHAMP

What rumors? Colonel Sharp is a gentleman.

LOWE

He is a man. Like you and I.

43

BEAUCHAMP

What rumors?

LOWE

That there was a child that died.

BEAUCHAMP

A child?

LOWE

And he abandoned her.

BEAUCHAMP

Surely you don't believe such a thing!

LOWE

I don't know.

BEAUCHAMP

It is not possible!

LOWE

I said I did not know. He may have gotten carried away by her charms.

BEAUCHAMP

Those are lies you heard! He is a grandson of the Archbishop of York. Be still! -- it comes again!

ANNA

"And is thy heart so strong
As for to leave me thus
Who hath loved thee so long
In wealth and woe among?
And is thy heart so strong
As for to leave me thus?
Say nay -- say nay!"

LOWE

I have heard it before but never so plaintively. It is English poetry—

44

BEAUCHAMP

Shhh! Listen! It comes again!

ANNA

"Is it so strong
As for to leave me thus
Who hath loved thee so long
In wealth and woe among?
And is thy heart so strong
As for to leave me thus?
Say nay -- say nay!"

LOWE

It's hushed and all is still!

BEAUCHAMP

All is not still! I must meet her.

LOWE

She loves to read. She speaks the poetry of Sir Thomas Wyatt. Perhaps you could call upon her and inquire about her library. Let us go down.

BEAUCHAMP

Go on down, John, go. I will follow shortly. Go!

LOWE

The hour is growing late. What's the matter, Jerry?

ANNA

"Who hath loved thee so long
In wealth and woe among,
And is thy heart so strong?
Say nay -- say nay!"

LOWE

Let's go! Jerry, give these fancies to the wind. Come on! We are expected and cannot be late. It would be rude. Don't you remember?

BEAUCHAMP

Remember? I do. Lead on! I do remember.
[As they start to leave]

45

Believe me I would give, freely would give, the broad lands of all my successes to look upon the face hidden away upon that farm. To gaze upon that veiled face, and hear once more that silent tongue.

                    LOWE
For God's sake, let's go——

                    ANNA
              Say nay! -- say nay!

                    BEAUCHAMP
It's so strange. Very strange. I thought that the voice chimed in with my own desires and invited me to stay! Sweet voice! I hear you and will surely stay! Now be this Fancy, by Heaven, or be it Fate, still I won't leave. John, please make my apologies, I can't go with you tonight.

                    LOWE
Have it your way. Good-night, Jerry.

                    BEAUCHAMP
Good-night, my friend, good-night.
              [LOWE exits. BEAUCHAMP watches him go, and then turns
              and faces the direction of the voice. He heads towards the
              Cooke plantation, Retirement.]

Act Two
Scene Four

[In the house at Retirement, Glasgow, Kentucky. HYACINTH ushers him
into the library where he is seated. She returns with a bowl of fruit, offers
it to him, sits it near him and leaves.]

                    POE
A phantom voice in the wind? Jereboam Beauchamp fell in love with Anna Cooke even before he laid eyes on her; the erotic mystery of love awakening his heart from an endless slumber. He rode up to her farm pretending to be interested in her romantic library. Due to the scandal of her accusations toward Solomon Sharp, Anna Cooke sternly refused to make new acquaintances or receive the visits of former friends--she said she could never be happy in society again.

HYACINTH

[Returning with his hat.]

Madam has retired. She refuses to see you.

[She gives him back his hat and gestures for him to follow her out to the door. Dejected, he starts to follow her but then stops.]

BEAUCHAMP

Please send for her.

[He returns and sits defiantly on the sofa. HYACINTH huffs and exits. In a moment, ANNA Cooke walks into the room. BEAUCHAMP stands and bows]

I'm Jereboam Beauchamp.

ANNA

Are you?

BEAUCHAMP

Good afternoon.

ANNA

Good afternoon.

BEAUCHAMP

I'm Jereboam Beauchamp.

ANNA

So, you have said.

[BEAUCHAMP is speechless.]

Mr. Beauchamp—

BEAUCHAMP

Jereboam Orville Beauchamp.

ANNA

Jereboam *Orville* Beauchamp—

BEAUCHAMP

--Not to be mistake with my uncle Jereboam Beauchamp. Colonel Jereboam Beauchamp. My namesake. Are you acquainted with him?

47

ANNA

Yes. The same Colonel Beauchamp who was accused of treating an entire battalion with *spirituous liquors*?

BEAUCHAMP

That's right!

ANNA

A member of the General Assembly. He has a character of deep intrigue. He introduced the bill in the State Senate for the Relief party.

BEAUCHAMP

That's right!
> *[He is pleased that they have struck a familiar chord.]*

ANNA

Our family is Anti Relief.

BEAUCHAMP

> *[Discouraged.]*

That's right.

ANNA

Mr. Beauchamp, I am disinclined to make acquaintances.

BEAUCHAMP

Oh, I know.

ANNA

You do? Then why, may I ask, are you here?

BEAUCHAMP

I don't want to make your acquaintance. I mean—I have a friend who has made your acquaintance—or, at least he knows of you. Yes, he knows of you—I guess that he is acquainted with you . . . in that sense—and he speaks highly of you! Oh, yes! In fact, he has so heightened my anxiety to meet you that I had resolved to hazard the mortification of you refusing my acquaintance. I don't want to intrude upon your acquaintance--

ANNA

But you have, Mr. Beauchamp.

48

BEAUCHAMP

Oh, no! I don't want to make your acquaintance—I mean, I do, but I don't. I don't want it for myself—no, no! I want it for my sisters. I have two sisters. And they so much want to make your acquaintance . . .

ANNA

Where are you from, Mr. Beauchamp?

BEAUCHAMP

Jereboam Orville—

ANNA

Mr. Jereboam *Orville* Beauchamp. Where did you come from?

BEAUCHAMP

The front door. Your servant let me in.

ANNA

Yes, I know, but before that?

BEAUCHAMP

My father has a farm just over the ridge. That's where my sisters live. And it can be lonesome, without books or society—that I thought, . . . you would see fit to . . . favor me with the benefit of your library. While I remained in the country? For my sisters?
[*He takes a deep breath and, pleased with himself, smiles.*]

ANNA

You encourage your sisters to read?

BEAUCHAMP

How else can they be prepared for the world? My uncle, Colonel Beauchamp, never learned to read. I don't want that for my sisters.

ANNA

Most women are ignorant of books.

BEAUCHAMP

If they are ignorant then the men have made them so.

49

ANNA

Women are expected to be the gentler sex.

BEAUCHAMP

By books written by men.

ANNA

[Impressed with his way of thinking, she shows him her library.]

As to my society, I have retired to this secluded spot never again to mix with the world. But as to my library, it is at your service. It would give me pleasure to loan you whatever books you like for them.

BEAUCHAMP

For *them?*

ANNA

Your little sisters, of course.

BEAUCHAMP

Oh yes, why yes, of course . . . Thank you.

[As he searches the shelves.]

Romances, mysteries, murders . . . Keats, and Byron, and Shelley. *I met murder along the way—He had a mask like Castlereagh—*

ANNA

Very smooth he looked, yet grim;
Seven bloodhounds followed him . . .
[She chooses a book and hands it to him.]

BEAUCHAMP

Wollstonecraft. *"A Vindication of the Rights of Woman."*

ANNA

She is the mother of Mary Shelley.

BEAUCHAMP

She wants to change the fabric of our society. So that women would have power over men.

ANNA

Not power over men. Power over ourselves. Your sisters should read it. You might want to read it. Become "acquainted" with it.

BEAUCHAMP

Thank you.

ANNA

What work do you do, Mr. Beauchamp?

BEAUCHAMP

I am an attorney.

ANNA

Ah. I am in need of a new attorney. Tell me, do you get to Frankfort much?

BEAUCHAMP

Not often, my lady.

ANNA

But you must. It is important for a young attorney to know the works of the Legislature there at our state capital.

BEAUCHAMP

Yes, my lady.
            [He stands admiring her. An awkward pause lapses.]
Now, it is late and I must release you to your evening.

ANNA

Wouldn't you like to take more books?

BEAUCHAMP

I think tonight, only this one.

ANNA

            [Smiling at his design to frame an excuse for another visit.]
When you've finished, I want to hear all your thoughts of it.

BEAUCHAMP

Good night.

[BEAUCHAMP bows and exits. ANNA watches him leave and then disappears into the house.

[A few days later, at Retirement. HYACINTH leads BEAUCHAMP into the house as before, she leaves, and he waits for ANNA. He reads some books. HYACINTH comes in with his hat, and with frustration, he leaves, for ANNA has declined to see him once again.]

POE

I probably should explain something about this mess of Old Court and New Court. It began with the Panic of 1819. After all, we were our own country for the first time, and that independent economy came with a price. Unfortunately, banks loosely began to print their own money and this led to a bankruptcy in the country where money was loaned that could not be paid back. So, a "Relief" program was designed to forgive the debts leaving those who had lent out the money holding the bag. This idea won the majority in the Kentucky General Assembly, so that Legislature abolished the Old Court of Appeals and created a New one. But the Old Court supporters were not going anywhere—they wanted their money back.

[Another day. HYACINTH leads BEAUCHAMP into the house. She stares at him and leaves. BEAUCHAMP waits and reads.]

Sharp and Beauchamp are of the New Court crusading for the destitute so that their poverty might be shared by the richer folks and bring them down a notch or two. John Lowe and Anna Cooke are of the Old Court—Ant-Relief--not wanting to switch places with the poor. It makes for strange bedfellows.

HYACINTH
[Reentering with his hat.]
She cannot see you today.
[She stares at him.]

BEAUCHAMP
Miss Hyacinth, why do you keep staring at me?

HYACINTH
I had a dream about you last night.

BEAUCHAMP

Did you? Strange how anyone may conjure one up in his dreams without one's permission.

[Humorously]

Was I as handsome there as you see me now?

HYACINTH

[She looks at him hard.]

You was ugly.

[She hands him the hat again as though tired of holding it.]

Madam sends her apologies . . . again.

BEAUCHAMP

Tell your Madam I will wait for her.

[He sits. HYACINTH huffs and starts to leave. She stops and looks back.]

HYACINTH

Ugly!!

[She throws him his hat and is gone. Soon ANNA appears.]

BEAUCHAMP

It is not your books that lead me here. I come to see you.

ANNA

I cannot return the visits of your sisters. I am happy for them to read any of my books.

BEAUCHAMP

I seek only your conversation of an evening, as a friend.

[They sit and the time passes.]

POE

Three months and a week did not escape without him seeking her conversation of an evening. A mutual friendship was born between them such as mortals seldom feel. But soon there was kindled in his heart a feeling and a flame he had never felt before. "That sweetest of all passions which, reciprocated, happily turns earth into heaven."

ANNA

[Turning from him in tears.]

Do you speak to me of love, Jereboam Beauchamp? Oh! This mockery is most cruel. Most cruel indeed.

BEAUCHAMP.
Don't cry, dear Anna. Please don't cry. Your bitter tears will drive me mad. Oh, don't mourn, Anna. Be comforted. I know -- I know it all, and still, I speak of love. Look at me, brightest and beautiful, Anna. Turn your eyes to mine. You ask me if I could speak of love, knowing what I know, and seeing what I have seen. You ask me that and yet I answer you. On my bended knee I answer you.
[He kneels]
Sweet Anna, I love you. Love you. Love you through good and ill, through wound and woe I love you. No mother, with her first-born on her knee, thrills with more intense love than I for you. Not on God's altar, in any time or place, has burned there a holier fire than burns now within my spirit for you.
[He rises]
Even for your hardships I love thee. Even for your griefs. Your beauty and your woes.

ANNA
You forget yourself, remembering me. Of all the young girls your age, pure and without reproach, why would you choose someone like me? I am dishonorable. I have a tainted reputation. My name is seared and blighted, how would it tally with the ancestral honors of your family and your professional success?

BEAUCHAMP
Don't speak to me of success! What is the New Court with its Relief measures but a robbery of payments due to you, from credit you have given in good faith. I hate--I loathe the name; I do abhor the unsatisfactory and ideal thing that brought me success. Are you not a woman and I a man? Do I not love? Are you not beautiful? What more do we need? Ha! Success! Don't speak of it.

ANNA
I am Old Court . . .

BEAUCHAMP
And what is Old Court wanting back but what is theirs, but what had been given in good faith!

ANNA

What are you saying?

BEAUCHAMP

That I refuse to be on the opposite side of the fence from you. I've been New Court long enough. Now I will die an Old Court man.

[She moves across the room. He follows behind her.]

By all I hold most sacred and most solemn--by all my wishes now--my fears--by all I scorn on earth and hope in heaven--there is no deed I wish more to succeed in, than in your cause to scoff at this same success and trample it under foot.

ANNA

Jereboam! You love me. In my heart of hearts, I feel that you truly love me.

BEAUCHAMP

Oh, Anna!

[He grabs her and kisses her.]

And you love me?

ANNA

Shh! Hush!

[She pulls away]

I thought I heard a figure pass through the gloom of those trees. A spectral figure, solemn, and slow, and noiseless. Like the grim shadow of conscience, solemn and noiseless.

[She walks across the room and returns.]

I was mistaken. It was only a giant bough stirred by the autumn wind. Jereboam!

BEAUCHAMP

My Anna, my love! What is the matter? Why are you suddenly so pale? Conscience will never cast a shadow nor shake your spirit. It's only that the night wind is chilly and these melancholy boughs throw a gloom over all things.

ANNA

Jereboam Beauchamp! You speak to me of love. I believe there is a Heaven . . .

[She looks at their stacks of books. Stories she has read.]

---A land that is new and undiscovered—only spoken of in books and songs--A thousand leagues within the golden west? A fairy land of flowers, and fruit, and sunshine, and crystal lakes, and over-arching forests, and mountains, around whose towering summits the winds of Heaven flow free. Which air to breathe is Happiness now, and will be Freedom hereafter in days that are to come?

BEAUCHAMP
Oh, will you – will you fly to that Paradise -- my Anna, will you fly to that Paradise with me? There Care shall be forgotten, and Sorrow shall be no more, and Eros be all. And life shall then be mine, for I will live for you, and in your eyes. And you shall no longer be a mourner. But the radiant Joys shall wait upon you, and the angel Hope shall attend you forever; and I will kneel to you and worship you, and call you my beloved, my own, my beautiful, my love, my wife, my all. Oh, will you, will you, Anna, fly there with me?

ANNA
My father is dead. My brother is dead. There is no one to avenge my honor. And so, I hide here away from the world for all eternity. A deed is to be done –

BEAUCHAMP
What is this deed you speak of?

ANNA
Colonel Sharp has blighted all my happiness and while he lives I will feel unworthy of your love. But I will kiss the hand and adore the person who would avenge me. Solomon Sharp lives to tell the vilest stories against me.
[She takes out a handkerchief and begins to weep]

BEAUCHAMP
Tell me.

ANNA
His friend John Waring is spreading the story that my child . . . my poor blessed little child that was denied this life . . . that my poor angel *was the child of other men*!
[Her face hot with tears, she faces BEAUCHAMP]
It has killed me! And my baby, buried in the cold ground, is silent to defend its honor. And yet Solomon Sharp lives!

56

BEAUCHAMP

And he shall die!

> *[In an explosive rage, he exits out of the house with his quest to avenge her honor.]*

ANNA

> *[After a pause.]*

"And he shall die!" At last!

> *[But relief fades to conscience]*

Solomon Sharp die? Who spoke the words? Where am I? What was it he said?

> *[She looks for him.]*

Jereboam! You are not gone--you are not gone, Jereboam! I feel you are not gone. Yet I cannot look, in case I don't see you; you can't go with those words upon your lips. O, speak to me! Let me hear your voice: one word, one word, to say that you are not gone. One little sentence, to say how you do scorn, how you do hate my womanly weakness.

> *[Thinking him to be outside in the garden]*

Ha! ha! You are not gone. O speak to me! I knew you wouldn't go! I knew you wouldn't. Couldn't. I knew you dared not to go. Villain, you are not gone. You mock me! And so, I stop you. Stop you!

> *[The room seems to tilt.]*

Where am I? It is well. It is very well! So that the blade be keen. The blow be sure. It is well.

> *[She breathes a deep sigh of relief. Things are about to change. And where she will be at least will not be where she has been.]*

It is very well. At last! At last!

Act Three
Scene One

[Sometime later. A street in Frankfort. BEAUCHAMP enters.]

BEAUCHAMP

This weakness grows upon me. I am faint. And much more I fear I am sick. It will not do to die before I have lived! Keep your hands from me for a while, Satan. Have pity on me, Prince of the Powers of Darkness and Death. Stay from me yet awhile! Oh, pity me! Let me not perish now, in the budding of my hope for Paradise! Let me live, yet a little while longer. It is I who pray for life. I who recently demanded death.

[To LOWE who enters]

What did Leander Sharp say?

LOWE.

Solomon Sharp told his brother that he has no cause for quarrel or a feud with you. He refuses a duel.

BEAUCHAMP

What did you say? What answer did you bring me, John? With what excessive fragrance does the wind bring, is it weighed down from bowers! A fairer day or one worthier of Kentucky that no mortal eyes have seen! What did Dr. Sharp say?

LOWE

That his brother, Solomon Sharp will not and cannot accept the challenge. He has no quarrel with you.

BEAUCHAMP

So, it is most true. All this is very true. On a day like this when the skies are so calm and utterly free from the evil taint of clouds, what reason did he give?

LOWE

Some years ago, Solomon Sharp passed a bill to stop state officers and attorneys from dueling. So, you see, even if he wanted to, he cannot duel.

BEAUCHAMP

I will make him break the law he created and show him for the hypocrite that he is!

LOWE

Solomon Sharp has no cause for quarrel. He only wants to be left alone. The man has a wife and children at home. He gave up his campaign for the Kentucky Senate because John Waring ran him into the ground over this whole thing!

BEAUCHAMP

Yes, and where did it leave him? Governor Adair appointed him Attorney General! Like a cat he always comes up standing on his feet!

LOWE

You think he will give in to you the way he did to that hothead John Waring?

BEAUCHAMP

Yes, I do.

LOWE

John Waring only seeks to destroy the character of a man who he cannot intimidate. I can't help but wonder . . . if someone else—or maybe more than one—have offered you a better price for Solomon Sharp's pound of flesh? Have they? Have they?

BEAUCHAMP
[Ignoring the remark]

Do me a piece of service; go back and say to Dr. Sharp, that I, that Jereboam Beauchamp, hold his brother a villain! Tell him that it is exceedingly just he should have cause for a duel with me.

LOWE

I was your friend once. When we differed on the most crucial positions with the Relief. You were then a member of the New Court wanting Relief and I a member of the Old Court against it. Funny. Now that Miss Cooke has turned your head to our side, I find us more at odds. I warn you; it is too easy a sin to try and destroy what you cannot have.

BEAUCHAMP

What? What does that mean?

LOWE

Unrequited love.

BEAUCHAMP

He rejected her—

LOWE

I do not speak of Anna.

BEAUCHAMP

The villain robbed her of a good name!

59

LOWE

He is no more a villain than you or I. You've been reading too many of her romance novels. What was there to rob had long been taken by half the men in town twice as many times—

[BEAUCHAMP hits him. LOWE falls.]

BEAUCHAMP

Will you tell him?

LOWE

Tell him yourself.

[He gets up and walks away. BEAUCHAMP exits while bumping into a drunken HUGO. LEANDER enters and addresses HUGO.]

LEANDER

Hugo, my man, what storm has befallen you?

HUGO

The storm of love, Sir. You see before you the flat works of what love can do to a man. I'll be hanged for the woman I love. I'm damned if I do, and damned if I don't. In short, I'm flat damned.

[HUGO falls flat on the ground faceup.]

LEANDER

Damned if he does, that's flat! Why, yes, that's flat. Extremely flat, and candid, and so forth and sociable, and all that kind of thing. Damned if you do? Look you, you ignoramus. What do you mean? Is it your fixed intention to lie all day in that especial manner? If so, then tell me!

HUGO

I'll let you know nothing about it, and for the best of reasons. In the first place, Sir, I did not hear a word your honor said, and in the second, Sir, I cannot talk about it. It's very strange: can't you see that I'm dead!

LEANDER

It's very strange I can't perceive you're dead? Soho! I see! I've heard before that the dead sometimes wander the earth not knowing that they have died. Ha! ha! I have it! I wish to see my brother Solomon, but he won't see me. Jereboam Beauchamp is stalking him and he has fallen back into doom and gloom. But I know my brother, and if I can get him to laugh, he'll forget all about this foolishness. I'd bet a trifle now I'll make this idiot go and tell my brother that he's deceased. And if it works, the game is up.

[To HUGO]

So. So, You're dead, eh? Come now, come now, Hugo! Be candid with me: is it indeed a fact and are you really dead?

HUGO

No, Sir, not exactly. Dead, so to say, but having just committed sooicide, I'm what they call *deceased*.

LEANDER

Ah! I see. It is positively so. Poor soul he's gone! Sooicide, indeed! But now that I think of it, *deceased* is not the word. What do you say, Hugo? "Deceased" is not the proper word to express your case with due exactitude. Perhaps *defunct* would suit it better.

HUGO

Sir! I'm defunct.

LEANDER

Ah, very well! Then I shall tell your master that you're defunct. Or stop, suppose I say— I think there would be more dignity in saying, "Dear brother, your worthy servant Hugo, not being dead, nor yet to say deceased, nor yet defunct, but having unluckily made way with himself — that's *sooicide* you know — your worthy servant Hugo has now <u>departed</u> this life."

HUGO

Say that, Sir, say that! For now, upon consideration, I think I have. . . departed this life.

LEANDER

I will. I'll say it! I will inform Solomon. But not so fast. I'm wrong. I must not do it; it is against all rules of etiquette. This is a matter demanding due consideration, Hugo, one of a lasting importance. Do you not think-- You see I yield unto your better judgment--Do you not think it were more fitting, Sir, more decorous, you know, you understand me, more delicate, more proper, and all that: that <u>you</u> should tell the circumstance yourself unto Colonel Sharp? Ha! Ha! Do you understand me, Sir! That's the better plan, isn't it?

HUGO

Why yes, it is.

LEANDER

Undoubtedly, it is. You are right, get up! And lose no time about it. Be quick. Get up!

HUGO

Get up? I can't. Sir, I've been dead an hour and am stiff as you can see.

LEANDER

Well, yes, I do. You are a little . . . stiff. All very true. I most sincerely pity you; but, Sir, could you not, do you think, by a desperate effort, attempt to stir a little? Let me help you? Damnit! This will never do! Why, bless me, Sir, perhaps you're not aware that . . . that in short today is very hot . . . and that a corpse in very hot weather won't keep. Do you understand me, Sir? My nose is delicate, and to be plain: you smell. Sir, yes, you smell. Come now, be quick! Indeed, I cannot, will not, answer for the consequence of staying any longer. Sir, you might drop to pieces!

HUGO

Good God! That's true! Give me your hand, Sir!
[LEANDER helps HUGO stand]

LEANDER

Ah, that is well! Extremely well attempted! Sir, I am glad to see you on your legs. A little stiff, no matter! Not ungraceful in a corpse. Now, Sir, this leg . . . a little farther . . . that's it! Most excellent! Ah! That is exquisite! Now, Sir, the left . . . You have a genius, Hugo, for putting out a leg! Now, keep it up! Excellent! Now, that's what I call walking! Magnificent! A little farther, Sir! Farewell! Now remember to tell Colonel Sharp as I directed: you've departed this life. You're dead. Deceased, defunct, and all that sort of thing.
[He pushes HUGO toward the direction of his brother and exits laughing.]

Act Three
Scene Two

[Another day on the streets of Frankfort. SOLOMON Sharp encounters Jereboam BEAUCHAMP who carries with him a dueling box.]

SOLOMON
Jereboam Beauchamp, you are here!

BEAUCHAMP
I am Jereboam Beauchamp, and you see me, don't you? Yes, I am here.

SOLOMON
Sir, some strange, some singular mistake -- misunderstanding --has no doubt arisen: you have been urged in the heat of anger to address a letter with some strange words. I am aware of nothing which might warrant you in this thing. I have given you no offense. Am I right? Was your letter a mistake? Undoubtedly it was. We all do make mistakes.

BEAUCHAMP
Draw, villain, and jabber no more!
[He offers two dueling pistols from a box.]

SOLOMON
Ha! Draw? You call me a "villain?" You would duel? What have I ever done to you?
[He examines the guns from the box.]

BEAUCHAMP
The grave awaits you. A tomb to atone your sins—I offer it to you in the name of Anna Cooke!

SOLOMON
In the name of Anna Cooke? You can't be serious.
[He closes the case of dueling pistols.]
Stop it. I will not fight you. I dare not fight.

BEAUCHAMP
I pity you.

SOLOMON

And do you pity Anna?

BEAUCHAMP

Now is Death and Hell! Mark me, sir, do not think that you will get away from me like this. Prepare for public insult in the streets – before the eyes of the citizens. I'll follow you like an avenging spirit; I'll follow you even unto death. Before those whom you love, before all Kentucky, before all the world I'll insult you, villain. I'll humiliate you, do you hear me? You would be a coward and not fight me? You lie! For you shall. If I have to horsewhip you across this good state and back, you will dual with me!
[He exits in a rage.]

SOLOMON

Now, this indeed is justice. Most righteous, and most just, for Heaven comes to judge me.
[He suddenly sees HUGO walking in a daze.]
Hugo, there. What's the matter?

HUGO

I have a message from your brother, Leander.

SOLOMON

A message from Leander? I could use one right now. What message is that?

HUGO

That your faithful servant, Hugo, has done departed this life. Deceased, defunct, and . . . all that sort of thing. He dead.

SOLOMON

I wish I could join you. But wait. Hugo? Dead? But are you not Hugo?

HUGO

Do you mean the one Hugo that belonged to your father Captain Sharp was given to you? That groomer of the stable, that cares so carefully for your horses, that . . . that one strong and handsome—is it that Hugo of you speak? No, I am not that precious soul. I am but a ghost of such a great one as he. A shadow that is passing. A big big shadow, mind you, but just that . . . . a mist.

SOLOMON

This is strange. You look like Hugo. But you are a ghost?

HUGO

Yes. The storm of love has killed me. I have committed the sooicide. I shall
never rise again!
>[He prostrates himself on the ground, arms and legs
>stretched, face down.]

SOLOMON

>[Starting to laugh]

Suicide? This is serious. Tell me, how did you do it?

HUGO

>[Remaining unmoved on the ground. And this is the way that
>SOLOMON feels!]

By wishing.

SOLOMON

Wishing?

HUGO

Yes. Wishing 'she loved me. Oh, I climbed the tree with the rope around my
neck. But then I saw a crow flying by and remembered that if you made a
wish and if he did not flap his wings before he went out of sight, that wish
would come true.

SOLOMON

Did he . . . flap his wings?

HUGO

I don't know. I fell out of the tree.

SOLOMON

And that's how you died?

HUGO

I might have. But at that very moment I landed on my feet. It was a small
tree, see. A bush really. But then I saw a hay wagon--and remembered that
if you make a wish and count thirteen and turn away, that wish will come
true--if you don't see the hay wagon again!

SOLOMON

What happened?

HUGO

The hay wagon ran over me! I only got to ten.

SOLOMON

Oh! And that's how you died!

HUGO

I might have. But at that very moment I bent down: because I heard the
first whippoorwill--and remembered that if you make a wish when you
hear the first whippoorwill of the year and walk three steps backward and
pick up whatever's under your left foot and spit on it, that wish will come
true and Hyacinth will love me—so, I bent down and picked it up. It was
a horseshoe, and you know what I remembered?

SOLOMON

Enlighten me.

HUGO

That if the toe is pointed towards you, you can make a wish if you spit on
it and throw it over your shoulder.

SOLOMON
[Confused]
But how was it that you came to die?

HUGO

At that very moment Ben found a horse shoe pointing towards him and
threw it over his shoulder: it hit me right between the eyes! Sooicide! I
perished.

SOLOMON
[Laughing]
So, Hyacinth has slain you at last! Tell my brother Leander he has succeeded
in making me laugh today!
[But HUGO is not laughing]
Hugo, dying is no way to win a woman's heart. You don't want her pity.
You want her respect! You have to show her that you love her.

66

HUGO

But how can I do that?

SOLOMON

What does she ask of you? But to stop drinking. She wants a sober man who thinks straight about things. Who can be a good husband and father.

HUGO

That's asking a lot.

SOLOMON

Tell me about it. But I did it for my wife, and you can do it for Hyacinth. And I've been a better man for it. And husband. And father. I was a fool before.

HUGO

You think Hyacinth would have me if I sobered up?

SOLOMON

I know she would. It's worth a try, isn't it?

HUGO

[Getting up]

That's cause for an 'erection!

SOLOMON

I think you mean *resurr*ection.

HUGO

That too!

SOLOMON

This must be our lucky day, Hugo. There goes a white horse.

HUGO

Quick! Make a wish and spit over your little finger.

[HUGO does this. They exit, SOLOMON laughing.]

67

Act Three
Scene Three

[Outside Retirement in Glasgow. BEAUCHAMP has been packing his horse.]

POE
Jereboam Beauchamp waited two days for Solomon Sharp, then discovered he had escaped to Bowling Green. There he moved his law practice to lie in wait for Sharp who never appeared. A letter from Anna was ignored. In June of 1824, Jereboam and Anna were married, the promise still to be fulfilled. The deed still to be done.

The threshold of a house and its safety is full of superstition. A groom carries his bride over the threshold so that her foot does not touch the floor and bring bad luck to their marriage. So that the house is a fresh haven of peace and happiness. So that the house becomes their home. The threshold of a house is sacred. And the threshold of this house, the home of Colonel Solomon and Elizabeth Sharp, was the threshold that faced the second Capitol building when it went up in flames and fell into a pile of smoking rubble.

These crumbling walls — these tottering arcades
These moldering plinths — these sad and blackened shafts
These vague entablatures: this broken frieze
These shattered cornices, this wreck, this ruin,
These stones, alas! these grey stones are they all
All of the great and the colossal left
By the corrosive hours to Fate and me?

The Marquis de Lafayette, our hero from the American Revolution, was celebrated from river town to river town. Up the Kentucky River to the town of Frankfort, with its Capital building in ashes, he arrived. And at the banquet was toasted by Colonel Solomon: "To the people: Liberty will always be safe in their holy keeping."

BEAUCHAMP
She comes.

ANNA
[Entering wildly, carrying a scarf and the mask]

If Patrick Darby has been stirring up trouble, it will work to our advantage. If only you can get someone to have him to go to their house and ask questions. It will cause suspicion. He will leave his footsteps in the yard.

BEAUCHAMP

Darby is a vindictive and unrelenting monster. A fool that needs to be gotten rid of, and no one will object. The perfect suspect for us and he hates Sharp.

ANNA

It will be the night before the Legislature meets. Solomon will be making his rounds chatting everyone up in town. He will probably get home late. You will just have to follow him around. That's why the mask.

BEAUCHAMP

It may be late when he retires, then. I'll stay hidden across the street at the ruin of the Capital. They still have not rebuilt it.

ANNA

If his brother is still living in the house with them, make sure he is home and not out with a patient: you wouldn't want him to come home and find you.

BEAUCHAMP

I'll kill the bastard first!

ANNA

No! Not his brother!
        [But this is an odd request. She struggles to explain.]
You will . . . destroy Dr. Leander Sharp by killing his brother. He worships his older brother.
        [She is calmer]
Trust me, it will be enough to kill him when you kill Solomon Sharp.
        [This sounds strange to BEAUCHAMP but he accepts it.]
You will have to listen carefully and find out where they sleep. The house is large. You want to find the door nearest their bedroom. It may be that if they have guests for the Legislature, they have moved to a different room. Be sure all in the house have gone to bed. And now the hour is come for vengeance or will never come again.
        [Quickly and wildly, she dresses him: the scarf to hide his forehead, the minstrel mask to hide his face. She raises the

mask atop his head. She hands him the dagger with the cross handle.]
Jereboam, are you ready?

BEAUCHAMP

As ready as I should be! By the God of Heaven, I'll destroy his blessed threshold and at the foot of its altar leave him dead.
[She pulls the mask to his face. She kisses the mask on the mouth. He exits for his horse.]

ANNA

Now go. Fly away. Farewell! Farewell, Solomon, and farewell my hope in Heaven!
[She exits back into her house.]

POE

And so, we return, where we began, to that haunted November night. Jereboam Beauchamp stabbed Solomon Sharp to death at his own threshold, his bride of seven years standing by helplessly. The ashes of the Capital building watching silently in the shadows.

$5,000 was raised for the reward for the arrest and conviction of the killer— offered by the Governor, the trustees of the city, and friends of Sharp.

There were two Old Court suspects. The first was John Upshaw Waring who had publicly threatened to kill Sharp and had circulated handbills of the Sharp scandal with Anna Cooke. But Waring was recuperating from a gunshot to the hip the day before the murder. And the second was no other than Patrick Darby, the land speculator.

Patrick Henry Darby. Every town has one. That troublemaker who doesn't know he is alive unless he is in the middle of a conflict, stirring it up. They make messes everywhere they go and leave them behind for others to clean up, but go to bed each night enjoying restful sleep. Such a fellow is so loathed that even our playwrights here refuse to portray him—the world is polluted enough without adding to it.

When the New Court Relief members were pointing their fingers at Darby and shouting conspiracy, he quickly began his own investigations. They led Darby to a certain Captain John F. Lowe, who confessed that Beauchamp had told him all about the planned assassination.

Jereboam spent the night after the murder with relatives in Bloomfield, then he made his way to Bardstown for a night, then to Bowling Green before returning to their farm in Glasgow. He and Anna were preparing to flee to Missouri, but a posse from Frankfort arrived at their threshold.

[It is the doorway of Retirement in Glasgow. MCINTOSH, the jailer and others appear to make arrest.]

MCINTOSH

Jereboam Beauchamp. We are here to arrest you for the cold-blooded murder of Colonel Solomon Sharp. And your wife Anna, as your accomplice! *[All disappear as POE enters]*

POE

The trial began on the eighth day of May, 1826. Testimonies against Beauchamp:
[ELIZA passes by on her way to court.]
Eliza Sharp, the widow, who had witnessed the murder herself in their home. **Joel Scott**, the prison warden, who had rented a room to Jereboam that night and found his room empty between the hours of the murder. **Patrick Darby**, who claimed that the Beauchamps demanded from Solomon Sharp the following goods: $1,000.00 in cash, 200 acres of land, and a slave girl in exchange for leaving him alone; and that Sharp had refused to pay, and so they wanted him dead. Of course, the only problem with this story was that Darby had never met the Beauchamps until after the murder.
[HYACIHN passes by, stops and sneers.]
Others suggested that the murder was politically motivated by Darby and his Old Court members. And it didn't work in Darby's favor when he lost control and attacked the defense counsel with his cane! Beauchamp maintained that he was innocent. Things were going well for him. The trial seemed to lean in Beauchamp's favor. Until finally there came the testimony of:
[LOWE passes by on his way to court.]
Captain John F. Lowe, who was able to produce a letter from Beauchamp concerning the planned assassination. And Lowe had witnessed Beauchamp waving a flag with shouts of victory on his return home from the murder. After thirteen days, the jury returned their verdict.

[It is the courthouse in Frankfort, Kentucky. BEAUCHAMP is on the stand. POE speaks for the voice of the judge:]

Jereboam Beauchamp! The Commonwealth of Kentucky finds you guilty for the cold blooded murder of Colonel Solomon Sharp and confirms that on the night of November 6, 1826, on the very doorstep of Colonel Sharp's home, you disguised and armed, did stab Colonel Sharp with a poisonous knife through the heart until he fell dead. You will be taken to Gallows Hill June 16 and hanged until dead. Has the guilty party anything to say?

BEACHAMP
Your Honor. I request time to write something for the benefit of those nearer and dearer to me than life itself. I am innocent. If you say I am guilty, it is for killing out of love.

Act Four
Scene One

[Madison street in front of the house of Captain Sharp. The day of the hanging July 7, 1826. Bells ringing and shouts heard in the distance. Several persons cross and re-cross the stage rapidly. Enter BEN walking quickly. RUPERT enters from the other direction. The two collide. They comically fumble about, compose themselves, and head off in the wrong directions. They stop and turn.]

RUPERT.
Hey there, Ben! Did you say today? Is it today — the hanging?

BEN.
Today I believe.

> *[They continue their exit, realize that they are headed in the wrong direction, turn, pass each other and exit off. HYACINTH sashays in, fantastically dressed, and carrying a large hatbox, almost collides with BEN. She enters at first quickly, then sauntering, and finally stops near the middle of the stage. She is lost in the contemplation of the jewels upon one of her hands, which is ungloved. She at length sets down the hatbox and looks at the watch hanging around her neck.]*

HYACINTH.

It aint late. No! It aint late at all. What need is there of hurry? I'll answer for it. There's time enough to spare. Now, let me see! The hanging is in the hour, and the morning is not half done. I can tell how many minutes there are between then and now: ten, twenty, thirty, forty, fifty, sixty! Sixty minutes! Why I can very easily get all my errands done in half an hour at the most! What better time to go shopping than during a hanging. The shops will be empty! Who'd be without a watch? These are pretty gloves! I won't walk myself to death. I won't. I'll take my time.

[She seats herself on a bench and kicks the hatbox to and fro
with an air of nonchalance. BEN rapidly crosses the stage.]

Hey, Ben! Ben! Ben! Can't you hear? How dare that sassy slave not answer Hyacinth! The wretch won't stoop to even see Hyacinth. And as she sits upon the bank looking so like a lady! She *is* a lady! Hyacinth is indeed! But after all, she thinks there is a difference between some ladies and others. The ignorant, the stupid, the villains! Between her former mistress, Anna Cooke, for instance, and her present noble mistress, the lady Eliza. She made a change for the better she thinks. Indeed, she is sure of it. Besides, you know it was impossible for Hyacinth to stay there when such reports have been circulating about Miss Cooke. Miss Cooke has nothing of the lady about her. Not a tittle! One would have thought Miss Cooke was a peasant girl. Miss Cooke is so humble. Hyacinth hates all humble people! And then Miss Cooke talked to Hyacinth with such an air of hatefulness. Miss Cooke has no common sense, of that Hyacinth is sure. I ask you now, Hyacinth, do you, or do you not suppose your mistress had common sense or understanding when she gave you all them jewels?

[RUPERT rapidly crosses the stage and without noticing
HYACINTH.]

Am I invisible?! That man's a fool or he would not be in a hurry. He would have stopped. If he had not been a *fool* he would have stopped, took off his hat, and, making a low bow, said "I am most superlatively happy to see you, *Madam* Hyacinth." Well, Hyacinth just don't know. Some people are fools by nature. Some have a talent for being stupid. Look at that ass now, Hugo, he thinks Hyacinth will have him. But, oh no! She couldn't. He might just as well--for all the use he makes of it--have been born without a head.

[She looks down at the ring on her finger. There is a premonition
with it that makes her slowly remove it from her hand. She
looks at it and makes a fist around it with her fingers. She
pauses, then moving quickly exits in the direction that it seems
to lead her. From opposite directions, BEN crosses carrying

a bundle and RUPERT crosses with a bundle: the two collide. Unknowingly, they have exchanged bundles and start to exit. Realizing the problem, they clumsily return each to its proper owner.]

RUPERT

I beg your pardon—

BEN

Forgive me—

RUPERT

Have you seen Hugo?

BEN

Undenounced.

RUPERT

Unbeknown.

BEN

Unbelievable!

RUPERT

Where are you going in such a rush?

BEN

To the hanging procession. Isn't it exciting!

RUPERT

I look forward to a good hanging.

BEN

Oh, yes! Me, too.

RUPERT

Still, it's a terrible shame—

BEN

Oh, yes, shocking—

RUPERT

Only one hanging.

BEN

Yes, only one.

RUPERT

The jailer heard Beauchamp tell his uncle, the Colonel, that there were several accomplices in the murder. The New Court suspects Patrick Darby. The Old Court thinks Beauchamp acted alone. I think we shall never know.

BEN

We shall never know.

RUPERT

Darby says that it would not have been such a crime if only Beauchamp had challenged Sharp to a duel in the broad daylight, not killing him in the dead of night. On his own doorstep.

BEN

With a wife and three poor children!

RUPERT

Darby thinks Beauchamp the most abandoned young man he has known. I heard him say he hoped he would die because he knew he was unfit to live!

BEN

The kettle calling the pot black!

RUPERT

I think it's the other way around.

BEN

[BEN turns around]
The kettle calling the pot black!

RUPERT

Darby seems to have riled Beauchamp by telling him that Colonel Sharp had forged documents about the child. Claiming the child was, well, *you know.*

                          BEN

Oh, yes! I know. Oh, yes, how I know.
          [He pauses]
What do I know?

                        RUPERT

          [Whispering]
That the child was born . . . . *colored.*

                          BEN

Goodness, me. *[He pauses.]* What color was it? I love chartreuse. Although
fuschia--

                        RUPERT

          [In a loud whisper]
Negro! And you know what that means!

                          BEN

Oh, yes! I should say I do! What should I say I do?

                        RUPERT

The child could not have been Colonel Sharp's child!

                          BEN

Of course not! Not if it were a girl! Everyone knows that Colonel Sharp
were a boy!
          [Laughing]
Was it a boy?

                        RUPERT

The baby was stillborn!

                          BEN

It makes no never mind, as long as the child is still healthy!

                        RUPERT

The baby's dead!

                          BEN

You mean it's still dead?

RUPERT

Oh, forget it! Besides, I don't think you can trust anything Patrick Darby says. The man's a damned scoundrel.

BEN

Scourge!

RUPERT

A scamp. One of his clients that he was representing was a young free black woman. He took her money and sold her back into slavery! Why, he tried to corrupt the land titles in Clarksville, that they gave him an hour to leave town or they'd take him over the river and beat him as long as there was a beech limb in the bottom!

BEN

The scallywag! Do you think it's true what Beauchamp says: that Darby put him up to the murder?

RUPERT

I think Beauchamp just enjoys tormenting the wretch a little while longer. A very little while longer: Beauchamp and his wife, they poisoned themselves in the cell.

BEN

Aint it dreadful?

RUPERT

Delinquent.

BEN

Delirious--

RUPERT

Short of disastrous: they're still alive. Now! To the hanging—

> *[Once again, they make their exit in opposite directions but collide, this time with RUPERT's bundle dropping letters to the ground. BEN stoops down to gather up the letters for RUPERT. RUPERT is impressed by this and we see admiration in his eyes as he looks at BEN. BEN hands the letters to RUPERT tenderly. RUPERT receives them*

77

affectionately. The two slowly walk together side by side enjoying each others' company as they exit.]

HYACINTH
[Entering with the list Eliza Sharp has given her]
Heigho! What's this? Oh! It's the paper that my lady gave me, with the list of articles she wants: ten yards of taffeta, sixteen of gold brocade, and ten of Genoa velvet. One, two, three, . . .
[As she counts, she tears a slip from the paper at each number, and arranges it on the ground in an abstracted manner, proud of her ability to read.]
Four, five, six, seven. That's it. Now eight, nine, ten . . . ten yards. I can't forget it now. Ten yards: ten yards of velvet. Hyacinth must try and get her a dress of Genoa velvet. It's so becoming. And she would look so much like her lady in it! I think I see her now. Oh! She's a lady worth serving indeed. Oh, she has airs and graces and dignity. Yes! She has dignity, Mrs. Eliza Sharp.
[Arises and struts affectedly across the stage.]
And then she has a voice. Heavens! What a voice! So loud, so lady-like, and so commanding! "Hyacinth, get me this." "D'ye hear?" "Bring that." Then "Yes, ma'am," Hyacinth replies, and curtsies thus meekly and daintily thus. Oh! Hyacinth is a maid of one in a thousand for a dainty curtsey. But when Hyacinth gets to be a lady . . . When she weds the apothecary . . . oh, then it will be a different thing. A different thing indeed! She'll play her lady to a T, that she will. She'll be all dignity, and talk thus: "Hugo, you villain!" Hugo shall be her slave.
[During this part of the soliloquy Hugo enters unperceived and watches. He is well dressed and handsome as a respectable groomsman.]
She will say to him at last, "Hugo, you villain! Look you here, you rascal! You good-for-nothing, idle, lazy scoundrel! What are you doing here? Be gone you ugly, you silly, sulky, dirty, stupid idiot! Begone, Hyacinth says this minute. Get out of her, you viper. Get out, you jackass! 'Out you vagabond!" And *then* if he's not gone in half a minute, Hyacinth will turn about and let him have it!
[Swinging with her fist]
It's as well now as any other time. Thus. Thus . . .
[She strikes again and again]
I'll let you have it thus — thus — thus
[She has stepped on the hatbox and her foot has gone through it!]

78

Look what you made me do, you wretch! I'll let you have it thus--thus —
thus —
> *[She throws the box at him and puts the ruined hat on her
> head, then turns to see HUGO and is stupefied.]*

HUGO

I am most superlatively happy to see you, Madam Hyacinth.

HYACINTH

I'm sorry, I didn't see you standing there.
> *[She adjusts her hat]*

Hugo?

HUGO

How beautiful you look today, my Lady.

HYACINTH

My Lady? Oh, this old rag? It's just something I had—Hugo? That can't
be you?

HUGO

> *[Bowing]*

At your service, Madam.

HYACINTH

But you've changed. You're so handsome—
> *[Suddenly back to her old humor]*

Where the hell have you been lately?!

HUGO

I have gone respectable, my Lady. And high time too, I must say. Master
Leander has promoted me as head groomsman over all the stables of the
estate. And you, I understand have new arrangement with Mrs. Elizabeth
Sharp.

HYACINTH

Yeah. She bought me from Miss Cooke. So, I could be here and . . . well, . . .
So, I could be here.

79

And I was never happier. She was not good enough for a Lady's Maid such as yourself.

HYACINTH

Hugo, are you drunk?

HUGO

I never touch the bottle now. It is not respectable. Maybe for some but not for Hugo.

HYACINTH

I can't believe my eyes—

HUGO

The shops are quite empty now. Might I escort my Lady around the town to finish her shopping? I might be of some help to direct her to the choicest shops with the very best prices?

> *[He bows and offers her his arm. Dazzled, she takes it. They exit together, HYACINTH not taking her eyes off HUGO.]*

Act Four
Scene Two

[It is the prison cell in the cellar of John McIntosh's house, Lewis and Clinton Street, Frankfort, Kentucky. The only entrance is a trap door in the ceiling, and the only outside light is from a grate to the street above. ANNA reads from their writings. July 15, 1826.]

ANNA

"After we had taken the laudanum last night at about 12 o'clock, we remained on our knees some hours at prayer, and then laid down and placed our bodies in the fond embrace which we wished them interred—"

BEAUCHAMP

"--My wife laid her head on my right arm, with which I encircled her body, and tied my right hand to her left upon her bosom . . ."

ANNA

"Thus, we lay in prayer for hours in momentary expectation of dropping to sleep, to awake in eternity . . ."

BEAUCHAMP

Lord Byron would be proud!

ANNA

It is good, isn't it?
                        [She hands him back the journal. He continues to write.]

BEAUCHAMP

It is our love letter to the world. It will sell thousands of copies—people are hungry for this. And it will buy us our freedom!
                        [Eagerly he continues to write. John MCINTOSH, the jailer, lifts the trap door and speaks.]

MCINTOSH

Mr. Beauchamp, there are preachers here to see you.

ANNA

Good God, will they never leave us alone.

BEAUCHAMP

Tell them to go away. We can't be disturbed right now.

MCINTOSH

I'll tell them to speak to you through the grate.

ANNA

No! Damn them. I'll cover that window. Can you see well enough with the candle, my love?

BEAUCHAMP

Yes. Cover it.
                        [ANNA goes to cover the window with a blanket, but the ministers are already there. We hear only their voices.]

PREACHER

Mrs. Beauchamp, Good morning. Brother Clay and brother Noel and brother Waller are all here with me. May we come in and talk with you?

81

ANNA

I was just about to cover the window. We are not well—

PREACHER

Yes, we were told that you had taken poison. Let us come in and pray with you—

ANNA

Brother, my husband regrets it more than any other act of his life. Now, please, the light hurts his eyes--

BEAUCHAMP

Tell them to come back this afternoon.

ANNA

Did you hear? My husband says to come back this afternoon. We will talk with you then.

PREACHER

But Mrs. Beauchamp, your immortal soul—

ANNA

We are both confident, Brother, that our sins are forgiven and we will be happy beyond the grave.
                    [While continuing their pleas she covers the window]
May we see you there as well.
                    [We hear MCINTOSH, the jailer, from above]

MCINTOSH

The governor has ordered your removal, Mrs. Beauchamp. You must come with me.

ANNA

What?!

MCINTOSH

He has heard of the poison you took and wants you removed. You are not guilty, Mrs. Beauchamp, the court acquitted you. It is only your husband who is guilty—

ANNA

No! Tell the Governor that I will not leave my husband. I don't care what he was told, it is all lies. Lies to separate us. I won't leave my husband if you drag me out of here. I tell you, I won't!--

MCINTOSH

Mrs. Beauchamp, I'm coming down there—

ANNA

Come then. Beat me. Drag me. I will fight you off with every ounce of energy I have left. I will, I swear it! I am not leaving this cell!

BEAUCHAMP

Would you drag an innocent woman against her will? How cruel can you be, man?

MCINTOSH

[Resigning.]
All right then.

ANNA

[To BEAUCHAMP]
"You shall never be buried until I am dead also. Even if I have to starve myself to death."
> *[BEAUCHAMP looks to her with tenderness, but her words*
> *are meant for him to write: she indicates the journal, for him*
> *to record her dictation.]*

MCINTOSH

Mr. Beauchamp, your father is here to see you, with your uncle, the Colonel.

BEAUCHAMP

Tell them we cannot see anyone.
> *[He continues to write.]*

ANNA

Will they never leave us in peace!
> *[She continues to dictate. He writes.]*
"I commit myself for forgiveness upon the mercy of an all merciful God, who has forgiven all the sins of my life . . ."
> *[THOMAS Beauchamp is descending the ladder.]*

BEAUCHAMP

Father, ...You have brought word from the Governor? He has issued a pardon?

THOMAS

I told you that he will not.

BEAUCHAMP

But an exile? He will permit me to go into exile?

THOMAS

No. I told you. Under no conditions. He is most resolute.

BEAUCHAMP

But when the public reads my *Confessions*, they will force him––

THOMAS

I told you, no one will touch it. They will not publish it, no one will! What about this do you refuse to understand?! You are going to be hanged in a few hours!

> *[BEAUCHAMP backs away from him. We hear drums in the street.]*

My son. I know that you did not act alone with this. But you are the one they will hang.

BEAUCHAMP

We will spare them that. Anna and I have already taken poison.

THOMAS

No! My son, no––

BEAUCHAMP

It is too late. Last night in prayer we lifted the fatal cup to our lips.

THOMAS

You are not in possession of your proper reason--

BEAUCHAMP

I did it with the clearest dictates of my judgement, asking forgiveness from our Father in Heaven. But heaven has been silent. Give me your dagger, Father!

84

THOMAS

You know that I do not carry one——

BEAUCHAMP

But my uncle, he carries a dirk——

THOMAS

No! He would feel himself an accomplish in the crime. No. You must prepare for death, my son, death at the gallows.
> *[THOMAS embraces his son and weeps. He holds the face of his son in his hands and whispers something to him that we cannot hear. Something that ANNA tries to hear but cannot. Something between father and son and their God. The drums stop. BEAUCHAMP hands his father the manuscript, now with additional pages.]*

BEAUCHAMP

Take it anyway. It has no purpose here.
> *[THOMAS takes the manuscript of his son's Confessions. He looks to his son, but cannot speak for the emotions choke him; he ducks his head and climbs up the ladder with the manuscript. BEAUCHAMP returns to the desk and sits. He sits in silence.]*

ANNA

[Sarcastically]
So, it's a sin to take one's life. But not a sin to be hanged by the neck. Hanged, drawn and quartered!
> *[Still silence.]*

BEAUCHAMP

You should not have come here.

ANNA

You have my heart, where else would I go? You are the lord of my bosom's love. I will rise with you and roam the starry and quiet dwellings of the blest! In Heaven!

BEAUCHAMP

If not Heaven, then Hell. You had no one to avenge your honor. Your father had died. Your brothers all dead . . .

ANNA

Yes—

BEAUCHAMP

So, I took their place. You said that all your brothers are dead?

ANNA

Yes, all of them. And we will join them now, my love—

BEAUCHAMP

How did they die? The War?

ANNA

Yes, the War.

BEAUCHAMP

After that night--the night I knocked at his door and avenged your honor--a few nights later, I lodged at a tavern. The man there said he was your brother.

ANNA

What? You never told me this—

BEAUCHAMP

He claimed to be your brother.

ANNA

He lied.

MCINTOSH
[From above.]
They are coming for you. I will come down.

ANNA

No! Wait! Please. I am not dressed.

MCINTOSH

All right. Then hurry.
        *[ANNA reaches inside her bodice and reveals the bottle of
        poison. She uncorks it.]*
Let us finish this.

[She recites Romeo's words from Romeo and Juliet:]
Come, bitter conduct, come, unsavory guide!
Thou desperate pilot, now at once run on
The dashing rocks thy sea-sick weary bark!
Here's to my love!
[She hands him the bottle. He takes it and pretends to drink.
He hands it back to her.]
O true apothecary!
Thy drugs are quick—Thus with a kiss I die!
[She pretends to drink and quickly corks the bottle. She
kisses him while hiding the bottle back inside her dress.]
There is a land, my love——

BEAUCHAMP

A thousand leagues within the golden west? A fairy land of flowers, and fruit, and sunshine,

ANNA

And crystal lakes, and over-arching forests,

BEAUCHAMP

And mountains, which air to breathe is Happiness now,

ANNA

--and will be Freedom hereafter in days that are to come. Fly to that Paradise with me!
[There is a pause. He pulls away from their embrace. She waits]

BEAUCHAMP

It does not work. . . . . . Its antidote stops it.

ANNA

What antidote?

BEAUCHAMP

Yes, what antidote?

ANNA

[She hands him the cross handled dagger, something she has cleverly kept hidden for the right moment.]

87

Hurry. Take this. Join me.

*[He holds the dagger. They hear a noise and look up. She
recites the words of Juliet:]*

Yea, noise?--Then I'll be brief. O happy dagger! This is thy sheath--

*[She snatches the dagger from him and aims it at her heart.
But he stops her and takes the knife.]*

BEAUCHAMP

What antidote?

ANNA

There is no antidote—

*[She reaches for the knife but BEAUCHAMP moves away
from her. He produces a ring, the same ring that HYACINTH
wore.]*

Where did you get that?

BEAUCHAMP

Your slave girl, Hyacinth, passed it to me through the grate. While you
were sleeping. You recognize it?

ANNA

No . . .

~ BEAUCHAMP

Sure, you do. He gave it to you. Now, why would a man give a woman a
ring that was glass? It is, you know. Just glass. Now, if it were real, it would
pledge his love. But it's not real. So, why would a man be wearing a ring
such as this . . . but that it must have had sentiment. Yes. Sentiment only.

[She reaches for the dagger but he moves away from her.]

And what does the sentiment represent if he gives it to her? Not love. No.
But a promise. A vow to keep. To keep . . . . a secret?

*[He turns his back to her and moves to the desk. He takes
an empty sheet of paper left behind from the manuscript and
positions it on the table by the pen.]*

My father spoke with your brother.

ANNA

He is a liar! A coward!

88

BEAUCHAMP

My father or your brother? Just how many liars and cowards are there? He spoke with two of them. Are there two of your brothers still living? Or are there more?

ANNA

They are dead to me.

BEAUCHAMP

And neither would avenge your honor? Neither of them?

ANNA

Hurry, my love, take the dagger now—

BEAUCHAMP

No. The antidote stops it. The antidote of truth.
            [ANNA buries her face in her hands and cries.]
What is that truth, Anna? Before God in heaven who will soon be receiving our souls, what is that truth?!

ANNA
            [Weakly]
Solomon Sharp . . . is an honorable man.

BEAUCHAMP

He was guilty!

ANNA

He was guilty, yes, guilty of being my lawyer. And guilty of coming to my house upon my request. Over legal matters with the farm and nothing more.

BEAUCHAMP

It is the poison that speaks. He is a villain!

ANNA

Solomon came that night because I sent for him. The night when I— delivered my child.
            [The thought of the child provokes great sadness and regret within her. She smiles with tenderness when remembering its brief life.]

89

Another man might have left, but he in his chivalry meant to stay to see that I was safe. And he learned from the midwife--I was in no position to stop her, you see, to keep him from knowing--

BEAUCHAMP

That the child was his bastard—

ANNA

No. No.
[She pauses. She looks at him.]
It was not his.
[He sees the truth in her eyes.]
And being the man he was, he told no one. He gave me that ring as a vow.

BEAUCHAMP

No . . . . No . . . !

ANNA

Yes, my love. I am the villain. Forgive me—

BEAUCHAMP

No! You can't be saying that those rumors—those terrible lies—
[Her eyes burn with tears of regret]
No! Tell me the truth. Tell me the truth!
[He grabs her violently for a confession. He shakes her, but realizing that the jailer might hear him, covers her mouth. He waits to hear any approach of the jailer. None.]
I have killed an innocent man?!
[Violently nodding her head, he throws her to the floor where she huddles and weeps.]
You whore!
[The phantom secret that has haunted him for months now steps out from the shadows revealing itself as their constant cell companion. To himself:]
That's why you didn't want me to kill his brother . . . because you knew he was innocent.
[BEAUCHAMP paces the cell. Trying to understand what she has told him. Trying to picture it all in his mind. This portrait of blatant betrayal. This stranger that has long awaited introductions.]

90

ANNA

[Sitting up, she adjusts her hair. To herself.]

They said that chivalry was dead. And then you came. 'Defended me against those terrible rumors. Oh, they were terrible. As terrible as a *dragon*. In this day and time, there is nothing worse. Nothing so fierce. So, men say. The ones who make the rules. You came and defended my honor. Or was it your own that you defended?

> *[ANNA gets up and uncovers the window. The light comes inside.]*

You accuse *me*.

> *[ANNA watches the traffic of feet as they pass the ground window grate]*

This double standard of yours. It's all right for a man. But not a woman. No, not a woman. Sure, he can take to his bed as many slave women as he likes and increase his surplus property value. But dare a woman look longingly at one dark skinned man—one beautiful young man . . . I was lonely. Long before I met you. And he was kind. What of *you*?

> *[Puzzled, he looks at her.]*

You . . . so eager to kill.

BEAUCHAMP

Because I *loved*!

ANNA

[She is not afraid of him.]

But you could not have the one you *loved*. Nor could I. And so, you did what you had to do, what I had to do, the only thing to do, the only way to deal with it: to kill it.

> *[BEAUCHAMP trembles; his nakedness revealed.]*

We wanted the same thing. We are guilty, don't you see, of the same crime? For loving the one we had to kill.

> *[BEAUCHAMP is silent.]*

Can you deny it?

BEAUCHAMP

[She has silenced his rage. With a dagger to the heart.]

Then this love of ours was only the love for . . .*[SOLOMON]*

ANNA

Love and hate. Two sides of the same coin.

BEAUCHAMP

Now he is gone. And what have we left between us? Oh, my God!
[He falls to the floor. There is a silence. The drums begin again.]

ANNA

[She kneels beside him.]
At last the poison begins its work. Oh, hold me, Jereboam. Tell me that you forgive me.
[She falls into his arms.]
Do you hate me?

BEAUCHAMP

This thing between us has been nothing less than a fever. A power beyond our control. If I blame you, I must blame myself . . .

ANNA

Then you love me? Tell me you love me. That you love me still--

BEAUCHAMP

Have I a choice?

ANNA

[Pulling away, desperate to be seen clean before him]
I never took the poison.

BEAUCHAMP

[Holding back his laughter]
Neither did I.
[He bursts into laughter. She laughs. All of the anger, rage, deceit, and fear is released as loud as—no louder than--the drums from the street. When they stop laughing, they are both out of breath. The drums stop. He pushes her hair aside and holds her face. He looks at her as he has never looked at her before.]
I think I am meeting you for the first time. And . . there are no words.

ANNA

Had I met you long ago, I would never have been so lonely. If only we had met ten years earlier!

BEAUCHAMP

Yes. I would have been twelve.
> *[They laugh. We hear footsteps from above. The two quickly rise. The drums start again. Desperately, he kisses her. With the knife, he stabs her. She falls.]*

With your blood I am killed.
> *[He stabs himself with the bloody dagger. He falls. ANNA reaches for her husband but can only reach the knife from the floor. Immediately MCINTOSH and others enter down the ladder.]*

We have killed ourselves.

Act Four
Scene Three

[Upstairs, a bedroom in the house of John McIntosh, just hours later. HYACINTH, simply dressed, watches at the window. ELIZA is kneeling, attending to a dying ANNA.]

HYACINTH

Stabbed, yet they do not die. They'll be taking him to the gallows now. Hyacinth never seen so many people. People pourin' in from every direction. Must be thousands.

ELIZA

As many as were here for the visit of Lafayette.

HYACINTH

More.

ELIZA

That's a sad commentary on our people.

HYACINTH

Give them what they want, they'll believe any lie. The truth aint so easy.
> *[ANNA moves. ELIZA attends.]*

ELIZA

Her breathing is slow. But still she breathes.

93

HYACINTH

You should have refused her when she called for you. She just done it to ease her conscience, you know. Hyacinth would have refused her. Hyacinth hate her.

ELIZA

Hate is the worst of daggers. And hurts worse the one that strikes with it. The Samaritan stopped and helped the man on the road to Jerusalem, and that man was his enemy.

HYACINTH
[As MCINTOSH and PREACHER enter with BEAUCHAMP]
They are coming here.

MCINTOSH

You see her. Now, let's go.

BEAUCHAMP

She is not better. You lied to me! No, she is dying!

MCINTOSH

I said only that you could see her. Now, come——

BEAUCHAMP

Let me go to her!

MCINTOSH

No. Now, come——

BEAUCHAMP

This is my wife! My wife who is dying, and you refuse her husband a decent farewell? Let me just go to her for a moment.

PREACHER

He is about to be hanged. What harm can it do?

MCINTOSH
[Releasing him.]
Very well, then. For a moment——

94

BEAUCHAMP
[Stumbling to ANNA's side. ELIZA recoils.]
Does she live?

ELIZA
*[How dare he have the audacity to speak to her! Her eyes
burn with emotion.]*
As well as she deserves.

BEAUCHAMP
*[In removing his hand from his side, we see the blood from
his stabbing. He cradles ANNA's face with his hands.]*
My dear, do you know that this is the hand of your husband?
[But there is no response. To ANNA]
Farewell, child of sorrow— Farewell child of misfortune and persecution—
you are now secure from the tongue of slander—
[But there is sarcasm in his words, bitterness]
For you I have lived; for you I die.
*[BEAUCHAMP kisses her twice. Once for the blind love he
once bore for her. Another for their new acquaintance.]*
I am now ready to go.
[HYACINTH grunts. He turns to ELIZA and HYACINTH:]
From you, ladies, I would expect a tear of sympathy!
*[MCINTOSH pulls him away. LOWE enters with LEANDER
and a hush falls over the room. LEANDER is almost
unrecognizable: tired and worn, his grief has changed him,
aged him. If there is sympathy in the room, it is felt for him.
Avoiding LEANDER, BEAUCHAMP offers his hand to LOWE
who refuses it. BEAUCHAMP addresses the PREACHER:]*
Preacher, I want you to know that I have found salvation.
[MCINTOSH takes BEAUCHAMP out.]

LEANDER
[Acrimoniously]
How convenient.

HYACINTH
He's getting what he rightfully deserves.

95

PREACHER

If we all got what we rightfully deserved, there would be little hope for any of us.

>[He exits with LOWE following. ELIZA goes to LEANDER and embraces him. We hear the pounding of drums from the street. POE appears at the side and takes up the end of the poem as the drums sound.]>

POE

"Not all our power is gone; not all our Fame;
Not all the magic of our high renown;
Not all the wonder that encircles us;
Not all the mysteries that in us lie;
Not all the memories that hang upon,
And cling around about us now and ever,
And clothe us in a robe of more than glory."

HYACINTH

>[She watches as LEANDER exits; she goes to the window.]>
The wagon done stopped. He's calling for somebody . . . Good Lord, it's Patrick Darby! That devil! **He wants him to acquit him.**
>[She laughs]>
Oh, the words!

ELIZA

What are they saying?

HYACINTH

You being a good Christian woman you wouldn't want to hear! Darby's face is as red as a poker, and Beauchamp just a wavin' him off.
>[She imitates the wave like a queen.]>

ELIZA

They tell me you were there that night. The night when all of this began. The night she gave birth.

HYACINTH

Hyacinth was there.

ELIZA

Was there really ever a child?

HYACINTH

Oh, there was a child all right. Your Colonel was there. He were only there as a gentleman. Because Hyacinth called for him, he came. He were a honorable man, ma'am, to a dishonorable woman.

ELIZA

You speak harshly of your mistress. The child was born dead. Such a thing is hard for a woman.

HYACINTH

That child weren't born dead.

ELIZA

What are you saying?

HYACINTH

How we know that woman didn't kill that child, as good as you'd kill a fly in the ointment. She killed it because it was--.

ELIZA

Dear God in heaven. How can you say such a thing! Did you see it?

HYACINTH

No, they rushed the little thing away and buried it. But I wouldn't put it past her. No, I wouldn't!

ELIZA

I guess . . .

HYACINTH

Such baby has no chance in this life. No. Better off it be dead. I could almost feel sorry for Miss Anna, if I knowed it was true. I only know what I believe. I know that none of this murder would've happened had your husband not a-been there and seen it for hiself. Been a witness to it all. He knows the truth. That's why Hyacinth speak so harsh to her. She force Hyacinth to keep her ugly secret. She bribed Hyacinth with all those jewelries. But they was only paste! Hyacinth should have knowd it was coming. She should have knowd.

ELIZA

How could you have known?

HYACINTH

Hyacinth see things.

ELIZA

Ah, yes. So, I've been told.

HYACINTH

Hyacinth aint ashamed of it. She was just too tempted by that jewelry, that's all. She couldn't see straight.
        [Carefully]
Hyacinth saw the murder too.

ELIZA

Did you?

HYACINTH

'Before it happened.

ELIZA

Did you, really? Why didn't you tell someone?

HYACINTH

Hyacinth did. But no one listened. Who gunna listen to a slave girl?
        [She looks out the window]
Hyacinth see a good future for you and your children, ma'am. What don't destroy us make us stronger.

ELIZA

Thank you, Hyacinth. You are kind to say that. Tell me. Can you see the gallows?

HYACINTH
        [Watching from the window.]
Up there on the hill? Too far away to see.

ELIZA

But you can.

HYACINTH

'You makin fun of Hyacinth?

ELIZA

No. Not at all. I believe you.

HYACINTH

*[She sees the sincerity in ELIZA's eyes. Turning back to the
window, she focuses on her gift.]*
Hyacinth will try. For you she'll try.
[As she concentrates]
Yes, a good future for you, ma'am. The . . . President, yes, . . . he is going
to ask for your hand . . . My! My! Hyacinth has seen it.

ELIZA

*[Such weird ideas make her almost question HYACINTH's
abilities.]*
The gallows?

HYACINTH

[Now, back to BEAUCHAMP. Aware of something]
They's asking if he wants to speak to the crowd. He says no. He is ready
to go to his wife. Go to the devil, he means!

ELIZA

Tell me more. All that you see.

HYACINTH

He asking to change the music. Wants a livelier tune. Napoleon . . .

ELIZA

I hear nothing from here.

HYACINTH

He's askin' for water. Now, they be putting the noose around his neck—
they got to hold him up from falling. Two men it take to hold him up. Two
Negros. There, it is on.
*[ANNA reaches for her neck. Then she is heard giving a
heavy sigh.]*
There, the deed is done.

*[ANNA dies. ELIZA and HYACINTH look at the same time
to ANNA realizing that she has died the very moment of
BEAUCHAMP's death.]*

99

ELIZA

It is well. It is very well. At last. At last.

POE

It put Kentucky on the map of the world; they named it, "The Kentucky Tragedy." For some, it was the first time they had heard of the state. This tragedy. This great tragedy.

What made it "great?"
Was it the murder for love of a husband avenging the honor of his wife?
Was it the death of an innocent man—in the prime of his life—murdered in cold blood on his own doorstep while his wife watched and his children slept?
Or was it the hunger of the world for romance as entertaining as the murderous games in the Colosseum?

> *[RUPERT, HUGO, BEN, ELIZA, and HYACINTH enter as narrators.]*

RUPERT

Beauchamp's *Confessions* were finally published and became enormously popular across the country and the oceans. Its publisher, however, was sued for $40,000 from John Lowe and others, and had to flee to Mexico where he became a priest.

HUGO

Leander Sharp spent the rest of his life vindicating the tarnished good name of his brother; his *Vindication* was never published in his lifetime for fear of Patrick Darby's threat of libel.

BEN

And President-elect Harrison, whose wife was ill, did ask for Elizabeth Sharp to preside with him over the White House in Washington; but she refused, content to rear her children and remember her late husband.

ELIZA

The resting place of Solomon Sharp and his wife is honored with a marble shaft reaching to the heavens, inscribed with the words: *"Solomon P. Sharp was assassinated while extending the hand of hospitality . . ."* And beneath it: *"What thou knowest not now, thou shalt know hereafter."*

HYACINTH

Thomas Beauchamp had the bodies of Jereboam and Anna buried in a single grave; beneath the soil there, in one casket, two skeletons are entwined. Their stone bears these words:

Entombed below in each other's arms
The husband and the wife repose,
Safe from life's never-ending storms,
And safe from all of their cruel foes.

[RUPERT, HUGO, BEN, ELIZA, and HYACINTH exit as a mist approaches.]

POE

On those cold gray days of autumn, if late at night there comes a knock at your door, don't answer it. Around the bonfires in Kentucky, they say that it may be the knock of Jereboam Beauchamp, who has left the entwined embrace of his love to search the thresholds for a victim. With a knife he travels from the grave, going door to door. Waiting for someone to answer and come out. It matters not that you be guilty or innocent. What matters is that his lover be avenged. Out of honor for love. Or maybe, . . . maybe it is just the wind that we hear? And *nevermore*? This was an unfinished play. I'd keep my door locked at night.

[POE turns, walks down the street, and disappears in the mist.]

CURTAIN

Postscript

Figure 1
Solomon Porcious Sharp by
Matthew Harris Jouett

Solomon Porcius Sharp
[August 22, 1787—November 7, 1825]

Solomon Sharp was born in Abingdon, Virginia, son of Revolutionary War veteran Thomas Sharp who participated in the Battle of King's Mountain. The Sharp family moved to Russellville, Logan County, Kentucky in 1795; Kentucky previously part of Virginia became its own state in 1792. Admitted to the Bar in 1806, he relocated to Bowling Green, Warren County, Kentucky where he and brother, Dr. Leander Sharp, partnered in land speculation.

Solomon served in the Kentucky House of Representatives from 1809 to 1811. During the War of 1812, he moved from private to major in just twelve days, and later to colonel. He was elected to the Thirteenth and Fourteenth Congress of the United States House of Representatives, lost his seat in 1816 over his support for the Compensation Act, but was reelected the following year. He advanced in place in Frankfort society by marrying the daughter of a physician and officer in the War of 1812, Eliza T. Scott, who bore him three children. They moved to Frankfort, the capital of Kentucky in 1820, to further his political career.

Figure 2
Home of Solomon Sharp, Madison Street, Frankfort, Kentucky

President Madison said that he "was the ablest man of his age who had represented the west." But his 1821 campaign for the Kentucky Senate was plagued by violent altercations from John U. Waring, which drove him to accept instead an appointment as attorney General of Kentucky by Governor John Adair. He sided with the Debt Relief Party that favored debtors over creditors to the exclusion of Old Court supporters such as Kentucky favorite Henry Clay, and supported Andrew Jackson in the 1824 presidential election. He was elected to the House during this bitter controversy, a dangerous position for Solomon Sharp.[4]

During the early morning of November 7, 1825, twenty-three-year-old Jereboam O. Beauchamp knocked at the Madison Street residence of the Sharp family and stabbed Solomon Sharp to death. The following year Sharp's brother Dr. Leander Sharp wrote his own book to defend his brother's honor, *Vindication of the Character of the Late Col. Solomon P. Sharp,* where he named Patrick Darby, Anti-Relief partisan, a conspirator with Beauchamp. Due to threats, Leander did not publish his *Vindication,* although it was discovered years later.[5]

Jereboam Beauchamp
[September 6, 1802—July 7, 1826]

Named after his uncle the Kentucky State Senator, Jereboam O. Beauchamp was educated at Dr. Benjamin Thurston's academy in Barren County, Kentucky. He pursued law after being influenced by Glasgow and Bowling Green attorneys such as Solomon Sharp but became disillusioned by Sharp when the scandal arose that accused Sharp of fathering Anna Cooke's illegitimate stillborn child. Beauchamp fell in love with Anna

Figure 3
Jereboam Beauchamp stabs Solomon Sharp; illustration from *The United States Criminal Calendar*, 1835.

Cooke, and married her with the promise that he would avenge her honor. She was sixteen years his senior. Together they plotted the murder of Sharp which after several attempts took place on November 7, 1825.

---

[4] L. F. Johnson, *Kentucky Tragedies and Trials*, (Lexington, Kentucky: Henry Clay Press, 1972), pp. 44-45.
[5] "Squire" J. Winston Coleman, Jr., *Sketches of Kentucky's Past*, "The Beauchamp—Sharp Tragedy," (Lexington, Kentucky: Winburn Press, 1979), pp. 129-33.

Tried and condemned to hang, Beauchamp was granted a stay of execution during which he wrote his book *The Confession of Jereboam O. Beauchamp: who was hanged at Frankfort, Ky., on the 7th day of July, 1826, for the murder of Col. Solomon P. Sharp.* Both Jereboam and Anna attempted suicide in prison but Jereboam was hanged on July 7, 1826, and Anna died in her cell. The two were buried by Beauchamp's father together in a single grave at Maple Gove Cemetery, Bloomfield, Kentucky. His book was published and the tale of murder to avenge love was a national sensation with the public.

Anna Cooke
[February 6, 1786—July 7, 1826]

Anna Cooke was thought to be from a fine family in Tidewater, Virginia: her father Giles Cooke owned twenty-two slaves and thousands of acres of land while her mother, Alicia Payne, was related to First Lady Dolley Payne Madison and her uncle had been a pallbearer to President George Washington.[6] She was the fifth child between nine brothers and one sister. She was remembered as being educated, a reader and discusser of books, and a poet. Her refusal to marry suggests she was strongly influenced by her reading of Mary Wollstonecraft, the great advocate for women's equality and mother of authoress Mary Shelley. Leander Sharp wrote that she denounced organized religion. Although never referred to as a beauty, she was remembered with "a sprightliness and gaiety, which once made her the delight of the social circles in which she moved, and commanded the admiration of her acquaintances."[7] She married Jereboam O. Beauchamp in June 1824, under the agreement that he would avenge her honor by killing Colonel Solomon Sharp, the man she professed had abandoned her unmarried with his child. After her death, *The Letters of Ann Cook* was published gathering the sympathies of a romantic hungry public.

---

[6] Dr. and William Carter Stubbs, *Descendants of Mordecai Cooke, of "Mordecai's Mount," Gloucester Co., Va., 1650, and Thomas Booth, of Ware Neck, Gloucester Co., Va., 1685,* (New Orleans., 1923), pp. 102-11, Brooke Payne, *The Paynes of Virginia*, 2nd ed. (Harrisonburg, VA: Carrier, 1977), pp. 244, 246.

[7] Christine Jacobson Carter, *Southern Single Blessedness; Unmarried Women in the Urban South, 1800-1865* (Urbana: University of Illinois Press, 2006).

Edgar Allan Poe
[January 19, 1809—October 7, 1849]

Edgar Allan Poe was born into a theatrical family. Due to alcoholism and the hard criticism he received for his stage talent, his father, David Poe, Jr., disappeared a year after his birth. His mother, the English actress, Elizabeth Arnold, died of tuberculosis the following year, the Richmond Theater of Virginia giving a benefit performance on her behalf as she lay dying. Her children were separated with Edgar taken into the family of John and Frances Allan. Edgar attended the University of Virginia for one year but due to financial reasons in 1827, withdrew to

Figure 4
Edgar Allan Poe, daguerreotype, by photographer Edwin H. Manchester, 1848.

be enlisted in the United States Army. His *Tamerlane and Other Poems* was published under the pseudonym "a Bostonian." Failing as an officer cadet at West Point, he pursued a career as writer, editor, and literary critic.

Edgar Allan Poe wrote his only known drama in 1835, centered around the then popular Solomon Sharp Kentucky murder, an event that seemed to catch the hearts of the nation less than ten years before. As many of the figures were still living and the embers of the horrific event still moldering, he chose to disguise the historical figures and location and set his play in 16th Century Rome, naming and fashioning its main character after the Italian poet during the Florentine Renaissance, "Poliziano." The beginning of his play appeared in the December issue of the Southern Literary Messenger entitled *Scenes from Politian, an Unpublished Drama*. The play continued in the next month's edition but then stopped.

Poe found that the "the real events were more impressive than the fictional ones." But "the real events" were scripted by Beauchamp and Cooke who in their own writings contrived the tale. "They concocted all of this, years earlier, for the two, steeped in the literature of the era, knew exactly what Americans wanted and expected to hear, and with that knowledge, they tapped into the cultural touchstones of the era's literature: seduction and honor and reckless heroism."[8] The unfinished Poe play has since been referred to as *"Politian."*

---

[8] Matthew G. Schoenbachler, *Murder and Madness, the Myth of the Kentucky Tragedy*, (Lexington: The University Press of Kentucky, 2011), pp. 235, 243-4.

Bibliography

Beauchamp, Jereboam O. *The Confession of Jereboam O. Beauchamp : who was hanged at Frankfort, Ky., on the 7th day of July, 1826, for the murder of Col. Solomon P. Sharp. 1826.* Gale, Sabin Americana, February 22, 2012.

Carter, Christine Jacobson. *Southern Single Blessedness; Unmarried Women in the Urban South, 1800-1865.* Urbana: University of Illinois Press, 2006.

Coleman, Jr., "Squire" J. Winston. *Sketches of Kentucky's Past*, "The Beauchamp—Sharp Tragedy." Lexington, Kentucky: Winburn Press, 1979.

Johnson, L. F. *Famous Kentucky Tragedies and Trials.* Louisville, Kentucky: The Baldwin Law Book Company, 1916, Lexington, Kentucky: Henry Clay Press, 1972;   *The History of Franklin County, Kentucky.* Frankfort, Kentucky: Roberts Printing Co., 1912.

Payne, Brooke. *The Paynes of Virginia*, 2nd ed. Harrisonburg, VA: Carrier, 1977.

Poe, Edgar Allan. *Broadway Journal*, March 29, 1845; *Complete Poems*, edited by J. H. Whitty, Boston and New York: Houghton Mifflin Company, The Riverside Press Cambridge, 1911, second edition 1917; *Edgar Allan Poe, Essays and Reviews*, Literary Classics of the United States, Inc. New York, N.Y.: The Library of America, 1984; *Scenes from Politian, an Unpublished Drama.* Original manuscript, 1835, the Pierpont Morgan Library, the William H. Koester Collection at the University of Texas; *London Magazine of Light Literature*, November 1875; *Southern Literary Messenger*, December 1835 and January 1836;   *Southern Magazine*, Baltimore: November 1875; "The Philosophy of Composition," *Graham's American Monthly Magazine of Literature and Art.*   Philadelphia, April 1846; *The Poems of Edgar Allan Poe*, edited by Floyd Stovall. Charlottesville: 1965. *The Poetical Works of Edgar A. Poe*, edited by J. H. Ingram, London and New York: 1888; *The Raven and Other Poems*, Sahara Publisher Books, 1845; "William Gilmore Simms," from *Godey's Lady's Book*, January 1846.

Schoenbachler, Matthew G. *Murder and Madness, the Myth of the Kentucky Tragedy.* Lexington: The University Press of Kentucky, 2011.

Sharp, Leander J. *Vindication of the Character of the Late Col. Solomon P. Sharp. Frankfort, Kentucky: Amos Kendall and Co., 1827.*

Stubbs, Dr. and William Carter. *Descendants of Mordecai Cooke, of "Mordecai's Mount," Gloucester Co., Va., 1650, and Thomas Booth, of Ware Neck, Gloucester Co., Va., 1685.* New Orleans, 1923. Allen County Public Library Genealogy Center, Contributor.

Botherum

Introduction

Richard Cavendish's short play, based on an authentic Lexington lawyer and banker, Madison Conyers Johnson (1806-1886), is a probing analysis of his character. Johnson built the notable Gothic/Greek revival cottage, Botherum, in what is now known as the Woodland Heights neighborhood of Lexington.

The play dives into Johnson's essential goodness of heart, while accentuating his importance to his city. Botherum takes on a wonderful life of its own and is a central character in this play. This was an enjoyable read, and I hope someday to see it produced.

Richard H.C. Clay

Botherum

We see the inside of an old stone farm house. Lexington, Kentucky nearing the middle of the Nineteenth Century. MADISON Johnson enters carrying his rifle, saddlebag, and a whip. A man in his thirties, dressed in riding clothes of the period. He puts the saddlebag and rifle on a nearby table; with his whip, he examines the intruders to the house: the furniture, stoneware, papers, etc. strewn across the room. He is wearing leather gloves that he never takes off and carries with him a saddlebag. FISH, an African living on the farm, wearing work clothes of the period, enters and waits to be addressed.

MADISON

So, this is all there is? The three rooms?

FISH

Yes, sir. There is the winter kitchen underneath. The summer kitchen in the back.

MADISON

Your master lived an austere life.

FISH

Yes, sir. At one time there were eight people living here. The young ones grew up and left. The old ones died. Then there was only him.

MADISON

I was surprised by the turn out at the funeral, and in the rain. He must have been well liked.

FISH

Yes, sir. He was. He was a fine man. He was always good to me. I understand that you bought the place?

MADISON

Yes. We have a lot in common, this old house and I.

FISH

I heard that it sold. 'That Mister Madison Johnson bought us.

113

MADISON

"Us?" What do you mean?

FISH

We come with the house, sir. Me and the wife.

MADISON

What?

FISH

It should be in the deed.

[MADISON rummages through the saddlebag and pulls out
the deed. A rope falls to the floor. A rope tied as a noose.
MADISON reads over the deed.]

MADISON

It would help if people would learn to write! This handwriting is atrocious.
How is one expected to read this? I've never studied Sanskrit. I don't want
any slaves!

FISH

You don't want us?

MADISON

I don't agree with slavery. The ones I've got, well, they are like family.
They need to be free but the minute I free them, someone is out there just
ready to sell them down south.

FISH

Do you want us to leave?

MADISON

I didn't mean that.

FISH

We have no place else to go, sir.

MADISON

Nor do I.

[His words leak a melancholy loneliness that he is quick to conceal.]
Don't every refer to yourself as a slave. You are a man. The same as me.

[He continues to be enthralled with the paper and disappointed by it.]
I'm looking to get away from town. Thirty-five acres is large enough. At least they got that right. What do they call you? Do you have a name?

FISH

Fish.

MADISON

Fish?

FISH

They call me Fish.

MADISON

What is your name?

FISH

That's the only name I've ever known.

MADISON

Why "Fish?"

FISH

I'm the best fisherman in the county, so they say. I can show you the best spots. And . . . they say I look like it. A fish, that is.

MADISON

Then I hate to think what they would call me.

[He sees that the rope has fallen from his saddlebag and quickly retrieves it]
I wish to be left alone now.

[Thinking that FISH has left, MADISON sits in an old cane chair, the rope huddled in his lap. From a silver flash he takes

115

a heavy drink. He suddenly is aware of FISH's unwavering presence.]

That will do for now. Thank you.

[FISH, aware of MADISON's disturbed state, hangs back.]

FISH

I could bring you some coffee, sir.

MADISON

I don't want coffee. I want to be left alone. Close the door. On the other side. What is it?

FISH

You seem upset.

MADISON

Do I? What gives you that idea? I don't want to be bothered.

FISH

Shall I put the rope away for you, sir?

MADISON

Rope? What rope?

[But the presence of the rope is obvious. MADISON laughs at himself.]
Oh, this rope.

FISH

You have a good laugh.

MADISON
[Suddenly angry]
What? I never laugh. I don't want to be bothered. Did you hear me?

FISH

Yes. You don't want to be bothered.

116

MADISON

Don't bother me, now! I want to be left alone. I want to be left alone.

FISH

We are never alone, sir. God is always here.

MADISON

Is He? Do you think? I used to think as much. But not anymore.

[Lying about the rope]
I saw an old mule outside the fence. I thought I would go get her . . .

[FISH reaches for the rope. But defensively, MADISON hugs
it to his chest.]

FISH

I'll get her for you.

MADISON
[Suspecting that FISH senses correctly:]
How old are you, Fish?

FISH

Thirty-eight, sir.

MADISON

Are you? Then we are the same age. Isn't that strange? We are men of
the same years but God has dealt us different hands. Me in my place, and
you . . . in yours. You with a wife, you say? And me . . . Leave me alone.

FISH

I'm sorry to be a bother, but I'm afraid of what you will do.

MADISON

That is none of your business. It does not affect you.

FISH

Pardon me, but it does. They will use that noose on me for what you are
about to do. And my wife will have no husband. How will she fend for
herself?

117

MADISON

Are you mad? What makes you think you'll be hanged?

FISH

If you destroy yourself, I'll be the one to blame. They'll say I did it. And I'll hang from the nearest tree.

MADISON

That's nonsense.

FISH

You must have loved your wife very much.

MADISON

[Rudely]
Did I mention a wife?
[Then softly]
She was my reason for living. She is gone and our baby with her. I have nothing to live for. Please, leave me alone. Don't bother me.

FISH

Where shall I bury the body?

MADISON

What?

FISH

I will be the one left burying your body. Where would you like to be buried? On the property I would guess.

MADISON

In the church graveyard, of course.

FISH

They will not let you be buried there.

MADISON

Why not? I am a member.

FISH

Not if you take your own life.

MADISON

Oh, that's right. You could say I had a heart attack.

FISH

But they will see you hanging there dead.

MADISON

That's right. From a heart attack.
    [But he shakes his head, realizing the absurdity of it.]

FISH

There is a fine spot where the pinks grow. You would like it there.

MADISON

    [These words are old friends of his, lost for too long. The sound of them awakens him from a stupor. A sound that alarms, yet comforts.]

The pinks?

FISH

They were beautiful this year. Perhaps I could cut them and bury you there.

MADISON

No! Don't cut the pinks. It will kill them. They won't come up next year if you cut them now.

FISH

Why would you be concerned about the pinks coming back? You won't be here.

MADISON

I see what you're trying to do.
    [He laughs at what he interpreters to be a cunning plan at
      play]
But it won't work. Who told you about the pinks?

FISH

I don't understand.

119

MADISON

That was her favorite flower. She loved them. Pinks. She loved flowers. And life. And laughter. There is none of that now without her.

FISH

But there are pinks. Carnations. I can show them to you. Your life is precious. Your body is the temple of the Lord. He is not through with you. You are young, sir. You will marry again . . .

MADISON

No. Not I.

FISH

Give it some time, sir.

MADISON

Time? Oh, I see.

> [He gets up from the chair, walks the room, looks out the window.]

You think that I've come from burying my wife and child. Come in time to see your Master buried?

FISH

So, it seems, sir.

MADISON

And what if I were to tell you that her grave is not as fresh as that of your old master?

FISH

Even if weeks have passed—

MADISON

Weeks?

FISH

Months, then . . . It takes time. But time heals all things.

MADISON

It has not been a week or a month. Or a year, even. It has been *years*.

My Sally died *eleven years ago* today. This very October day. We were married before Christmas and she was dead before All Hallow's. Eleven years. There has been no healing. Don't you know that Death is no respecter of time? Every morning when I get out of bed without her it is like that first morning. Just as fresh a grave . . .

Have you ever seen wild dogs chase a deer? Oh, that deer can be strong and fast. But the longer they chase it, the farther they go, the weaker that deer gets until it finally falls. No, the face of my clock has passed its eleventh hour; and past midnight, there are no numbers left.

It would be so easy to join her. I've been just existing all these years. Going through the motions. I've not been alive. Why not bury the dead?

FISH

Don't you believe in an afterlife, sir?

MADISON

Oh, yes, that. It would be my luck.

FISH

Don't sell your soul to the devil.

MADISON

He would be shortchanged, believe me. You think if I put myself down—like we do an injured animal—that I will wake up tomorrow in hell?

FISH

An eternity in hell seems a long time.

MADISON

Yes. It has already. There is a type of grief—I never knew this before. Where people grieve themselves to death. It doesn't heal with time. Every day you just have to decide to live again . . .
[He returns to the chair, sits, leans back.]
I must have been insane to have bought this old place. It's useless. What was I thinking?
[The chair cracks, he jumps out of it before it collapses]
This place is more a ruin than I.

121

FISH

It was a fine farm once. It could be again. There are wonderful fruit trees and good pasture for livestock. The soil is so rich you could eat it. I could help you, sir.

MADISON

Bring this farm back to life again?

FISH

I would be honored.

MADISON

Do you think we could? I bet McMurtry could to do something with this old place. He does a fine job with the Gothic Revival.

FISH

Make it anything you want.

MADISON

"Anything I want." All I wanted left me years ago. And now, all I want is not to be bothered. But you say there are pinks?

FISH

Yes, sir.

MADISON

I had forgotten. She would love them. Don't cut them. Not now. They need their foliage to nourish their roots. So, they will come back . . .

FISH

Next Spring they will be beautiful.

MADISON

Next Spring . . . And the Spring after . . . You and I will grow older. And this old farm . . . Do you and your wife have children?

FISH

No, sir. The Lord has not granted them to us.

MADISON

He keeps much in reserve, doesn't He? No children. And if she were to die, your wife, you will be left alone just like I. And we will be two old gentlemen together on this old place. From the old school. It needs a proper name. Does it have a name?

FISH

No, sir.

MADISON

Your Master never named the place? The house? The farm?

FISH

No, sir.

MADISON

That is not good. A house should have a proper name.

FISH

Like Ashland?

MADISON

Yes, like Ashland.

FISH

And Claremont?

MADISON

Not Claremont.

FISH

Master Clay was by to see you.

MADISON

Cassius? I don't want to see him.

FISH

He is concerned about you, sir.

MADISON

For eleven years I've avoided him and his concern for me.

FISH

But why?

MADISON

Isn't it clear? He was her brother. To look at him is just to remind me of her. Of what I had taken from me. Of what I will never have again.

Listen, I've known Cassius a long time. We were in school together. In fact, he burned the place down. Although he always says it was his boy shining his boots and knocking over the candle.
[He laughs]
You have to know Cash.

FISH

He is what they call an Abolitionist.

MADISON

Yes, he wants to see slavery abolished. I didn't say he wasn't a good man. He is. I just can't see him.

FISH

His heart mourns her in much the same way as yours. She was his sister.

MADISON

Yes. And lived such a sad life, my Sally. She was a few years older than I, you'd think wiser, but she married an ass hole.
[He plays with the whip]
Who went out and got himself shot and killed. I had hoped to come into her life and bring her some happiness. Instead, I killed her.

FISH

You did nothing of the kind, sir.

MADISON

It was my baby that killed her. Had I left her alone she would be with us still.

FISH

With all due respect, sir, every wife wants to give her husband a child. No matter what the risk.

MADISON

It would have been nice to have been a father. To have a wife and a child and a home. Don't pity me. And don't admire me. I am a sinner if ever there was one.

FISH

You are hard on yourself, sir.

MADISON

No, I am honest.
[In anguish he rubs his hands through his hair]
Please! Don't bother me! I don't know what's wrong with me. When I was growing up on the farm I wanted to be in school. When I was at university, my mind kept wandering to the farm. When I was single, I wanted to be married. When I was married, I couldn't help but wonder what I was missing by not being single . . . And now, with Sally gone, I wish she were here. Human beings are such fickle creatures. We are never pleased with what we have at the moment.
[He chuckles, remembering something.]
She bought me a very funny print. The painting of a Doctor "Botherum."

FISH

"Botherum," sir?

MADISON

Yes. Botherum. He was a medicine man that preached in the streets of London: a cure for every ailment.
[Of the way he remembers the print:]
In this painting, that she gave me—a painted lithograph—this Dr. Botherum stands on a wagon or a pile of something, enraptured in his preaching, while people all around him are doing the most comic antics-- paying no attention to him!
[He laughs, remembering how they both had enjoyed the print, remembering the sound of her laughter.]
The very thing they needed was right there in front of them and they were all too busy with the silliness of their lives. And he was just as silly not to know that he was not being heard. Oh, but the things that stare us in the face and we do not see.
[Thinking of her, he speaks softly]
My Sally . . . she knew me too well.
[This sparks an idea]

125

There's a name this old place could fit into! "Botherum!"

FISH

There's a book about a law suit between Counsellor Bother'um and
Bore'um.

MADISON

The Pleader's Guide.

FISH

Yes, by John Surrebutter.

MADISON

I've read it—a poem. And a play. So, you can read? How did you learn to
read?

FISH

I taught myself. I love to read.

MADISON

Me, too. I don't mean I taught myself, too. No, I went to school. Something
you would have loved. I didn't. But I do love to read. So, we have that in
common as well? Have you read many books?

FISH

Everything I can find. It's just that they are very expensive.

MADISON

That they are. I must loan you some books.

FISH

That's very kind of you. May I put the rope away for you, sir?

MADISON

Yes, Fish. Thank you.
          [He releases the rope to FISH who takes it. He takes hold of
          the rifle.]

FISH

The mule belongs to our neighbor.

126

MADISON

No doubt you are a treasure here.

FISH

And the rifle?
            [MADISON clutches it, rethinks it and releases it to FISH]
I'll put them away.

MADISON

Then you must show me around old Botherum. Help me see what I've been missing. Now—I can tell you don't warm up to the name? It's a painting and a play.

FISH
            [With a twinkle in his eye:]
I'd be afraid people will walk by and, respecting your privacy, say, "Don't bother 'him.'"

            [MADISON finds this very funny and laughs. It is a hearty
            laugh. A healthy laugh. One that has not visited him for some
            time. And like Doctor Botherum's concoctions, it brings a
            cure of healing. He takes a deep breath of it.]

MADISON

Will you show me those pinks?

FISH

Yes, sir. They will be beautiful next Spring.

MADISON

You must show me the best spots for fishing. And afterwards, maybe we'll ride down to Claremont and see Cassius.
            [He laughs again.]
"Don't bother 'im!"

            [MADISON throws his arm across FISH; the two men laugh
            and exit.]

CURTAIN

Postscript

Madison Conyers Johnson

Madison Conyers Johnson was born Sept. 21, 1806, near Georgetown, Ky. He was the son of William Johnson and Elizabeth Payne Johnson, the grandson of Col. Robert Johnson.

He entered Transylvania University in Lexington, Kentucky and graduated as head of his class in 1823, and from its Law Department in 1825. He was admitted to the Bar in 1825, and joined the faculty of the University.[9]

Figure 5
Madison Conyers Johnson by Matthew Jouett. Sixteen years old. Graduation portrait, Transylvania University.

Johnson married Sally Anne Clay, daughter of Green Clay and Sally Lewis Clay, widow of Edmund Irvine, December 23, 1828. It is believed that Sally died in childbirth at the age of 26, that following October 13, 1829. Johnson never married again. In 1844, he bought an old farm at the edge of Lexington and in 1851, remodeled its old stone house into a Greek Temple designed by John McMurtry. He named his thirty-acre plantation, "Botherum," and lived there the rest of his life.[10] It was named after a painting *"Doctor Botherum, The Montebank"* by Thomas Rowlandson, 1800. There was also a book and play, *The Pleader's Guide*, that spotlighted two characters, Counsellors Bother'um and Bore'um, 1803.

In 1837, when the Northern Bank of Kentucky was formed on the ruins of the old Bank of Kentucky and the Bank of the Commonwealth, Johnson was made director. Johnson was a member of the commission to prepare the Kentucky code of practice in 1850; and was a representative in the

---

[9] John D. Wright, Jr., *Transylvania: Tutor to the West*, The University Press of Kentucky, Lexington, Kentucky, 1975, p. 143.
[10] Kentucky Historical Society, "Historic Botherum," Kentucky, Frankfort.

Kentucky Legislature in 1853-54, and 1857-58. He was elected president of the Northern Bank of Kentucky in 1858. At his suggestion, made to Secretary Windom in 1890, the three per cent U.S. bonds were issued which resulted in a saving of millions of dollars to the government.[11]

In 1849, Madison C. Johnson, along with M.T. Scott, Benjamin Gratz, and Richard Higgins started the Lexington Cemetery by raising subscriptions the sum of $12,000.

Figure 6
"Doctor Botherum, The Montebank" by Thomas Rowlandson

Johnson was a Board member of Transylvania 1833-56, and again in 1865-67. In 1838, he was one of the donors of the Transylvania Institute of "One Hundred Gentlemen Citizens of Kentucky and Graduates of Transylvania University" under Henry Clay's leadership to rescue and sustain the school with a permanent endowment.[12] Johnson was on the faculty 1850, 1858, and 1865-81. He served on the newly-structured Board of Trustees when on March 10, 1856, the University was reorganized as a school for teachers.[13] In 1860, when Cassius M. Clay lost his life estate to public auction, Johnson and three others joined together to assume all his debts and buy back the homestead, allowing Clay to live there until he was able to pay them back.[14]

[11] Rossiter Johnson. Editor, *Twentieth Century Biographical Dictionary of Notable Americans.* Vol. I-X. The Biographical Society, Boston, Massachusetts, 1904.
[12] John D. Wright, Jr., *Transylvania: Tutor to the West*, The University Press of Kentucky, Lexington, Kentucky, 1975, p. 152.
[13] John D. Wright, Jr., *Transylvania: Tutor to the West*, The University Press of Kentucky, Lexington, Kentucky, 1975, p. 180.
[14] Cassius Marcellus Clay, *The Life of Cassius Marcellus Clay*, Volume 1, Cincinnati, Ohio: J. Fletcher Brennan & Co., 1886, p. 538.

Johnson served as chairman of the board of trustees of Transylvania University and president of the law department in 1865-86.[15] In 1864-65, Madison Johnson met with John Bryan Bowman before the Kentucky Legislature to merge Transylvania with Kentucky University. Kentucky University was to be the consolidated university and Transylvania was to maintain its corporate identity. President Abraham Lincoln's Morrill Act of 1862, endowed public lands for establishing an Agricultural and Mechanical college. Receiving this donation, the Agricultural and Mechanical College became one of the colleges of Kentucky University, later to be known as The University of Kentucky[16]

Madison C. Johnson died Dec. 7, 1886, at the age of 80, at Botherum and was buried in the Lexington Cemetery. Kentucky author James Lane Allen immortalized Johnson as the character of Colonel Romulus Fields in his short story, "Two Gentlemen from the Old School," which in 1891, was published in his book of short stories, *Flute and Violin and Other Kentucky Tales and Romances*, under the title,

Figure 7
Botherum Hall by Russell Richard Reichenbach Cavendish

Two Gentlemen from Kentucky. In the introduction to the 1919, MacMillan Company printing, Allen wrote of his childhood visits to Botherum, the home of the wealthy gentleman, Madison C. Johnson, who spent his days in down-town Lexington at the banks and courts of law. He also remembered the old African gardener who was devoted to Johnson, who was called "Fish" because of his piscatorial countenance, who would load Allen down with the flowers from the estate.

---

[15] "Index to Transylvania University Students from early 1800s – 1970s," Transylvania University, Lexington, Kentucky; Walter Wilson Jennings, *Transylvania Pioneer University of the West*, Pageant Press, New York, 1955, p. 233

[16] John D. Wright, Jr., *Transylvania: Tutor to the West*, The University Press of Kentucky, Lexington, Kentucky, 1975, p. 197.

"When the author was a lad he was much used to frequent, by permission, the private grounds of a wealthy gentleman living alone on the edge of Lexington. Those grounds— were there ever any others like them?— lawns, hedges, forest trees and evergreens, vines, fruits, flowers, birds, sun and shade, songs and quiet! They are all mirage now, lifted away from the earth."[17]

Botherum was built in the style of a Grecian temple. The entire house was stuccoed as was the Athenian style, but with time and as parts of the cement started to fall, they revealed the beautiful limestone bricks beneath that could no longer be hidden. Only the front portico entrance remained stuccoed when we bought it. The original roof was a slate pattern and I am ashamed to say we replaced it with modern roof shingles due to leakage. There was a colonnade of Corinthian columns at each end and one at the entrance. These columns were set on the brick pavement that surrounded the house. Clever brick guttering directed rainwater away from the house.

John McMurtry designed the house in a U-shape with a courtyard in the middle, a ladder that led up to the captain's walk. The summer kitchen was separated from the house and there was a winter kitchen in the cellar with steps leading up to a courtyard entrance of the house. The Foyer was a cloistered vaulted hall with skylight below the captain's walk used as a Dining Room. To the right and left, double doors have lozenge panes of colored glass, many of which were broken and I had recreated.

The showroom of the house was the drawing room with vaulted ceiling of gold leaf plasterwork, four alcoves, and bay windows on each side, one overlooking the courtyard. These windows were adorned with wooden shutters inside and out. As architect Clay Lancaster described it:

"Also vaulted, the finest room in the house was the octagonal drawing room, whose ceiling is enhanced with ribs, bosses, and a centerpiece of vines and gamopetalous flowers modeled in plaster. The same floral motif enframes the Tudor arch of the mirror over the marble chimney piece; and there are four niches, a doorway opposite the fireplace, and two side, arcuated semihexagonal bay windows, each forming a low pointed arch in the wall."[18]

---

[17] James Lane Allen, *Flute and Violin and other Kentucky Tales,* New York and London: Harper & Brothers, 1899, p. xi

[18] Clay Lancaster, *Back Streets and Pine Trees, the work of Jon McMurtry, nineteenth century architect-builder of Kentucky,* Lexington, KY: the Bur Press in Kentucky, 1956, pp. 35-37.

Botherum was a marriage of Gothic on the inside and Corinthian on the outside. Johnson wrote, "All styles may be divided into two classes. One derived from the post and lintel and the other from the arch; the Grecian being the type of the first and the Roman or Gothic of the second."[19]

There were six exits from the house as if Johnson was afraid of fires after the Principal Building of Transylvania had burned where he had studied.

In 1980, after I graduated from seminary and was ordained, my savings was burning a hole in my bank account and I was determined to purchase real-estate for the first time. My father, John Cavendish, recommended Botherum which was for sale due to zoning failure for commercial use. He agreed to loan me the money at no interest. So, I bought Botherum, not very keen on its style but respectful of Father's business advice. Almost immediately, I was called to take a church across the state and sold it instead to him. I would go on to purchase The Robert Peeples House in Shawneetown, Illinois and successfully got it on the National Register. Father moved into Botherum. I will never forget returning for the first time after starting the new pastorate so far away. It was late. His family antique furnishings, Federal and Victorian, all had found their place in the house; every lamp and chandelier was lit, with every light over every oil painting. It was a spectacular welcoming that I will always cherish. And I felt like one of the "Two Gentlemen from Kentucky."

Father Cavendish lived there much as had Johnson, a widower entertaining fine people of Lexington and especially the good members of Walnut Hill Church. One of the many colorful escapades that happened there was an elegant formal dinner party for the Bishop and friends when the dining room table collapsed in the middle! Yet, not a one of his grandmother's priceless crystal goblets had been damaged! He put them on a tray and headed to the kitchen to wash and return them while the guests cheerfully put the table back together. Unfortunately, he tripped and the goblets went crashing to the floor again, this time not a one was saved!

Elizabeth Simpson wrote in *Bluegrass Houses and Their Traditions* a story of Dr. Horace Holley refusing to allow Johnson to participate in the Transylvania University graduation commencement service because of his looks. Father knew Ms. Simpson and insisted that she had fabricated the

---

[19] Clay Lancaster, *Antebellum Architecture of Kentucky*, Lexington, KY: The University Press of Kentucky, 1991, p. 270; "Observations on Architecture," *Lexington Daily Press*, May 27, 1887.

story for her own interests and there was no truth in it whatsoever. Wild stories easily become legend, and the more dramatic the more entertaining. The idea that Johnson built the house as a shrine to his dead wife is one of those legends, but a creative one. A truer one was that Henry Clay planted the Ginkgo in the front yard that, among others, had been brought over from China.

For years, a large Victorian mansion had stood in the front yard blocking the front door and, being inaccessible, many people thought the left side of the house facing Madison Street was the front. Don and Gail Henry, from whom we bought the house, had the Victorian house torn down, and to their credit incurred the incredible costs, so that the public could enter the front of Botherum. Inside the double doors to the library were two Ionic columns, the Henrys had removed the doors and wall in hopes of making the front room more spacious for public events; often visitors would remark about the appearance of the ionic order after entering through the Corinthian. The foyer, which Father always called "Entrance Hall," has a large brown antebellum marble fireplace the Henry's had rescued from the cellar and returned to its former glory.

Don and Gail also regaled to us the story that Johnson had possibly built a passageway under the house that extended to the front end of the farm at the creek below High Street. Prior to our sell of the house, a sinkhole fell beneath what had once been the courtyard exposing a brick arched ceiling underneath. We had the collapse filled in with gravel. Had this been the secret passageway of "underground railroad," or a cistern? I do remember that there had been an outhouse near the right side of the house and a cistern there was dug up for plumbing purposes, so why would there have been an additional cistern just feet away under the courtyard?

The rest of the story of Botherum is history, "happily ever after," as garden architect Jon Carloftis bought the house from us, restored it with his own creative mark and glorious landscaping, and has hosted innumerable events for charities and historic preservation. A visit to Lexington, will not be complete without a stop at historic Botherum.

Bibliography

Allen, James Lane. *Flute and Violin and other Kentucky Tales.* New York and London: Harper & Brothers, 1899

Clay, Cassius Marcellus. *The Life of Cassius Marcellus Clay, Memoirs, Writings, and Speeches, Showing His Conduct in the Overthrow of American Slavery, the Salvation of the Union, and the Restoration of the Autonomy of the States.* Volume 1. Cincinnati, Ohio: J. Fletcher Brennan & Co., 1886

Estersohn, Pieter, *Kentucky Historic Houses and Horse Farms of Bluegrass Country.* New York, NY: The Monacelli Press, 2014.

"Index to Transylvania University Students from early 1800s – 1970s." Lexington, KY: Transylvania University.

Jennings, Walter Wilson. *Transylvania Pioneer University of the West.* New York, NY: Pageant Press, 1955.

Kentucky Historical Society. "Historic Botherum." Frankfort, KY. https://history.ky.gov.>markers>historicbotherum.

Lancaster, Clay. *Antebellum Architecture of Kentucky.* Lexington, KY: The University of Kentucky Press, 1991.

Lancaster, Clay. *Back Streets and Pine Trees, the work of Jon McMurtry, nineteenth century architect-builder of Kentucky,* Lexington, KY: the Bur Press in Kentucky, 1956.

Rossiter Johnson. Editor, *Twentieth Century Biographical Dictionary of Notable Americans.* Vol. I-X. Boston, Massachusetts: The Biographical Society, 1904.

Wright, John D. Jr. *Transylvania: Tutor to the West.* Lexington, KY: The University Press of Kentucky, 1975.

Beating the
Dark Home

Introduction

Most of the performers who appeared in theatres across the country in the 19th Century and beyond are barely known today. The theatrical years before sound films, radio, and television are murky at best. Faded newspaper clippings, programs, a few scratchy recordings and photos are all we have to remember them by. Some of the top stars like Joseph Jefferson wrote autobiographies but the majority are unknown except to a small band of collectors and theatre historians.

And that is why we have to research and write articles, books, plays, etc. to show the full range of performers, authors, theatre owners, designers and others who toiled across the country bringing their talents to millions across the country and even to Europe. Their lives could be tough but they themselves romanticized their love of the stage. To paraphrase the mail carriers, "neither snow nor rain nor heat nor gloom of night" stayed these performers from theatres across the country.

And one of these is Andrew Tribble. Not well known today but he exemplifies the 19th Century actors' life upon and off the wicked stage. His story is important for our understanding of our theatre's past, present and future. We all owe a debt to Mr. Tribble and his theatrical world and to Mr. Cavendish for bringing it alive for readers now and in the future.

Ken Bloom

Ken Bloom is a Grammy Award winner, author, director, record producer, and playwright. Ken's books include: *American Song: The Complete Musical Theatre Companion; Hollywood Song; Tin Pan Alley; Broadway: An Encyclopedic Guide to the History, People, and Places of Times Square; Broadway Musicals: The 101 Greatest Shows of All Time with Frank Vlastnik; Sitcoms: The 101 Greatest Comedies of All Time; The American Songbook: The Singers, the Songwriters and the Songs; Jerry Herman: The Lyrics: a Celebration* with Jerry Herman; *Remember How I Love You: Love Letters from an Extraordinary Marriage* with Elaine Orbach; *Hollywood Musicals: The 101 Greatest Song and Dance Movies of All Time; Attending and Enjoying Concerts* with Josh Wellman; *Show and Tell: The New Book of Broadway Anecdotes; Eubie Blake: Rags, Rhythm, and Race* with co-author Richard Carlin; *The Complete Lyrics of Sheldon Harnick*. For a decade and more he has been editor of *Marquee*, Journal of the Theare Historical Society of America. If you're curious, look Ken Bloom up on Wikipedia.

Beating the Dark Home

CHARACTERS

ANDY Tribble	the vaudevillian
AMOS Tribble	the brother
OPHELIA	the charwoman
BESSIE Tribble	the wife

SETTING
A dressing room, Pekin Theater, Chicago, Illinois

TIME
Evening, winter, 1906

Scene One

An upstairs dressing room on the top floor of the Pekin Theater, Chicago 1906. In the corner of the room is a dressing screen; the room acts also as a janitor's closet with mops and brooms. ANDY Tribble, African American vaudeville actor in his twenties, sits at his makeup table in his undershirt before a mirror taking off the black makeup from his face. The table is cluttered with his shirt, a towel, a candlestick, a cork, and makeup; there is a wastebasket nearby. ANDY stops to ponder the person under the mask in the mirror. It seems to stare back at him as a stranger, lost to an uncertain future. A child's drawing is attached to the mirror, and ANDY takes it and looks at it. It is a picture of him, his wife Bessie, and their son Atwood. The thought of the child brings a troubled smile to his face.

> [AMOS, his brother, African American in his twenties, enters the room silently. He is dressed in his Sunday best coat and tie, holding his hat he stands at the door. To disguise his nervous anxiety, AMOS recites lines of the "interruptive" routine they performed a few years earlier.]

AMOS
Where you been, brother Amos?

> [ANDY looks up and sees the reflection of his brother behind him. Immediately, he stiffens, unable to turn and greet him.]
I've been to races, Brother Andy.

> [ANDY continues to remove the make-up. Their estrangement is almost hostile.]

ANDY
Again? What track did you play at?

AMOS
I played over at —

ANDY
[Finding safety in the mask of a comic:]
That track's no good, Brother Amos! Why, you should of played over at—

AMOS

'Never goin' back there, Brother Andy. That's where I lost all my money!

ANDY

How much did you lose?

AMOS

Oh, I lost—

ANDY

Was it that much?

AMOS

I bet on a horse, and that rascal —

ANDY

Was he that far behind? Now, the horse you should have bet on—

AMOS

He had a bad leg.
> [But the vaudeville routine stops here. ANDY does not
> continue.]

It sure is good to see you, brother.

ANDY

Is it?

AMOS

It's been too long.

ANDY

Has it?
> [AMOS fumbles with his hat, not sure how to continue.]

How is Cora and the baby?

AMOS

They are doing good. Thanks.

ANDY

That's good. And life on the farm?

AMOS

It's going good.

ANDY

That's good. So, what brings you back to Chicago? Did you see the show?

AMOS

No.

[There is an awkward silence. AMOS approaches him, stands over him at the table. He sees two rubber balls in the waste basket and takes them out.]

You still do our old routines? 'Can't juggle with just two balls, you know.

ANDY

[Lying, but not convincingly. Referring to AMOS:]

The other one must have got away.

AMOS

[Overlooking the double meaning.]

No, I didn't see the show. I lived that applesauce too many times.

ANDY

They loved us on stage.

AMOS

[He walks the room, playing with the balls]

They loved *you*. We were always just the olio act. A fish.˙

ANDY

You don't remember.

AMOS

I was the second banana. I remember being pelted with tomatoes.

[He throws a ball at his brother. ANDY misses it.]

ANDY

Once——

AMOS

Not once

[He throws the second ball. ANDY catches it.]

ANDY
[Placing the ball on the table]

Twice. Maybe——Okay, a few times. I see you've kept your old moods.

AMOS

Maybe it's the smell of the cork. It always kind of made me sick. Making fun of our people like we were plantation buffoons. Come home, Andy. I've got work on the farm for both of us.

ANDY

You don't understand.

AMOS

What? I don't understand how much you want that applause, that laughter, that reassurance that you are loved?

ANDY

It's not that--

AMOS

Your little boy loves you. Cora and I love you. Is that not enough? Is that not enough?

ANDY

No. No, it's not.

AMOS

That's what I was afraid of.

ANDY

Bessie and I are doing just fine, Amos. Couldn't be better. We've been treading the boards together.

AMOS

She took my place, huh? Did you know she's in jail?

146

ANDY

What?!

AMOS

She was with the other women parading for the vote.

ANDY

Good God--

AMOS

But they got mixed up with the strike that's going on. It got kind of rough, throwing things—

ANDY

Is Bessie all right? Where's the boy?

AMOS

She's fine. He's fine—he's with her parents. They said she wanted you to go on without her. I see you did.

ANDY
[Up from his chair]
They have her in *jail?!* I've got to go to her—

AMOS

No. They'll just arrest you and you'll end up losing your job. Just wait it out.

ANDY

"Wait it out?"

AMOS

Yes, that's all you can do right now.

ANDY

Good God.
[He sits. AMOS retrieves the other ball from the floor]

AMOS

'Seems she's always getting herself in trouble.

ANDY

She's just standing up for what she believes in. A better world for our children.

AMOS

They were bringing in truckloads of Negras to beat up the strikers.

ANDY

It'll be the death of her one of these days.

AMOS and ANDY

Just like Daddy—

ANDY

[They are silent, ANDY not wanting the memory of their
father to spark any feelings of tenderness.]

Folks that work the factories live like rats in the tenements. They can barely put food on their tables. The union is the only way they have a chance for a better life. And the vote is the only way women can have a voice.

AMOS

More reason to come away from this, Andy. This is not a safe place.

ANDY

I'm not going back—

[He turns back to the mirror. AMOS paces, plays with the
ball. He bounces the ball off the wall. Of the theater:]

AMOS

The new place looks great. It sure seats a lot more.

ANDY

Twelve hundred.

AMOS

No kidding? What was it when we played it? A couple hundred or more?

ANDY

It was a saloon then.

AMOS

It sure is fancy now. The first all-black stock company. 'Heard there's already been a fire . . .

ANDY

Nothing is going to happen to Robert Motts.
[He holds the ball from the table out to his brother]
These are yours, you left them behind.

AMOS

[Calmly placing the other ball on the table.]
I'm not a juggler.

ANDY

Is that why you ran out on me?

AMOS

I guess they didn't pay you—

ANDY

Hell, no, they didn't pay me.
[He pushes the balls back into the wastebasket.]
It's a wonder they even kept me on—

AMOS

I had to go. I couldn't stand it—

ANDY

My own brother! And not even a note to let me know if you were dead or alive?!

[They are quickly silenced by the arrival of OPHELIA, the charwoman who enters with her mop and pail. She is a spinster now, past her prime, living on tattered memories and unpromising dreams. But her countenance is brightened by the sight of AMOS Tribble.]

OPHELIA

Mr. Amos! My, it's sure good to see you again, Mr. Amos!

AMOS

'Evenin,' Ophelia.

OPHELIA

Why, it hasn't been the same around here without you! 'Come back to join your brother?

ANDY

He's come back to fetch me to his farm in Indiana. To rescue me from the circus. But I told him things are going just fine.

OPHELIA

Oh, really? Don't you miss the roar of the crowd, Mr. Amos?

AMOS

Like the plague.

OPHELIA

I was saying to your brother, Mr. Tribble, just the other day, "Have you heard from your brother Amos?" I always thought the two of you would go to Broadway.
            [OPHELIA, so glad to see AMOS again, cannot help but lean
            against ANDY and gaze again at his brother.]

ANDY

            [To OPHELIA:]
Don't you have things to do?

            [ANDY stares at OPHELIA. She stares right back at him.]
I have half a mind to remind you that its closing time.

OPHELIA

And what happened to the other half?
            [She goes about her business putting the cleaning things
            away.]

AMOS

I was just leaving. I guess there's nothing much more to say . . .

            [ANDY makes no response. AMOS sings *Give My Regards
            to Broadway* by George M. Cohan, 1904:]

150

Did you ever see two Yankees part upon a foreign shore?
When the good ship's just about to start for Old New York once more?
With tear dimmed eye, they say goodbye
They're friends, without a doubt;
When the man on the pier shouts, "Let them clear!"
As the ship strikes out.

Give my regards to Broadway!
Remember me to Herald Square!
Tell all the gang at Forty Second Street
That I will soon be there!
Whisper of how I'm yearning
To mingle with the old time throng!
Give my regards to Old Broadway
And say that I'll be there, 'ere long!

I best beat the dark home. Break a leg.

> [ANDY stares at himself in the mirror. AMOS exits.
> ANDY is silent. There is a sick feeling in his stomach.

> [Humor comes naturally to OPHELIA, but she has no desire
> to share it on stage. For ANDY it is mostly work, to be
> performed before an audience.]

OPHELIA
Well, I finally got that toilet unstopped.
> [Of the brother-to-brother relationship:]
One of them anyway.
> [She looks back to where AMOS has exited]
That sure was not a nice thing to say.

ANDY
I didn't say a thing.

OPHELIA
I meant what he said to you.

ANDY
Oh, that. When we were kids, back in Kentucky, we'd stay out playing ball
until it got dark. Our mama would call us to come in, but we'd stay out

151

there, with her just a yelling and mad as a hornet. Then we'd race home to get there before dark, cause after dark she'd tan our hides. "Beat the dark home," we'd say. We just wanted to hold on to that last bit of sunlight . . .

OPHELIA

Where I come from, 'weren't safe for any Negra to be seen on the street after the sun gone down.

ANDY

We figured that Mama's wrath was worse.

OPHELIA

No, I meant that other thing he said: hoping you'd break your legs!

ANDY

"Break a leg?" That just means he hopes I get work. If you break out on stage from the side curtains—the legs, we call them—you get paid. Surely, you've heard that.

OPHELIA

Why 'you call the curtains, "legs?"

ANDY

The side ones. They're long and slender, like women's legs.

OPHELIA

'Don't look like no legs on a woman I ever saw.

ANDY

I'm sure they don't.

OPHELIA

Don't look like my legs.

ANDY
[With reassured sarcasm.]
I'm sure they don't. The stage is a woman, that's what Amos always said. She has legs. She's a teaser. A tormentor. And she has an apron.

OPHELIA

Men wear aprons.

152

ANDY

Yes, but under her apron, there's a trap!
[He laughs at his wit]

OPHELIA

Lord, have mercy!
[Of his joke:]
There's another clogged toilet in here!

ANDY

It's just all vaudeville talk.

OPHELIA

[Of the downstairs toilet]
You should have seen that downstairs! It was so stopped up, I thought it
would never clear.

ANDY

Spare me the details . . .

OPHELIA

It so reminded me of that time that woman swallowed that hundred-dollar
bill.

ANDY

What?

OPHELIA

Oh, that's right, you weren't here then. I tried just about everything I could
think of to get that toilet cleared downstairs, and we did the same with her.

ANDY

Someone swallowed a hundred-dollar bill? Here at the theater? You lie.

OPHELIA

Don't believe me. It was before the fire. It was one of those gangsters' girls.
Drunk as a skunk, she was.

ANDY

And you were trying to get the money back?

OPHELIA

Is your cornbread half-baked in the middle? What goes in has to come out!

ANDY

You don't mean . . . you couldn't . . .

OPHELIA

Of course I was trying to get it back!

[ANDY shivers at the thought]

ANDY

Uhh! That's *nasty*!

OPHELIA

Listen to you, like you wouldn't? You's a hypocrite!

ANDY

[Proudly]
Greek word for the actor with the mask!

OPHELIA

That money was mine! I had a new dress all picked out, and a hat to match!
I fed that floozy prunes, and molasses, flaxseed oil--

ANDY

Well, did it work?

OPHELIA

I tried peppermint tea, chamomile tea, ginger tea--

ANDY

Did it?

OPHELIA

Castor oil, rhubarb, slippery elm, and laudanum—only a few drops, its
opium and can kill you if you aint careful—

ANDY

Well, did you get the money back or not?!!

OPHELIA

No. It was counterfeit and "didn't pass."
[She breaks into laughter! ANDY does not find it funny.]

ANDY

I guess you heard my brother Amos?

OPHELIA

Uh-huh.

ANDY

He wants me to give up all of this!

OPHELIA

Uh-huh.

ANDY

To raise chickens and goats. Like we did when we were kids in Kentucky.

OPHELIA

Uh-huh.

ANDY

You think I should join him, don't you?

OPHELIA

Uh-huh

ANDY

Is that all you can say is Uh-huh?

OPHELIA

Uh-huh. If ignorance is bliss, you must be the happiest man alive.

ANDY

You sound like you're still fighting that cold.

OPHELIA

It's hanging on like hair on a biscuit.

ANDY

You ought to take something for it. Some honey and whiskey

OPHELIA

You know I don't touch that stuff. That's the devil's drink.

ANDY

Well, maybe then, just the whiskey.
            [But she doesn't find this funny]
He was good on stage.

OPHELIA

You two were good together.

ANDY

We always seemed to play In One. The olio act.

OPHELIA

The *what*?

ANDY

Olio act. Olio. From the "oil" cloth curtain. The number one curtain. As you go on upstage you got your number one curtain, your number two curtain, and your number three--

OPHELIA

Yes, I know how to count. But do you know what your problem is? You ain't got the balls.

ANDY

I beg your pardon?

OPHELIA

Someone has thrown your balls away.
            [She has seen the balls in the basket, and now fishes them out
            and puts them on the table.]

ANDY

Must have been brother Amos. He aint got the balls.

OPHELIA

Where's the third one?

ANDY

Beats me.

OPHELIA

You can't juggle with only two. You know they want you to do the juggling act.

ANDY

I can't with one of them gone.

OPHELIA

How convenient for you.

ANDY

I'm not a juggler.

OPHELIA

I know all the things you ain't. I'm just trying to figure out the things you is.

ANDY

I *is* a song and dance man.

OPHELIA

Did he tell you about Bessie?

ANDY

Does everybody know about Bessie but me!!

OPHELIA

Now, you stay put. She said not to go down there to that jail until it all boils over.

[OPHELIA goes behind the screen to change into her street clothes. ANDY looks with disgust at the balls.]

ANDY

Are they all gone downstairs?

OPHELIA

Uh-huh. But the stage lights is still on.

ANDY

Did you watch the show tonight?

OPHELIA

I've seen it before.

ANDY

The audience was sitting on their hands.
[Of AMOS's sudden appearance.]
Can you believe that ugly bastard just showing up like that!

OPHELIA

Mr. Tribble, that kind of talk does you no good!

ANDY

'Sorry. Can you believe that handsome bastard just showing up like that?
Leaving me high and dry? Like a wagon with two wheels?

OPHELIA

He wrote you that letter—

ANDY

Yeah, after he'd been gone for weeks. I worried myself sick.

OPHELIA

There was no need to. You knew where he went.

ANDY

That doesn't matter. I was still upset. Then he has the impertinence to tell
me that "black face" makes our people look stupid. That I was making us
look like the poor dumb darkie from the fields of Kentucky!

OPHELIA

It *is* demeaning. It's just like the way they portray us women on the stage.

ANDY

What's wrong with the way they portray you women?

OPHELIA

What's wrong? The white men are all the time dressing up like us and making us out to be nothing but streetwalkers. We aint like that. Someone needs to go out there on stage and show them how we really are. We got brains. We got humor.

ANDY

You're absolutely right.

OPHELIA

We're not just a pretty face.

ANDY

[A double take at her]
You're absolutely right.

OPHELIA

Why **do** you wear the black face?

ANDY

The white ones was the ones that started it.

OPHELIA

Makin' fun of the Negra?

ANDY

Stealin' our fun. Because they couldn't laugh at themselves. When we wear the black face, we're pokin fun at them.

OPHELIA

Oh! So, it's kind of like stealing back the laughter that belonged to us.

ANDY

Yeah, stealing back the laughter. They put on the clown white in the circus and people laugh at *them*. Slip on a banana peel and the house roars. There's a little bit of buffoon in all of us. A fella's got to laugh at himself. You take yourself too seriously, you're done for.

OPHELIA

Tell that to those ones causing all the trouble against the union. If brains was lard, they wouldn't have enough to grease a pan! We women just got to get the vote so things can change in this world. Why does everyone want to fight about it?

[She sings *If the Man in the Moon Were a Coon* by Fred Fisher, 1906]

Say, Jasper, 'taint no use
Talking even though you talk from now till noon
Don't try to tell me, Mr. Know-It-All
A coon is up in the moon
Why! a Negra, with his brown figra
Certainly darkens up the silvery moon
Wake up! you're dreaming with your eyes aglare
You great big foolish coon

If the man in the moon
Were a coon, coon, coon
What would you do?
He would fade with his shade
The silvery moon, moon, moon
Away from you
No roaming 'round the park at night
No spooning in the bright moonlight
If the man in the moon
Were a coon, coon, coon

Most everyone has heard
Stories that a chicken is a coon's delight
Just think the dangers to a hen roost
With that good old moon out of sight
'Deed! chicken would be soft
Pickin' if the man up in the moon were black
Oh my! the harvest for that darkey with
That great big sack on his back

Why **do** they laugh when someone slips on a banana peel? It seems mighty mean to me.

ANDY

It aint right to use the word "coon" no more. It's hurtful.

160

OPHELIA

Says who?

ANDY

Says Bob Cole, that's who.

[Taking the shirt from the table, he smells it.]
I think maybe this shirt needs to be washed and ironed.

OPHELIA

Now, Mr. Tribble, you have no business doing that, after you've worked all day out there on that stage in those hot lights. Here, let me help you.

ANDY
[Deeply touched at the offer, he hands her the shirt.]
Why, thank you Ophelia. That's awful nice--

OPHELIA
[She takes the shirt]
I'll hang it on the back of the door, you can do it when you come in tomorrow.

ANDY

Gee, thanks.

OPHELIA

Don't you worry about Bessie none, she knows what she's doing. You did well when you married her. Don't know what she saw in you, though. Don't know how you ever had the kid—you on tour all the time. She' out there parading for the woman's vote while you in here just telling the same old jokes over and over. Wouldn't surprise me none if she weren't helpin' those poor strikers from the Montgomery Ward factories.

ANDY

Amos said they were sending in Negros to beat-up on the strikers. Those traitors.

OPHELIA

They got to feed their families, too.

161

ANDY

Yeah, but you don't do it like that. You don't turn on your own people.

OPHELIA

We can turn lots a ways when hunger beats at the door.

ANDY

Can you just for once take my side?

OPHELIA

Sure, where do you want me to take it?

[ANDY starts to throw the balls at the screen]

I say, let him without the sin cast the first stone!

[He thinks better of it.]

I just can't image what got stuck down that crapper . . .

ANDY

[Looking sheepishly at the balls that have one missing.]

Beats me.

[Joyfully, he dumps the two back in the wastebasket.]

I guess Bessie hates the theatre, too.

OPHELIA

She's got that theatre in her blood, just like you. You both stung by the same bug.

ANDY

Well, thanks, at least for that.

[OPHELIA has left her charwoman outfit hanging over the screen. Surprisingly, she emerges dressed elegant and sophisticated, in coat, hat, and fox furs.]

OPHELIA

Off in the snow I go!

ANDY

Where'd you shoot that? With that cold, you need to go to bed.

OPHELIA

Can't. 'Got to go get me a husband! A hunk!

ANDY

What about that church of yours? How come you can't find a nice respectable man there?

OPHELIA

I'm not lookin' for no nice respectable man, I'm lookin' for a husband.

ANDY

Rich and handsome.

OPHELIA

Did I say he had to be rich and handsome? As long as he loves me and cherishes me, he can be a little old frog, for all I care. But when I kiss him . . . Mmmm mmm. When I kiss him, he will turn into my hunk of a prince!

ANDY

And what will you turn into?

OPHELIA

The first chapel I can find!

ANDY

You need to muster up the gumption to speak to that new janitor you said was so lonely.

OPHELIA

Harry?! I'll have you know I already have.

ANDY

No kiddin'? Well, give me the hook!

OPHELIA

I'll wait in line. Yes, I am *so happy!* I found out why he looked so lonely.

ANDY

Why was that?

OPHELIA

He'd been to prison.

ANDY

Prison! Good God! For what? Stealing?

OPHELIA

Oh, no! What do you take me for? Harry aint no *thief.*

ANDY

Thank goodness. That's all we need around here. Where's my grouch bag?
Oh, there it is.

OPHELIA

'Was only for murder.

ANDY

Murder!?

OPHELIA

'Weren't his fault. He just gave his second wife a little nudge is all. *She*
fell off the bridge.

ANDY

What?! And that's why he was in prison?

OPHELIA

Oh, no, not for that! Good heavens, no. Harry was in prison because he
pushed his third wife out the window. But *she* opened it.

ANDY

What happened to his first wife?

OPHELIA

Oh, Harry drowned her. *She* couldn't swim--

ANDY

Wait a minute! I thought you said you were "happy" about him?

164

OPHELIA

I am. **He's *single*.**

> [She sings *I'm Just Wild About Harry* by Noble Sissle and
> Eubie Blake, 1921:]

There's some fellow for me in this world
Harry's his name
That's what I claim
Why for ev'ry fellow there
Must be a girl
I've found my mate
By kindness of fate

I'm just wild about Harry
And Harry's wild about me!
The heav'nly blisses of his kisses,
Fills me with ecstasy!
He's sweet just like chocolate candy,
Or like the honey from the bee
Oh, I'm just wild about Harry,
And he's just wild about me.

Now I'm just wild about Harry
And Harry's wild about me!
The heav'nly blisses of his kisses,
Fills me with ecstasy!
Say now he's sweet just like chocolate candy,
Or like the honey from a bee
Oh, I'm just wild about Harry,
And he's just wild about, cannot do without,
He's just wild about me.

ANDY

Get out of here!

OPHELIA
[Looking out the window]
It's still snowin' outside.

ANDY

Most vaudeville houses have a sleeper jump. It stays warm up there in the winter.

OPHELIA

Why do you call them a "sleeper jump?"

ANDY

Because it's so far up it takes about an overnight train trip to get here.

OPHELIA

I think the snow is beautiful. For a little while it makes the world clean. Covers all the dirt. I tell you: I can't keep up with all this showbiz talk of yours. Like "playing to the haircuts."

ANDY

That's when you're last on the bill. You have to play to the audience who's getting up and leaving. You end up playing to the back of their heads. "Haircuts," see?

OPHELIA

Maybe working on the farm is better than that.

ANDY

For some people.

OPHELIA

We wouldn't have food to eat if it weren't for the farmers. It aint such a bad thing.

ANDY

Not for Amos. He loves it. I guess. I hope he loves it.

OPHELIA

What do they mean when they talk about "takin' your pictures back?"

ANDY

You mean, "Give back your pictures?"

OPHELIA

That's it!

166

ANDY

The photos of you in the lobby, they give them back. That means you are fired. No. Amos wasn't fired. He took the veil--chose to leave the show.

OPHELIA

My, my. I'll just never learn how you show folks are talking these days.

[She has something on her mind. She disguises it:]

I had a friend 'wanted to sing at a wedding at church. Well, she croaked like a dead frog but no one would tell her for fear of hurting her feelings. What would you have done?

ANDY

Easy. I would 'of told her.

OPHELIA

And hurt the poor soul's feelings? And break her heart?

ANDY

I think it would be best. Sometimes it's best to know the truth, even when it hurts. Ophelia, what are trying to tell me? Have you heard something? About Amos?

OPHELIA

Yes. But no. Not about Amos. I . . . uh . . . overheard them in the office. I wasn't eavesdropping, no they were speaking pretty loud––

ANDY

What? Tell me. Was it about me? What about me? Tell me!

OPHELIA

[She pauses.]
You aint going to sing at no wedding!

ANDY

What?

OPHELIA

Well, . . . I don't think you have to worry about breaking your legs.

167

[ANDY sits at the mirror and looks at himself.]

At first, I thought they were saying you were nice and clean. "He's all washed up." That' what they said. But that means——

ANDY

I know what that means!

OPHELIA

I didn't want to tell you. They just got too much of the same thing--

ANDY

Just stop--!

OPHELIA
[She stops. Then carefully:]
Vaudeville ain't gonna last, you know. The "Two a Day" has done seen its day--

[ANDY throws his hands up for her to be silent!]

Those movin' pictures are going to take its place. They are small now but soon . . . It'll "Go big," isn't what you say?

ANDY

Yes. That's what we say. "Go big."

[They are silent. OPHELIA holds back her tears for him.]
What's the matter with *you*?

OPHELIA

Weddings always make me cry. 'You going to be all right?

ANDY

Why shouldn't I? I'm used to it.

When I was a kid, there was this white boy 'used to beat me up. My Daddy took it to the judge and filled suit. He was white, you see; he could do that. But the judge just said it was "a boy's fight" and left it at that. I had to face being small. Even when I tried being a jockey at the races.

OPHELIA

You'd of made a good jockey. The Kentucky Derby—

ANDY

The horse threw me and about killed me. I've had a yellow streak since.

OPHELIA

They say you just got to get back up on that horse when that happens.

ANDY

Yes. My Daddy did that. Like his grandfather, a Baptist preacher in pioneer Kentucky.

OPHELIA

You? The grandson of a preacher?

ANDY

Great grandson. Why, is that so surprising?

OPHELIA

No. I just find it hard to believe.

ANDY

He was friends with Thomas Jefferson. They called great granddaddy, "Old Ironside." Because he never backed down from what he knew was right. Daddy was the same.

OPHELIA

So, that's where you get your stubbornness.

ANDY

We get it honest. It's in our blood. Black or white we bleed the same.

Daddy married a freed Negra slave. He and Mama were so in love. 'You'd never seen two people devoted to each other the way Mama and Daddy were. And that love just poured out to Amos and me.

People in Kentucky didn't take much to it, so they left and went to Indiana. Lots of people goin' there at the time, I guess. Didn't care so much what color you were. Daddy was a preacher's son, see, and he believed in what the Bible said: that we's the same: no male or female, slave or free . . .

169

Problem is, not everybody knew their Bible. Daddy stood on its principals. And one day a man principally shot him for it.

OPHELIA

I'm sorry.

ANDY

Mama about grieved herself to death after Daddy was gone. Well, . . . until she married again. 'Course, she had to. Weren't no other choice. Not for a woman with two kids.

OPHELIA

Your momma and daddy must have loved you and Amos. I bet you was all the hugginest family!

ANDY

"Spoiled by love," people used to say.

OPHELIA

You'd never know it the way you and Amos act towards each other.

ANDY

We get that honest from Mom's mother.

OPHELIA

What do you mean? Your grandmamma wasn't a hugger?

ANDY

Oh, Grandmamma believed in hugging. Huggin' everybody! She always said, that way you knew how big to dig the hole.

OPHELIA

Huh! I know what she means.

ANDY

I guess. She had been a slave. Tough old bird. Trusted nobody. She was just different, I guess. Still . . . it used to worry us when grandmamma hugged us.

[He sings *Nobody* by Bert Williams and Alex Rogers, 1905]
When life seems full of clouds and rain

170

And I am full of nothin' and pain
Who soothes my thumping, bumping brain?
Nobody

When winter comes with snow and sleet
And me with hunger and cold feet
Who says, "Here's twenty-five cents, go ahead and get somethin'
To eat?"
Nobody

I ain't never done nothin' to nobody
I ain't never done nothin' to nobody, no time
So until I get somethin' from somebody sometime
I'll never do nothin' for nobody, no time

When summer comes all cool and clear
And my friends see me drawing near
Who says "Come in, have some beer"
Nobody

When I was in that railroad wreck
And thought I'd cashed in my last check
Who took the engine off my neck?
Not a soul

I ain't never done nothin' to nobody
I ain't never done nothin' to nobody, no time
Until I get somethin' from somebody sometime
I'll never do nothin' for nobody, no time

> [OPHELIA laughs. ANDY laughs. But ANDY's mirrored reflection brings him back to the present, and he groans at the darkened future it holds]

Damn. Now it's back to the auditions. I hate auditions.

OPHELIA
What you talkin' about?

ANDY
You got to prove yourself all over again. It always makes me so nervous.

171

OPHELIA

Even after all these years?

ANDY

Especially after all these years. I want to do my best. That's always been my motto.

OPHELIA

And that makes you nervous?

ANDY

Terrified.

OPHELIA

You show business folk are a strange lot! I sure wouldn't do something I hated. I say, if you can't do it with love, don't do it at all.

ANDY

I just want to "kill 'em!"

OPHELIA

I want to kill them too, especially those bullies fighting the union but it's against the Commandments!

ANDY

No. I mean kill 'em *with laughter*. We need to laugh at ourselves. When you laugh at yourself you see yourself for who you are. No better than anybody else. No bigger. No smaller. That's what makes the banana peel so funny: the high and mighty fall to the ground like the rest of us.

The "Two A Day" makes them laugh. Maybe for just a few minutes they can leave the burdens of this world behind and find some color, some joy. Some healing.

OPHELIA

You're here kind of late, aren't you?

ANDY

It's nice to have the room to myself for a few minutes.

172

OPHELIA

I always try and wait until the place clears out. 'You all getting undressed. Running around half naked.

ANDY

The dressing room is the one place where we take off more than we put on.

OPHELIA

Now, what are you talkin' about?

ANDY

You have to take off who you are. What troubles a man . . . Angers him. You always clean your face before you put the make-up on.

OPHELIA

I almost didn't recognize Mr. Amos without the makeup. Getting married and having babies has fattened him up some. He looked happy.

ANDY

I'll never forgive him.

OPHELIA

Oh, now, that's no way to be.

ANDY

I'm sorry but that's the way I am.

OPHELIA

Old Ironside, huh? You're just hurting yourself. When you forgive, it's like saying, "Evil, you can stay outside my doorstep. I aint having nothing to do with you no more!"

ANDY

Easier said than done. He hated the stage—

OPHELIA

You had good times together.

ANDY

Did we? I don't remember.

OPHELIA

Sure, you do. You said so yourself. Back in Kentucky when you was playing out there in the field until that last little glimmer of sunlight was gone . . .

ANDY

[Sings *Home Sweet Home* by Henry Bishop and John Howard Puyne, 1914]
Mid pleasures and palaces though we may roam
Be it ever so humble, there's no place like home
A charm from the skies seems to hallow us there
Which seek thro' the world, is ne'er met elsewhere
Home! Home!
Sweet, sweet home!
There's no place like home
There's no place like home!

[OPHELIA sings with him:]
An exile from home splendor dazzles in vain
Oh give me my lowly thatched cottage again
The birds singing gaily that came at my call
And gave me the peace of mind dearer than all
Home, home, sweet, sweet home
There's no place like home, there's no place like home!

OPHELIA

[She smiles at the thought, then with knitted brow:]
Your mama should have taken the switch to both of you!

ANDY

We just wanted a few more minutes. My, how we could squeeze the last drop out of a day!

OPHELIA

Don't let the sun go down on that anger.

ANDY

'Best to get mad after the sun done gone down. That way you have a full twenty-four hours to be angry before it goes back down again.

You say no one is out there on stage?

OPHELIA

Just the manager. Going through notes, I think. I bet your daddy made a difference in this world. And Mr. Andy Tribble will, too, if he'll ever stop and see that there's a light inside of him that needs to shine.

ANDY

If there's a light inside of me it's a *ghost light.*

OPHELIA

Hold on to that little bit of light before it's gone. It'll make a difference in this world.

ANDY

And *you* are making a difference?!

OPHELIA

I like to think so. In just a small way. In my way. If only to offer the world a clean floor. Kind of like the snow. Clean sheets. A clean toilet.

ANDY

That's not going to make a big difference to the world.

OPHELIA

Maybe not big. Maybe not the world. But it sure enough will to that person sitting on the crapper!
>[She throws her furs over the shoulder, heads to the door, and is gone.]

ANDY
>[Left now only with the reflection of himself in the mirror.]
This is the place where we take it off.

[He drops his head in despair. When he raises it:]
Any fool can play the lime light. That's what they called it, before electricity. They used to heat up a cylinder of lime and it would burn the brightest light onto the stage . . . they called it "being in the lime light." And it feels so good. Any fool can play it--

[He observes the darkened cork.]
If they would stop fighting, if they could laugh, then they could listen. Before the light goes out.

[He looks over at the screen where OPHELIA's charwoman outfit is hanging. What's he got to lose? He grabs the outfit and starts to put it on. He puts on her mob cap. Rubs on some rouge and lipstick, then the charcoal. He leans back from the mirror to admire his creation: The Charwoman.]

"I's got to find me a husband! A hunk!"

[As he exits for the stage, he stops, goes to the wastebasket and brings out the two rubber balls. He shoves them into his chest, adjusts his new found breasts, and with a twist of his hips exits with mop and pail as the lights go out on the scene.]

Scene Two

It is the empty stage at the Pekin. The curtains are open and the stage lights have been left on; besides the ghost lamp in the corner, the place looks deserted. ANDY, dressed as the Charwoman walks to centerstage and looks out over the lights. She plays at moping the stage.

ANDY

It's been a hard job cleaning this old place by myself. I wonder if they'll miss me? I never liked cleaning floors. I did it; but I still believe that "Floors . . . are *beneath me!*"

It's a hard job cleaning windows. I did 'em; cause I still believe, "It's the only job I can *see myself* doing."

It's hard to have a job and be a woman. Men don't like it. My girlfriend says her husband told her that a career and marriage just don't go together. That's what he said. "They don't go together." It's the truth, too: he hasn't had a job in years!

It's hard to find a good man. And to keep him happy. The other day my fella left a note on the ice box. It read, "This aint working, goodbye!" Can you image? I opened the ice box, it was working just fine.

[She looks out into the darkened audience]

You out there, do you think . . . maybe *you* . . . could like me? I like you.

[As the Charwoman, ANDY sings acapella *Under the Bamboo Tree* by Robert Cole and J. Rosamond Johnson, and James Weldon Johnson, J. W. Stern & Co., 1902]

Down in the jungles lived a maid,
Of royal blood though dusky shade,
A marked impression once she made,
Upon a Zulu from Matabooloo;
And ev'ry morning he would be
Down underneath the bamboo tree,
Awaiting there his love to see
And then to her he'd sing:

If you lak-a-me lak I lak-a-you
And we lak-a-both the same,
I lak-a-say,
This very day,
I lak-a change your name;
'Cause I love-a-you and love-a you true
And if you-a love-a me.
One live as two, two live as one,
Under the bamboo tree.

[Surprisingly, he is accompanied at the piano.]
Ah, yes, . . . the fancy fingers of Bob Motts! He knows my key.
Last time he played for me, the *black keys* stopped working.
[Beat]
It was a *flat-out disaster.*
[Piano rimshot. The piano starts to play again.]

Bob says he can play anything on that piano!
I says "Anything?" He says "ANYTHING!"
I says, "You can't play the trumpet on that piano!"

[Another rimshot. She sings to the accompaniment.]
And in this simple jungle way,
He wooed the maiden ev'ry day,
By singing what he had to say;
One day he seized her
And gently squeezed her.
And then beneath the bamboo green,
He begged her to become his queen;

177

The dusky maiden blushed unseen
And joined him in his song.

If you lak-a-me lak I lak-a-you
And we lak-a-both the same,
I lak-a-say,
This very day,
I lak-a change your name;
'Cause I love-a-you and love-a you true
And if you-a love-a me.
One live as two, two live as one,
Under the bamboo tree.

[She talks]
It's lonely being a Spinster. You don't want to go to things by yourself. So, I go out with my spinster girlfriend. Last week we went to the zoo. We were there, must have been five minutes, and one big gorilla pulls apart the bars, grabbed my friend, and ran off into the woods with her!
[She weeps.]
We couldn't find her for three days! Then they said she was in the hospital! I went to see her. She was bruised and scratched from head to toe! She was crying something awful. I said, "Honey, you're going to be okay; you've just got to pull yourself together!" She just sobbed and said, "He never visits, he never writes!"

[Piano rimshot. She sings and dances:]
This little story strange but true,
Is often told in Mataboo,
Of how this Zulu tried to woo
His jungle lady
In tropics shady;
Although the scene was miles away,
Right here at home I dare to say,
You'll hear some Zulu ev'ry day,
Gush out this soft refrain:

If you lak-a-me lak I lak-a-you
And we lak-a-both the same,
I lak-a-say,
This very day,
I lak-a change your name;

'Cause I love-a-you and love-a you true
And if you-a love-a me.
One live as two, two live as one,
Under the bamboo tree.

> [She takes a very dramatic curtsey. From the audience, there is some clapping. ANDY is taken by surprise. He shields his eyes with his hands to see through the stage lights out into the audience.]

Is that you, Bob?
> [From the darkened auditorium we hear:]

BOB
Yes.

ANDY
I can't see for the lights. Thanks for playing.

BOB
You're very talented.

ANDY
Well, thanks Bob. Who you got out there with you? I thought you were alone.

BOB
Just some friends of mine that happened to stop by.

ANDY
I'm sorry. I was told the place was empty.

BOB
We were happy to see you perform.

> [BOB walks up to the stage, we see him in silhouette.]

ANDY
You're not Bob Mott.

BOB

No, I'm not Robert Mott. Robert had to leave; about the time you came on. We just came to look at the place. Good timing if you ask me.

ANDY

I was just goofing off.

BOB

You like to entertain, I can tell. You work here for Robert?

ANDY

For about a year.

BOB

Do you juggle?

ANDY

[Sadly]

Yes.

BOB

Well, don't! You're too talented for that. I'd say Robert's mighty fortunate to have you. This is some place he's got here.

ANDY

They call it the "Temple of Music."

BOB

He's a pretty powerful politician around these parts. Since Mushmouth Johnson was killed, I'd say he's the number one Black power broker. Robert seems to know how to keep the police and politicians on his side. And he's bringing in the clientele.

ANDY

Mrs. Potter Palmer comes here quite a lot.

BOB

The wife of the millionaire who built the Palmer House?

ANDY

It was a wedding present to her.

BOB

I wouldn't mind a present like that, would you?

ANDY

No, I suppose not.

BOB

Well, I've got a present for you, Lawrence. I've seen your brother before, but I pictured you taller.

ANDY

"Lawrence?" I'm not Lawrence.

BOB

Of course not! My apologies. Larry.

ANDY

I'm not Larry.

BOB

You're not Lawrence Chenault, the performer?

ANDY

No . . .
                    [He thinks better of it.]
I get that all the time.

BOB

Oh. Well, us little guys have got to stick together. Do you often dress in drag?

ANDY

I just was trying something different. Its' . . . been a rough day.

· BOB

Well, it worked. I see a big future ahead of you.

            [BOB stops and stares at ANDY. There is an awkward
            moment that is too intimate.]
Are you here by yourself?

ANDY

Yeah-up.

[Nervous, ANDY does a time step.]

BOB

Are you free for dinner? I'd like to talk with you about your career. Or, better yet. We're headed for Europe in a few days, why not go with us? I'll show you around London.

ANDY

I'm . . . a married man.

BOB

Oh?

ANDY

She'll be here shortly. As soon as she gets out of jail.

[BOB, taking this as part of the act, laughs hysterically.]

ANDY

No, I really am married. And with a son. She's only in jail for protesting. She's no criminal or anything. She just has strong ideas—she thinks women should have the vote.

BOB

Oh. I see. Well, bring them along.

ANDY

Uh, I couldn't do that.

BOB

Attached to the floodlights here, are you? And the charcoal?

ANDY   .

You might say.

BOB

Well, I got a kick out of you on stage. You have a gift. To make people happy. I get rather blue at times, and tonight you got me laughing!

ANDY

Did I?

BOB

If you change your mind, here's my card. I can picture a beautiful future
for you.

    [BOB hands ANDY his card. ANDY reads the card.]

ANDY

All the big stars tell me the same thing. "Bob Cole," is it? As in, **the** Bob Cole?

BOB

Guilty. I didn't get your name?

ANDY

    [Convinced that he has been bamboozled]
J. M. Barrie. Now, if you'll excuse me, this little blackbird has got to fly
to Neverland.

    [He exits leaving a befuddled BOB Cole standing by the
    apron of the stage.]

Scene Three

The lights bring us back into the dressing room. More frustrated than ever,
ANDY returns OPHELIA's hat, apron and dress, tossing the juggling balls
back into the trash bin. There is a knock at the door. OPHELIA barges into
the room with a huff!

ANDY

Ophelia, I'm so sorry!

OPHELIA

After working all day, and me fighting this cold—

ANDY

I can explain—

OPHELIA

Sick as a dog, I got one foot in the grave and one on the banana peel—

183

ANDY

I know— I'm sorry—

OPHELIA

It's a sin for a man to dress up as a woman—says so in the Bible—

ANDY

Does it? Yes, well . . .

OPHELIA

I've never laughed so hard in my life!

ANDY

What?

OPHELIA

I laughed so hard, my sides is still achin.' And the sickness: *My cold, it just went away!* Laughed itself away, I guess! I've never felt better! You must of cured me, Mr. Tribble. I don't know who you was a'imitatin', but she must have been a'**scintillatin'**! I am so happy! I about peed my pants!
> [She grabs ANDY's face with both her hands and kisses him a little too hard and a little too long! BESSIE enters unannounced]

BESSIE

Should I be jealous?!

ANDY

Bessie!
> [ANDY runs and embraces his wife. Kisses her]

OPHELIA

Oh, Mrs. Tribble! Thank the Lord!

BESSIE

> [Protesting the fuss, she laughs. To ANDY:]
You're getting makeup all over me!

ANDY

I'm sorry! Are you all right?

BESSIE

I'm fine. I'm fine--

OPHELIA

They said you were in jail——

ANDY

The suffrage——the union strikers--

BESSIE

The officer saw you in the show. He came back laughing so hard he told them to let us all go home!

OPHELIA

I ran into Mr. Mott in the lobby——he says your job is *very* secure. He might raise your salary!

ANDY

Who else was in the audience!

OPHELIA

No one special. Just Cole and Johnson!

BESSIE

[Excited!]
Cole and Johnson!? Here?

OPHELIA

[Feeding off her excitement!]
Yes! Isn't it exciting? Who is Cole and Johnson?

ANDY

Bob Cole?
[He takes out the card and looks at it]

OPHELIA

Who is Bob Cole?

BESSIE

Who is Bob Cole? Just one of the most successful composers and producers around!

185

ANDY

No . . .

BESSIE

"Under the Bamboo Tree—"

ANDY

He wrote it.
[He drops the card and falls into his chair.]

OPHELIA

What did he say to ya? What'd he say?!

ANDY

He said he pictured a beautiful future for me.

OPHELIA

What did ya say to him? What'd ya say?
[She picks up the card]

ANDY

I told him I was busy.

BESSIE

Busy? Doing what?

ANDY

Committing suicide.

OPHELIA

You dumb ass!

ANDY

There is something wrong with me.

OPHELIA

Uh-huh.

ANDY

Something seriously wrong

186

Uh-Huh

ANDY

To throw away a chance like that!

OPHELIA

Uh-Huh

ANDY

I could cut my throat!

OPHELIA

Uh—can I get a knife?

BESSIE

Oh, sweetheart . . .

ANDY

How the hell did I know it was Bob Cole?

OPHELIA

Well, it says it right here on his card!

ANDY

So many big stars have told me the same thing, I didn't pay but little attention. Bob Cole wants to make me a star!

OPHELIA

And you flushed it down the crapper!

ANDY

Yes, I did.

BESSIE

Don't you see what this means? You finally broke a leg!
[She hugs and kisses him. He looks to OPHELIA]

OPHELIA

You're still a turd in my bowl!
[She exits laughing]

ANDY

Was there anyone else in the audience I should know about?

BESSIE

Your brother.

ANDY

Amos? Are you sure it was him?

BESSIE

He completely ignored me. It was him all right.

ANDY

I'm sorry—

BESSIE

He was laughing his head off. It was good to see him laugh.

[ANDY runs to the door]

Let him go, Andy.

ANDY

He was here earlier—

BESSIE

LET HIM GO.

[ANDY stops at the doorway, his back to his wife.]
I know. "He was never well." But he's a grown man, let him go. Love him enough now to let him go. Sometimes, Andy, I can't help but think this anger you have with him runs deeper, from something else--

ANDY

What do you mean? It's just that, well, he'll die on that farm--

BESSIE

And so will you, and so will I. He'll be in the field. You'll be on the stage. But he'll be doing what makes him happy.

ANDY

[He turns, admires his wife.]

What did I ever do to deserve you? Thank God they let you out and it's all over--

BESSIE

I'm afraid it's far from over. But *you* must have knocked 'em bowlegged out there. What did you do?

ANDY

I don't know. I just kind of let it all out of me. All the rage. And made it funny somehow. Whoever thought rage could be the fuel of funny?

BESSIE

They said you were screamingly funny—a shop stopper.

[Taking notice of their son's drawing]

Oh, look. How cute.

ANDY

Atwood's picture of the three of us. See? Me, Atwood, and you.

BESSIE

[Grabbing the picture.]

My nose is not that big!

ANDY

[Tearing up the card]

I don't know. And I don't care. Maybe it's Providence. Maybe the farm is calling us back—

BESSIE

The farm? But Cole and Johnson—

ANDY

I'm just glad to be center stage with you right now. Let's go out and have dinner and celebrate!

BESSIE

Let me at least stop and check on Atwood, and wash up. 'Get this prison smell off me. I need to get into a different skirt. Unless?

189

ANDY

Unless?

BESSIE

Unless, of course, I can borrow one of yours?

ANDY

Now, that's what you call "the tag line."

BESSIE

I'll meet you down at the café on the corner.

ANDY

Wait. I'll go with you.

BESSIE

Are you kiddin? Like that? They'll think I'm with my sister. And my sister aint that ugly!
[As she is going]
I'll be fine. I've already been to jail!

ANDY

[At the mirror, he looks at himself.]
Ugly? Ugly?! I thought I looked pretty good. Or good anyway.

[He admires the picture that Atwood drew. His thoughts return to AMOS.]
It looks a lot like Amos. I never noticed before.

[He sings *My Buddy* by Walter Donaldson and Gus Kahn, 1922]
Life is a book that we study
Some of its leaves bring a sigh
There it was written by a buddy
That we must part, you and I

Poor Amos. "Leave him alone." Let him die on the farm? He's doing what he loves to do?
[He sings:]

Nights are long since you went away

I think about you all through the day
My buddy, my buddy
Nobody quite so true
. *Miss your voice, the touch of your hand*
Just long to know that you understand
My buddy, my buddy
Your buddy misses you
Miss your voice, the touch of your hand
Just long to know that you understand
My buddy, my buddy
Your buddy misses you

[AMOS enters.]

AMOS

Knock knock?

ANDY

Who's there?

AMOS

Police.

ANDY

Police who?

AMOS

Police put your pants back on! May I come in?

ANDY

So, you were out there, too.

AMOS

In the back.

ANDY

They let Bessie out. Everything's okay. Well, for now, she says.

AMOS

I saw Cole and Johnson in the audience. I saw Bob Cole talking to you afterwards.

191

ANDY

Oh, yes. We're like that:

> [Sarcastically, showing crossed fingers, as if he and Cole are close and tight friends! ANDY goes to removing the face makeup.]

I thought he was kind of coming on to me, and well . . . The way he was looking at me—oh, damn, am I an idiot.

> [Disgusted with himself, he works at removing the makeup]

You are right. It's all about me. It always has been.

AMOS

Andy?

ANDY

Yes?

AMOS

I was thinking about the farm—

ANDY

Not another word about it, Amos! I've made up my mind. I'm leaving this hell hole and coming with you. We're changing shows too fast, and the ticket prices are way too high—

AMOS

I was thinking . . .

ANDY

I can't thank you enough. It's way too dangerous here in Chicago. Bob Mott is going to get himself killed the way that Mushmouth did. He's not well as it is. Then, do you think these elitists are going to stick around—you're darn tootin' they'll be out like lightening—it'll turn into burlesque with a black and tan café upstairs, painted ladies "dancing across the table," dancing the shimmy—

AMOS

I kind of forgot—

ANDY

Bessie will grow to love the open spaces and the fresh air will be good for Atwood. Like when we were kids in Kentucky--

AMOS

I made a promise to a friend who needs a job on the farm.

[ANDY stops and listens]
It skipped my mind. I'm really, sorry, I gave him my word . . . and well,
it's just that . . . well, a fella ain't much if he goes against his word . . . and
I . . . I--

ANDY

I see.

AMOS

It's just that he needs the job real bad. And, well, you've got a job . . .

ANDY

I understand. It's okay. Really, Amos, it's okay. I thought the house was
empty tonight. I learned something about myself, Amos. It took just their
applause to make me feel better about myself. To lift me out of the dark.
'Sure would like to learn how to do it myself—for when there's no one
sitting out there.

AMOS

[After an awkward silence, he notices the drawing.]
Your talent is sure not as an artist!

ANDY

It's Atwood's.

AMOS

Ahh!! . . . and beautiful, too. I—uh--knew it couldn't be yours.

ANDY

Don't you see? It's his drawing of the three of us. Look at all that detail.
He's got all the clothes, the features . . . Ha! He's got Bessie's nose just right.

AMOS

They have no feet.

ANDY

[His son has drawn the family with no feet.]
I hadn't noticed. They don't, do they?

AMOS

I'm glad they let Bessie out of jail.

ANDY

You are too hard on Bessie.

AMOS

I have my reasons.

ANDY

I wondered . . .

AMOS

Come on, Andy. We toured together during those months.

ANDY

[Nods to himself. He puts on a shirt.]
Our grandfather, they say, was friends with Thomas Jefferson. The writer of the Declaration of Independence . . . patriot of freedom--

AMOS

Yes, Daddy told us many a time.

ANDY

But Jefferson had slaves and took a young one for himself. It wasn't all that long ago, Amos. Not really. And the evils of slavery haven't stopped. Not for any of us. And not for Bessie.

AMOS

Do you know who it was?!

ANDY

Bessie never said. I'll never ask.

AMOS

The bastard who did it should be hanged!

ANDY

I agree. But the baby is not to blame. The child knew nothing of it.

AMOS

Spoken like a faithful husband.

ANDY

You always said that I kept a mistress. The stage.

AMOS

I said a lot of things I wish were forgotten.

ANDY

Then let it go with Bessie. He's my son. And who knows—maybe he'll grow up and be a giant to his little old dad.
[They laugh. ANDY admires the picture one last time.]
It is a giant of a love I have for that little guy.

AMOS

Daddy used to say that of us.
[He reaches out and takes hold of his brother's arm]
You're the only connection I have now with Daddy.

[The two men fall into a long-neglected embrace.]

ANDY

Are you feeling okay?

AMOS

I'm fine.

ANDY

You're going to die out there on that farm, you know?

AMOS

You're going to die out there on that stage, you know?

ANDY

Well then, . . . we'll go out doing what we love most. You need to eat something. Listen. I'm meeting Bessie down at the diner on the corner. Come join us. It's on me!

AMOS
[Falling into their old interruptive routine as they exit.]

195

Awww . . .Don't go out there, brother Andy, they filled up.

ANDY

But, brother Amos, they have the best––

AMOS

'Got food poisoned from it. I suggest you go to--

ANDY

Oh, I went there last time, brother Amos--

AMOS

How'd you go, brother Andy?––

ANDY

Driving-

AMOS

Driving what?--

ANDY

A brand new ––

AMOS

You'll never make it with that! What time is it?

ANDY

Its––

AMOS

Is it that late?

[As ANDY switches off the light, its last glimmer sees them out the door. Safely home, once more. And this theater is dark.]

CURTAIN

Postscript

Andrew A. Tribble 1876--1935

Before there were outrageous female Black comic characters of Tyler Perry, Eddie Murphy, and Flip Wilson, there was Andrew "Andy" Tribble, vaudeville song and dance man, and the father of comic female impersonations.[20]

Born 1876, in Union City, Madison County, he and his brother Amos were the sons of Alice Clutter and Andrew Tribble, a grandson of the Rev. Andrew Tribble.

The Rev. Andrew Tribble came to Kentucky in 1781, and had been friends with Thomas Jefferson in Virginia. Rev. Tribble served in the Revolutionary War as an American patriot and was imprisoned for his battle for freedom of religion. Thomas Jefferson attended Tribble's church in Albemarle County and is noted as crediting the Rev. Andrew Tribble with his plan for American democracy.[21]

Figure 8
Andrew A. Tribble *The New York Age*, Dec 24, 1908

"Andrew Tribble was the pastor of a small Baptist Church, which held its monthly meetings at a short distance from Mr. Jefferson's house, eight or ten years before the American Revolution. Mr. Jefferson attended the meetings of the church for several months in succession, and after one of them, asked Elder Tribble to go home and dine with him, with which he complied. Mr. Tribble asked Mr. Jefferson how he was pleased with their church government? Mr. Jefferson replied, that it had struck him with great force, and had interested him much; that he considered it the only form of *pure democracy* that then existed in the world, and had concluded that it

[20] Harry J. Elam, Jr. and David Krasner, *African American Performance and Theater History*, (Oxford, New York: Oxford University Press, 2001), pp. 179-80.
[21] Anna Berkes, "Andrew Tribble," *Thomas Jefferson Monticello*, (Monticello.org) March 25, 2008.

would be *the best plan of Government for the American Colonies*. This was several years before the declaration of American Independence."[22]

At the age of six, Andy Tribble and his family left Kentucky and moved to Richmond, Indiana. One would conclude that Andy was reared in a loving family, for at age twelve, his father filed an affidavit against Frank Haner, a small boy, for striking Andy. "It was a boy's fight, and Prosecutor Starr gave some good advice to settle the matter without resorting to the law."[23] Andrew tried his hand as a racehorse jockey but was thrown from a horse and developed a "yellow streak," as he put it, against riding. Then Amos and Andy ventured onto the stage as musicians.[24]

Figure 9
"In Old Kentucky" Strobridge & Co. Lith.; Cincinnati; New York: Strobridge Lith. Co., c1894.

The boys were members of The Original Pickaninny Band directed by Master Walter Brister sighted as "the youngest bandmaster in the world." They performed in the 1890s play *In Old Kentucky* by C. T. Dazey. These young African American musicians portrayed Negro children performing music before and during the play outside the theater with ragtime music. The band was to have been originally titled the Woodlawn Wangdoodles, organized by Master John Powell.[25]

The Tribble brothers outgrew the Pickaninny image and took their chance on the vaudeville stage, singing and dancing on the music hall stages of State Street, Chicago, and then left the stage. Andy worked as a hotel

---

[22] "Anecdote of Mr. Jefferson" *Christian Watchman* (Boston, MA.), July 14, 1826, pp. 7, 32.
[23] *The Richmond Item* October 30, 1888.
[24] "Well Known Character Comedian," *The New York Age*, December 24, 1908, p. 12.
[25] "Out of sight: the rise of African American popular music, 1889-1895," Notable Kentucky African Americans Database, accessed September 14, 2023, https://nkaa. uky.edu/nkaa/items/show/30000698; "In Old Kentucky," *Notable Kentucky African Americans Database*, accessed September 14, 2023, https://nkaa.uky.edu/nkaa/items/ show/47.

porter, married Bessie Ashbury on October 11, 1899, and their son, Atwood Alonzo Tribble, was born two years later. Amos, became a driver, changed his name to "Trible," returned to Richmond, Indiana, and married Cora Rile in 1901. But Andy's heart was in the theatre, and he returned to vaudeville in 1904, where he and Bessie sang and danced together and then joined the Pekin Theatre. The Pekin Theater was established in 1905, as the first black owned musical and vaudeville stock theatre in the United States. Amidst the struggles for women's suffrage, he donned a skirt one night and went out on stage comically hamming it up. From that day onwards, he brought laughter to a troubled world.[26]

"I never go on the stage unless I try to do my best. That, somehow, has always been my motto, and I have been well paid for sticking to it.

"One night to a very small audience, I was doing my best, not dreaming of anyone watching me but the manager. I was surprised to learn that among the few in the audience were Cole and Johnson. I was also told that they liked my work very much. They sent for me and gave me plenty of encouraging talk and pictured a beautiful future for me. Well, as all of the other big stars had told me the same thing, I paid but little attention to it.

"One day I received a letter bearing the postmark London, England. It was from Cole and Johnson, who were then in London. They reminded me of our agreement. My contract soon arrived. I had no idea what they had planned to do with me, but to make a long story short, they gave me the part of "Ophelia." If you saw the *The Shoo-Fly Regiment,* no doubt but that you remember the part. Now I am "Lily White" in *The Red Moon.*"[27]

"Vaudeville" comes from the French *"Val de Vire,"* the valley of the Vire River in Normandy, where songs were allegedly composed. In the United States, it grew as burlesque comedy, song, and dance from the Circus and Minstrel shows and became the most popular form of entertainment from the 1880s until the 1930s when motion pictures brought about its demise. Vaudeville spanned the life of Andrew Tribble. He was a member of The Colored Vaudeville Benevolent Association 1909.

Robert Cole had teamed up with J. Rosamond Johnson and his brother James Weldon Johnson to write popular songs such as "Under the Bamboo

---

[26] Thomas Bauman, the Pekin, *The Rise and Fall of Chicago's First Black-Owned Theater,* Urbana, Chicago, and Springfield, Illinois, (University of Illinois Press, 2014), pp. 23-26.
[27] *"Well Known Character Comedian,"* The New York Age, Dec 24, 1908, p. 12.

Tree." By 1901, Cole and Johnson had established a vaudeville of elegance and sophistication that catered to the elite classes, always performing in formal dress. In 1911, it was reported that Robert Cole at age 43, while walking with friends, waded out into the Catskill Creek fully dressed and drowned.

J. Rosamond Johnson went on to star in *Porgy and Bess* and *Cabin in the Sky*, and penned hundreds of hymns and songs for musical theatre which included *Lift Every Voice and Sing*. Brother James Weldon Johnson became an author and the U.S. consul to Venezuela. Cole and Johnson had "discovered" Andrew Tribble.

"The comedy of Flip Wilson's gender impersonation was similar to Tribble's in that it based itself in the social and political satire of gender. This type of humor was similar to that used by white minstrels in comic female impersonation and achieved like results: a determined break from the constraints imposed by political comment on the increasing ambivalence of men about the changing social roles of women."[28]

Tribble took charge of the Minstrel Show that adjoined the Boxing Carnival at the Richmond, Indiana Coliseum sponsored by the Colored Union Athletic Association of America March 29, 1918. The boxing match was between Joey Fox and Kid Hendricks with ten percentage receipts going to fund the Red Cross.

Andy Tribble's credits include:
The Man from Bam 1906, *The Red Moon* 1908, *Two African Princes* 1908, The Colored Vaudeville Benevolent Association 1909, *The Shoo-Fly Regiment* 1909, *The Smart Set* 1910, *His Honor the Barber* 1911, *Possum Hollow University* 1915, *Captain Rufus* 1914, *The Dark Spot of Joy* 1918, *Darktown Follies* 1920, *My Friend from Kentucky* 1920, *The Chocolate Brown 1921, Shuffle Along* 1921 and 1924, *Put and Take* 1921, *Oh, Joy!* 1922, *How Come?* 1923, *Tunes and Topics* 1923, *Hit and Run* 1924, *Struttin' Time* 1924, *The Red Moon* 1908 and 1925, *Get it Fixed* 1925, *Charleston Dandies* 1926, *4-11-44 1926, Lady Luck* 1927, *Watermelon* 1927, *Jazz Factory* 1928, *Ophelia Snow from Baltimore* 1928, *Bare Facts of 1928, Back Home Again* 1928, *The Jazz Regiment* 1929, *By Moonlight* 1930, *Brown Buddies* 1930, *A Wife for Sale* 1930, *Fast Life* 1930, *Club Saratoga Review* 1930, *Kilpatrick's Mammoth Minstrels* 1930, *Order in the Court* 1931, *Roof-Garden*

---

[28] Harry L. Elam, Jr. and David Krasner, *African American Performance and Theater History*, (New York: Oxford University Press, 2001), pp. 179-80.

Frolics 1931, Golden Girls 1931, Business Before Pleasure 1931, Roseland Revels 1931, SOB Sister 1931, Pep and Ginger 1931, Candyland 1931, Magnolia Time 1932, Harlem Scandals 1932, Miss Adeline 1932, Radioland Review 1932, Plantations Capers 1934, Brain Sweat 1934.[29]

Figure 10
Andrew Tribble post card with photos of two of his female characters on stage. Trav S.D. *Travalanche.* "Andrew Tribble: Drag Star of *"Darktown."* April 3, 2019

[29] "The Man from Bam," Chicago Tribune, April 15, 1906; Thomas Bauman, The Pekin, (Illinois: University of Illinois Press, 2014), p.144; "Two African Princes," The New York Age, July 9, 1908, p. 6.; "The Colored Vaudeville Benevolent Association", The New York Age, August 5, 1909, p. 6.; "The Shoo-Fly Regiment," The Oklahoma City Times, September 9, 1909, p. 12; "Smart Set," The New York Age, September 1, 1910, p. 6; "His Honor, The Barber," The New York Age, May 11, 1911, p. 6; "Possum Hollow University," Waukegan News-Sun, April 3, 1915, p.6; "The Chocolate Brown," The Chicago Whip, May 21, 1921, p. 6; "O, Joy," The Boston Globe, September 27, 1922, p. 4; "How Come," Press and Sun Bulletin, August 23, 1923, p. 10; "Struttin' Time," The Pittsburg Courier, July 5, 1924, p. 14; "The Red Moon," [Mr. and Mrs. Andrew Tribble] The New York Age, December 3, 1908, p. 6; The Pittsburg Courier, May 23, 1925, p. 10; "4 -11-44," St. Louis Globe-Democrat, December 19, 1926, p. 40; "Miss Ophelia Snow," The New York Age, December 29, 1928, p. 6; "The Jazz Regiment," The Baltimore Sun, March 10, 1929, p. 2; "By Moonlight," The New York Age, March 1, 1930, p. 5; "A Wife for Sale," The New York Age, March 8, 1930, p. 6; "Fast Life," The New York Age, March 15, 1930, p. 7; "Brown Buddies," Baltimore Sun, Sept. 21, 1930, p. 63; "Club Saratoga Review," The New York Age, December 20, 1930, p. 6; "Candyland," The New York Age, February 7, 1931, p. 6; "Order in the Court," The New York Age, March 28, 1931, p. 6; "Roseland Revels," The New York Age, May 2, 1931, p. 6; "Golden Girls," The New York Age, July 6, 1931, p. 6; "Roof Garden Frolics," The New York Age, August 8, 1931, p. 6; "Business Before Pleasure," The New York Age, October 3, 1931, p. 6; "SOB Sister," The New York Age, November 14, 1931, p. 6; "Pep and Ginger," The New York Age, November 7, 1931, p. 6; "Harlem Scandals," The New York Age, January 30, 1932, p. 6; "Magnolia Time," The New York Age, July 23, 1932, p. 6; "Brain Sweat," Times Union, April 5, 1934, p. 16.

On June 19, 1928, Andrew Tribble, along with entertainers like Eubie Blake, joined forces with Bill "Bojangles" Robinson who organized a midnight benefit at the Lafayette Theatre in New York City to raise money in helping a young African American boy return home who was a runner in the 1928 Bunion Derby. Fifteen-year-old T. Josephs was a member of a large family with a paralyzed father who was unable to support his family. T. Josephs finished 15th of 199 men in the Bunion Derby cross country race. The benefit raised money to purchase an automobile for the boy to get home to his family. The Bunion Derby race was a 3,400 transcontinental footrace from Los Angeles, California to New York City. It took eighty-four days. It was sponsored by Charles C. Pyle who promised a $25,000 grand prize as a way of making famous the 2,400 mile mostly unpaved road: U.S. Highway Route 66.

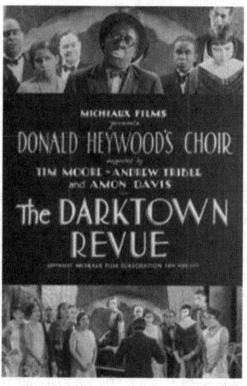

"In a wild grab for glory, a cast of nobodies saw hope in the dust: blacks who escaped the poverty and terror of the Old South; first-generation immigrants with their mother tongue thick on their lips; Midwest farm boys with leather-brown tans. These men were the 'shadow runners,' men without fame, wealth, or sponsors, who came to Los Angeles to face the world's greatest runners and race walkers."[30]

Andy left the New York stage to return home to Richmond, Indiana to be with his brother Amos who died of pneumonia

Figure 11
"The Darktown Revue" movie poster. Directed by Oscar Micheaux, 1931.

in July 1909.[31] Andy partnered on stage with Boots Allen 1909, Jeff DeMount 1911, Matt Marshall 1912, Charles Gibson and Blondie Robinson

---

[30] Charles B. Kastner, Bunion Derby: The 1928 Footrace Across America, (New Mexico: University of New Mexico Press, 2007).
[31] The New York Age, July 22, 1909, p. 6.

1916, Joe Henderson 1926, and Tim Moore, 1931. If Andy Tribble succeeded in keeping the memory of his brother alive in his vaudeville acts, having his partners play him, it was Freeman Gosden and Charles Correll, two white actors, who in 1928, took the two characters and created the *Amos 'n' Andy* radio show. Andy's partner Tim Moore would go on to star on television in *The Amos 'n' Andy Show,* that used black actors. Andy and

Tim had performed together one of the funniest haunted house routines, "Why Leave By the Window," in the Oscar Micheaux talking picture, *The Darktown Revue,* 1931.

The style of "buffoon humor" that emerged in the southern minstrel shows and then vaudeville, first played in black face by white actors, surfaced in the *Amos n Andy* radio and

Figure 12
Andy Tribble and Tim Moore performing "Why Leave By the Window," in the Oscar Micheaux movie *The Darktown Revue,* 1931.

television shows and has been criticized over the years. Yet, it is a style that has capitulated to stardom many white actors such as Jerry Lewis, Jim Nabors, Lucille Ball, Red Skelton, Gracie Allen and thousands of others. It is a style of humor that helps the human, regardless of race, laugh at oneself. The *Amos n' Andy* radio show ran from 1928-1960. The television adaptation ran from 1951-1966.

Andy Tribble suffered from a stoke while performing on stage in Baltimore, Maryland; he died at 61 years old, in his Baltimore home October 16, 1935. The funeral service was performed by The Rev. C. Watkins in the Richmond, Indiana home of his sister, Mrs. Cyrilda Davis, and burial on October 19 at the Earlham Cemetery where his brother Amos had been laid to rest. Surviving him was his wife Bessie; son Atwood; two sisters, Mrs. Cyrilda Davis and Mrs. Ellen Runyan of Richmond Ky; two brothers, Frank Dunbar of Richmond, Indiana and Fielden Dunbar of

Yellow Springs, Ohio. The papers wrote of him as "one of the first Negroes to gain fame as a female impersonator."[32]

Andy and Bessie's son, Atwood Alonzo Tribble, was much taller than his father. *The Pittsburg Courier* called attention to their difference in height and recorded the young son driving his father in a new sports car when Andy returned to Chicago in 1928.[33] He died in Oak Forest, Illinois 1983 at age 82 years old.

---

[32] *Palladium-Item*, October 18, 1935, p. 11, and October 22, 1935 p. 11; "Veteran Actor Dies," *The St. Louis Argus,* December 6, 1935, p. 10.

[33] "Andrew Tribble Back," *The Pittsburg Courier,* Saturday July 28, 1928.

Bibliography

Bauman, Thomas. *The Pekin, The Rise and Fall of Chicago's First Black-Owned Theater.* Urbana, Chicago, and Springfield: Board of Trustees of the University of Illinois, 2014.

Berkes, Anna. "Andrew Tribble," *Thomas Jefferson Monticello*, (Monticello. org) March 25, 2008.

Chicago Tribune. "The Man from Bam." April 15, 1906.

Christian Watchman. "Anecdote of Mr. Jefferson." Boston, MA., July 14, 1826.

Dicker/Sun, Glenda. *African American Theater.* Cambridge, U.K. and Malden, MA: Polity Press, 2008.

Elam, Harry J., Jr. and Krasner, David. *African American Performance and Theater History.* Oxford, New York: Oxford University Press, 2001.

Kastner, Charles B. *Bunion Derby: The 1928 Footrace Across America.* New Mexico: University of New Mexico Press, 2007.

Moran, Jeffrey P. "Tribble, Andrew A.," *Notable Kentucky African Americans Database*, accessed September 12, 2023, https://nkaa.uky.edu/nkaa/items/show/59. New York: Oxford University Press, 2012

Notable Kentucky African Americans Database. "Out of sight: the rise of African American popular music, 1889-1895," accessed September 14, 2023, https://nkaa.uky.edu/nkaa/items/show/30000698; "In Old Kentucky," https://nkaa.uky.edu/nkaa/items/show/47.

Palladium-Item, October 18, 1935 and October 22, 1935.

Press and Sun Bulletin. "How Come." August 23, 1923.

St. Louis Globe-Democrat. "4-11-44." December 19, 1926.

The Baltimore Sun. *"Brown Buddies."* September 21, 1930; *"The Jazz Regiment."* March 10, 1929.

The Boston Globe. *"O, Joy."* September 27, 1922.

The Chicago Whip. *"The Chocolate Brown."* May 21, 1921.

The New York Age. *"A Wife for Sale,"* March 8, 1930; *"Business Before Pleasure."* October 3, 1931; *"By Moonlight,"* March 1, 1930; *"Candyland."* February 7, 1931; *"Club Saratoga Review."* December 20, 1930; *"Fast Life."* March 15, 1930; *"Golden Girls."* July 6, 1931; *"Harlem Scandals."* January 30, 1932; *"His Honor, The Barber,"* May 11, 1911; *"Magnolia Time."* July 23, 1932; *"Miss Ophelia Snow."* December 29, 1928; *"Order in the Court."* March 28, 1931; *"Pep and Ginger."* November 7, 1931; *"Roof Garden Frolics."* August 8, 1931; *"Roseland Revels."* May 2, 1931; *"SOB Sister."* November 14, 1931; "The Colored Vaudeville Benevolent Association", August 5, 1909; *"The Red Moon."* [Mr. and Mrs. Andrew Tribble] December 3, 1908; *"Smart Set,"* September 1, 1910; *"Two African Princes,"* July 9, 1908; "Well Known Character Comedian." December 24, 1908; July 22, 1909.

The Oklahoma City Times. *"The Shoo-Fly Regiment."* September 9, 1909.

The Pittsburg Courier. "Andrew Tribble Back." Saturday July 28, 1928; *"Struttin' Time."* July 5, 1924; May 23, 1925.

The Richmond Item. October 30, 1888.

The St. Louis Argus. "Veteran Actor Dies." December 6, 1935.

Times Union. *"Brain Sweat."* April 5, 1934.

Trav S.D. *Travalanche.* "Andrew Tribble: Drag Star of *"Darktown."* April 3, 2019.

Waukegan News-Sun. *"Possum Hollow University."* April 3, 1915.

Day of Releasement

Introduction

In 1805, Shaker missionaries travelled to central Kentucky from New England. Within the year their converts, the first Kentucky Shakers, began to gather near what would become the village of Pleasant Hill.

The Shakers were a celibate, religious society, that aspired to live pure lives, and were known for their industrious nature, inspiring architecture and progressive social structure. This progressive social structure was evident in many ways, including the society's ready acceptance of Patsy Robertson and other African Americans as equals in their community at a time when so many other people of color were still enslaved in Kentucky.

Although the population of Pleasant Hill peaked near 500 in the 1820s, the community thrived well past the mid-19th century. However, the Civil War, Industrial Revolution, changing social attitudes and other factors began to signal the community's decline. By 1910 the remaining 12 Shakers at Pleasant Hill closed the community to new membership, and by 1923 the last Pleasant Hill Shaker had died.

In the first half of the 20th century, 'Shakertown' was home to general stores, gas stations, hotels, private homes and a Baptist Church. The highway and powerlines ran down the middle of the community. The history of this Shakers was being lost.

Then, a groundswell of private support led to the founding of a non-profit in 1961 that began to preserve the historic structures, repurchase former Shaker property, and interpret the incredible history of the Pleasant Hill Shakers.

Today, Shaker Village of Pleasant Hill is Kentucky's largest National Historic Landmark, sharing these 34 historic structures and 3,000 acres with guests from around the world. We invite you to visit during the day or for an overnight stay to explore, shop, dine and learn more about the incredible stories of over 2,500 people who once called Pleasant Hill their home.

Shaker Village of Pleasant Hill
3501 Lexington Road, Harrodsburg, Kentucky Shakervillageky.org
859.734.5411

Day of Releasement

CHARACTERS

1812

PATSY Roberts	African American woman, twenty one years old
BROTHER Elijah	forties *(also JOHN)*
SISTER Hannah	forties *(also SHARON)*
NAMON Roberts	sixties *(BERNARD)*
JINNY Roberts	sixties *(QWENDOLIN)*
EUGENE	African American man, thirties *(JEFF)*

SHAKER SINGERS AND DANCERS

1999

RANDY	late forties
JEFF	African American man, thirties *(also SHAKER ONE and EUGENE)*
JOHN	forties *(also SHAKER TWO and BROTHER)*
SHARON	forties *(also SHAKER THREE and SISTER)*
BERNARD	sixties *(also NAMON)*
QWENDOLIN	sixties *(also JINNY)*

SHAKER SINGERS AND DANCERS

Act One
Scene One

A room in the Office at Shaker Village of Pleasant Hill, outside of Harrodsburg, Kentucky. It is the year 1812. In one corner of the room, busy at a desk doing bookkeeping sits a male Shaker Elder, BROTHER Elijah; while at the other corner at another desk also busy with bookkeeping sits a female Shaker Elder, SISTER Hannah. Both are dressed in traditional Shaker dress. A young African woman in clothing of "the world" stands at Right looking out the window, watching something below. SISTER has just addressed the young woman, PATSY; but as though not having heard the SISTER, PATSY starts to hum a tune. It is a tune that she has never hummed before. As if it is forming a life of its own for the first time, she finds herself to be only an instrument for its music. The tune she hums will later be known as *Sweet Mother Home*.

SISTER

Young lady, the good brother asked you a question.

PATSY

I'm sorry?

BROTHER

Where did you learn that?

PATSY

Learn what?

BROTHER

That tune.

PATSY

I have never heard it before.

BROTHER

But you were singing it.

PATSY

Never sung it before.

213

SISTER

Brother Elijah and I just heard you.

PATSY

It just now came on me.

SISTER

But you must have heard it somewhere.

BROTHER

[He watches PATSY and sees her innocence.]
You were composing it, then?

PATSY

No, sir.

BROTHER

You didn't just think it up?

PATSY

[She laughs.]
Oh, no sir. It's been around a long time. I just now heard it. So, I hummed
it back.

SISTER

I didn't hear anything.
[She looks to the BROTHER.]
But if you never heard it before, and you weren't making it up . . .
[She and the BROTHER exchange looks.]

BROTHER

Does this happen often, child?

PATSY

Sometimes.
[BROTHER and SISTER look to each other again.]
Since the revival three years ago.

BROTHER

Would you say you were "gifted with the song?"

214

PATSY

I guess so.

BROTHER
[To the SISTER:]
I think maybe it's a gift.

PATSY

I sure like them better wrapped.
[The BROTHER chuckles.]
But I never had one. Can't miss what you never had. Wrapped, that is.

BROTHER

You may be an *instrument*.

PATSY

I'd love to be a flute.

BROTHER

I mean, our members can sometimes get messages from *above*. Do you think it came from Above?

PATSY

I know it didn't come from below!
[The BROTHER finds this amusing and chuckles.]

SISTER
Do you know any other tunes? That might be from Heaven?

BROTHER
It is our job to determine the visitations of the Spirit Land to our members. I must say that I am very taken by yours just now. It is true simplicity.

PATSY

What's that?

SISTER
True simplicity? The goal of all Believers. That's what we're striving for. To bow and to bend.

215

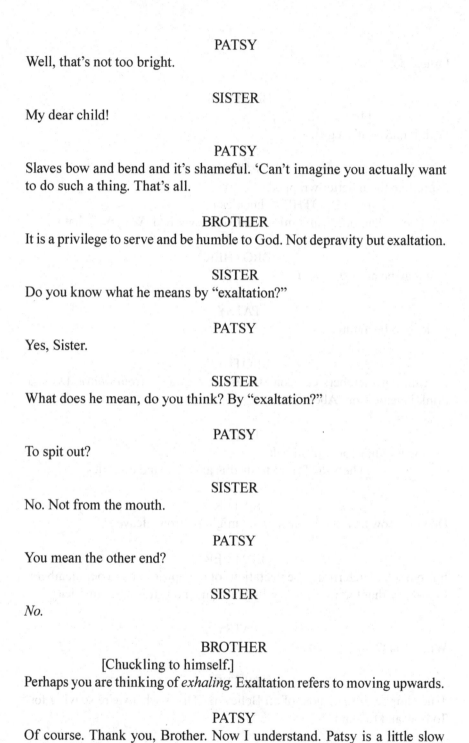

PATSY

Well, that's not too bright.

SISTER

My dear child!

PATSY

Slaves bow and bend and it's shameful. 'Can't imagine you actually want
to do such a thing. That's all.

BROTHER

It is a privilege to serve and be humble to God. Not depravity but exaltation.

SISTER

Do you know what he means by "exaltation?"

PATSY

Yes, Sister.

SISTER

What does he mean, do you think? By "exaltation?"

PATSY

To spit out?

SISTER

No. Not from the mouth.

PATSY

You mean the other end?

SISTER

No.

BROTHER

[Chuckling to himself.]

Perhaps you are thinking of *exhaling.* Exaltation refers to moving upwards.

PATSY

Of course. Thank you, Brother. Now I understand. Patsy is a little slow
sometimes. You mean "vomit!"

SISTER

No!

BROTHER

I mean that *exalt* is a different word altogether. To exalt is to move to the highest realm of happiness. Remember when our Lord said, "He who exalts himself shall be humbled. But he who humbles himself shall be *exalted!*"

PATSY

And all this time I thought He was going to spit us out. "Because thou art lukewarm, and neither cold nor hot, I will **spue** thee out of my mouth!" *Spue* that means spit.

BROTHER

Yes, the Good Book does say that. In Revelation.

SISTER

Forgive me, but are you waiting for someone?

PATSY

[She looks out the window.]
No, ma'am. I'm not waiting for no one.

SISTER

I thought that was why you were here?

PATSY

Oh, no! Can't be waiting for someone when they're already here.

SISTER

You have family who are Believers?

PATSY

Yes'm. There are two sisters.

SISTER

You have two sisters living here? At Pleasant Hill?

217

PATSY

No, ma'am. There are three here now. There's Susannah. I guess you could say she is living here. She's not dead. Susannah and me. We were born on the same day. The same year. But we aren't the same age.

SISTER

How is that possible?

PATSY

She is twenty. And I am twenty *too!*
[PATSY laughs at the riddle. BROTHER laughs with her]
Do you get it? I am twenty T-O-O. I can spell. Although you're not supposed to tell no one. I taught myself. No one is guilty for teaching me. Please don't say anything.

BROTHER

"Twenty, too." You have a good sense of humor, Patsy. Then there's four of you?

PATSY

There were two sisters born to the same mother, on the same day, at the same time, in the same month and year and they aren't twins neither. What are they?

SISTER

How can that be?

PATSY

They are two of a set of triplets!
[BROTHER laughs again finding this delightful]
They're here, too. Living--they aren't dead by no means!

SISTER

And you?

PATSY

I'm living, too. So, now you know why I come. We're here.

SISTER

I don't remember ever having seen you here before.

PATSY

No, you wouldn't.

SISTER

But I thought you said you were all here.

PATSY

We are. But I'm not one of them.

BROTHER

You're not one of them?

PATSY

That's right. I'm a slave.

BROTHER
[He smiles at her humility. With kindness:]
Mother Ann saw visions of slaves. Yes, she did. And the slaves were wearing crowns of gold. And their masters were serving them.

PATSY

I think I like your Mother Ann. I'd love to have a crown. A crown all my own. And just because I'm a slave? A gold crown. I sure would like a gold one!

SISTER

So, your sisters came here to follow the ways of our Mother Ann and The United Society of Believers in Christ's Second Appearing?

PATSY

No, they came to be Shakers. Of course, they are old maids, and don't have husbands and no place to go. I guess we are, too. Me and Susanna. But not the little ones.

BROTHER

The triplets.

PATSY

That's right.

219

SISTER

[A little frustrated, she changes the subject.]
The good Brother here has asked you if you have divine manifestations. If
you are what we call an "instrument." Have you had any experiences from
Heaven? Visits from angels, maybe?

PATSY

I once was sick with the fever. I felt a presence with me through the night.
Maybe that was an angel.

BROTHER

A good angel. It stayed with you until you were well!

PATSY

It might have been a better angel had it taken away the fever to start with.

SISTER

[Refraining from amusement.]
Have you come to make a confession?

PATSY

Oh, no, I made that three years ago. At the revival at Paint Lick. That's
where we live. That's where we used to live.

BROTHER

And where are you now?

PATSY

I told you. We're here.

BROTHER

That you did.

SISTER

And why are you here?

PATSY

I told you!

SISTER

Told us what?

220

BROTHER
[Humorously to the SISTER:]
She *told* you. To tell you. "They're here."

PATSY
Two of us have been here. Then there's the other seven. And their folks.
That makes eleven. Even I can add that together. But you're not supposed
to tell anyone.

SISTER
I'm not to tell anyone that there are eleven of you?

PATSY
No. That's not counting me.

BROTHER
And you. Why are you here?

PATSY
I told you! To tell you! The other ten are out on the street waiting to be let
in. But I'm not one of them because I'm a slave.

SISTER
Oh! My dear child, how long have they been waiting?

PATSY
Since I came up here.

SISTER
All this time? Why didn't you tell us?

PATSY
[PATSY can only roll her eyes.]
Mrs. Roberts said to keep my mouth shut and wait until I was asked.

[JINNY Roberts barges into the room: a woman of forty-
six, plump, wearing her best traveling clothes; her husband,
NAMON Roberts, following: the same age, wearing his
Sunday suit and hat.]

221

JINNY

Do you expect us to wait outside all day?

BROTHER

I am sorry. May I be of help?

JINNY

[To PATSY:]
Did you announce us, Patsy?
[PATSY ducks her head]
What have you been doing, girl?!

BROTHER

Patsy was having the best conversation with us just now. She was telling me about your arrival. That you are here. You must be Mr. and Mrs. Roberts. Welcome to Pleasant Hill. We've been expecting you. This is Sister Hannah and I am Brother Elijah. Please, won't you have a chair?

[The Roberts are seated.]

JINNY

We've come to join the Shakers.

SISTER

The world outside calls us that. We are the United Society of Believers of the Second Appearing.

JINNY

Why do they call you Shakers?

SISTER

Because we "exercise."

BROTHER

You may call it "dance."

NAMON

You exercise the demons out!

JINNY

Where I come from, we don't have demons and we don't believe in dancing.

222

SISTER

Here our dance is worship. Through the dance we are in union.

JINNY

With each other?

SISTER

With God and each other.

JINNY

We've come to join up. But we wouldn't have to dance if we don't want to, do we? If we don't believe in it?

SISTER

Why, may I ask, do you want to join the Believers?

JINNY

The war has taken our farm. My husband, Mr. Roberts has been injured and can't do any work. We had to sell all of our slaves, except for Patsy. Besides, it seems the thing to do.

SISTER

The thing to do?

JINNY

To be closer to God. We all need God, don't you think?

NAMON

She heard that Elizabeth Logan has joined your Shakers.

JINNY

That is not true!
        [She whispers:]
Do you have an Elizabeth Logan here?

BROTHER

"Logan," did you say?

SISTER

I'll check.
        [She looks through a registry.]

223

JINNY

She is the most beautiful, the most refined of ladies. We are good friends, you know—oh, yes, the best of friends. Her husband is a lawyer!

NAMON

We saw them at the revival here a few years ago. Here, when it was Mr. Thomas' farm.

JINNY

She took a liking to me right away. It was as if we had known each other all our lives. Or in another life, maybe. You may not believe in such things, but I do. At least, I think I do--

NAMON

She complimented her hat.

JINNY

Yes, he means to say that she admired my exquisite taste in style.

NAMON

She said she used to have one like it until it went out of fashion.

JINNY

Don't the men register somewhere else? I know that you separate the men and women. What my husband means is that Mrs. Elizabeth had an "Opening of the Mind," I believe that's what she called it.

NAMON

Yeah, all the sin just came right out. And from what I heard; she had a lot of it!

JINNY
[Whispering to SISTER:]
He doesn't know what he's saying half the time—the roof caved in on his head. If Elizabeth had an Opening of the Mind, then I'll have the same. But we don't have to give up all sin, do we? I mean, a little leaven helps the bread rise, don't you think?
[She gives the SISTER a wink.]

SISTER

Is that the reason you are here? To be like Mrs. Logan?

JINNY

Well, no. I want to be a Believer. Open my mind to God. Within reason.

NAMON

And have the Day of Releasement.

JINNY

Shh!

BROTHER

"Day of Releasement?"

JINNY

[She is suddenly cautious in her words.]
I heard some talk about it after the revival.

SISTER

The Day of Releasement is a day when everyone takes off work. Released from work.

JINNY

And you all work so hard here. Hands to work, hearts to God.
[She winks at her again. Another wink. Yet, another.]

SISTER

Have you something in your eye?

JINNY

[Composing herself.]
Uh, . . . no.

NAMON

She had an aunt that buried a lot of money back during the war—

JINNY

Will you shut up! *Please.*
[In an effort to quickly explain:]
We all need a day of rest. Isn't that the purpose of the Sabbath? And you have your own. A Shaker Sabbath!
[BROTHER and SISTER look at the couple with suspicion.]

225

Please, we want to be Shakers. We brought our children. Our whole family. We want to be "Believers," I mean. We are prepared to give up everything!

BROTHER

If you enter, you will do so as novices.

JINNY

We can't be Shakers right away?

SISTER

After a while here, if you choose, you will covenant with us.

JINNY

Do you think we could share the same room?

BROTHER

You will live with the novices. To the seekers who are new and are studying to become Believers.

NAMON

And we can leave at any time?

BROTHER

No one is kept against his will.

JINNY

But can I share the same room?

SISTER

Men live on one side of the building and women on the other. Each has their own doorway and stairs. You will not be allowed to share a room with your husband.

JINNY

I meant with Mrs. Elizabeth.

SISTER

She is no longer a novice. You and Mr. Roberts will become brother and sister. Even in the exercise.

JINNY

Fine, yes, fine indeed.

SISTER

We are a celibate community.

JINNY

FINE.

SISTER

Men and women may not touch each other.

JINNY

FIN--ALLY! I mean—That's just *fine by me*. If we have to make a sacrifice
for God . . .

SISTER

Our way of life was spelled out by Mother Ann Lee. She was born in
Manchester, England and her family were Quakers. It was revealed to her
that celibacy and confession of sin are essential for salvation.

NAMON

I heard that you're against the war. We've lost a lot of Kentucky men in
the war.

SISTER

We are against all forms of violence.

NAMON

But if we don't fight the British, they'll have the Indians scalp us.

SISTER

He who lives by the sword will die by the sword.

JINNY

They say that Mother Ann is Jesus come back from the dead. You don't
really believe all that nonsense, do you?

SISTER

Christ promised he would return.

JINNY

Yes, but as a woman?

SISTER

It is an indwelling of Christ. She was simply the helpmate. The embodiment of God in female form.

NAMON

Are you Catholic? Catholics worship Mary.

JINNY

They say that Mary was the Mother of God. Now, how can she be God's mother? If God is Jesus' father, that would make Mary Jesus' grandmother, wouldn't it?

SISTER

The Divine is a mystery to us. To be revealed later. Now we see in a mirror dimly.

JINNY

Well, it might be a good thing to clean the glass. I have plenty of questions when we meet face to face. But as for now, Namon and Jennifer Roberts want to be Shakers. Brothers and sister. At whatever cost. No dancing. No touching! Thank you, Jesus!

NAMON

They say the food here is real good, too!

JINNY

Hush.

BROTHER

We at Pleasant Hill share all of our worldly possessions. As did the early Christians. We are no longer burdened by the entrapments of this earthly life.

NAMON

Some of them worldly possessions ain't so bad.

BROTHER

Here your debts will all be paid.

NAMON

Oh, how we wish to be released from the burdens of this earthy life!

JINNY

And the kids won't be our responsibility?

SISTER

That's right.

JINNY

I'm having an Opening of the Mind already!

BROTHER

Now. What may I ask have you to share with our community?

NAMON

Nothing.

SISTER

A house?

JINNY

It burned.

BROTHER

A farm?

NAMON

The bank took it.

BROTHER

Livestock, maybe?

NAMON

There was a hog but we ate it.

SISTER

Any money?

NAMON

We don't have a penny to our name. That's why we're here!

JINNY

[Laughing.]
Don't misunderstand. It's not like we are poor or anything.

NAMON

It's just that we ain't got no money.

JINNY

That's not true! We have property! We have this slave girl you see before
you. Patsy. She is young and strong, and she has good teeth. Show them
your teeth, Patsy.

BROTHER

No, that will be fine.

JINNY

Patsy, get our luggage out of the carriage. Show this lady how capable
you are.

SISTER

You will not need those things. They are of your past life. Everything you
need here will be provided you.

JINNY

Everything?

BROTHER

Everything you need. Maybe not everything you want.

NAMON

I sure need some whiskey right now.

BROTHER

We are against such spirits.

NAMON

They told me you were big into the spirits.

BROTHER

Not that kind.

JINNY

Patsy, tell the driver that he can go now. Hurry, girl! Before we have to pay him.

SISTER

Patsy does not follow orders here.

JINNY

But I am her mistress.

BROTHER

Were her mistress. Patsy will be as one of us.

JINNY

But she is our Nego slave!

BROTHER

Not here. Here she is free. Free and equal, as we all are in Christ Jesus our Lord.

NAMON

But I paid good money for her!

SISTER

Then she is a *prized* possession; and you have freely donated all your earthly possessions.

PATSY

I don't mind. Did not Jesus order us to be servants to one another? I will go tell the driver—

BROTHER

No. From this day forward, you are no longer a slave. Thank you for your kindness. But we must all bow only to one Lord.

JINNY

Well, I never.

SISTER

If you would go downstairs, you will be instructed to the Family house of the novices.

231

JINNY

But without Patsy . . . who will do our cooking and cleaning?

BROTHER

We all equally share in the daily duties.

SISTER

Mrs. Elizabeth is partial to the washhouse.

NAMON

When will you talk to us about the Day of Releasement? She has an aunt, you see—

JINNY

Will you kindly be quiet? Things will be revealed in their own good time. Isn't that right?
                    [She winks again to the SISTER. Again. Again. She stops
                    herself and composes.]

BROTHER

I'll show you the way. Follow me.
                    [BROTHER leads them. NAMON and JINNY exit with him.]

PATSY

Is that true what you said? That I'm an equal?

SISTER

We all are equal in the Kingdom of God.

PATSY

Am I free to leave?

SISTER

Of course, at any time. But outside of these gates, you will be as you were. Only here will you find yourself an equal.

PATSY

This is all new to me.

SISTER

Well, the good Brother and I are also new here.

PATSY

Is that so? I would have thought you as old as Mother Ann.

SISTER

Since Mother Ann was born almost a hundred years ago, I don't see how
that's possible.

PATSY

I guess you don't look that old.

SISTER

Thank you.

PATSY

But some people can hide their age well, I knew this old Negro woman—

SISTER

I assure you, I do not.

PATSY

No, I guess you don't.

SISTER

[Not knowing how to take that last statement, she forges
ahead]
You will be with the novices for now. And when you become covenanted
with us, you will live in the Family house on the other side of the village.

PATSY

Away from the Roberts?

SISTER

Yes, indeed.

PATSY

With a free mind?

SISTER

With a free mind.

233

PATSY

I think I shall like your Pleasant Hill. I think now that I am free to speak my mind, I shall give a piece of it to that horrible Mrs. Roberts.

SISTER

Do not misuse that freedom. You will find that you get more flies with honey than with vinegar.

PATSY

Is that what Mother Ann Lee said?

SISTER

No, I think it was Benjamin Franklin. But you will find it always true. I have. You get more flies with honey than you do with vinegar.

PATSY

Unless they be fruit flies. They love apple cider vinegar. Besides, who wants more flies?

SISTER

Still, the basic meaning of the proverb is true. It pays to have a humble heart. A little kindness goes a long way, and is more effective than harshness towards the Mrs. Roberts of the world.

PATSY

The flies, you mean!
          [She commences to hum the tune.]

SISTER

You have never sung that song before?

PATSY

Never. I just remembered it.

SISTER

You *remembered* it? From years ago?

PATSY

No. I never knew it then. I remembered it from when I sing it years from now. In the years ahead, not behind. Won't you be singing years from now? I sure hope to.

SISTER

I think Brother Elijah might just be right about your singing.

PATSY

I never meant to say it was just me singing. He's singing with me.

SISTER

He?

PATSY

The boy.

SISTER

What boy?

PATSY

The boy I sing to. Who sings with me.

SISTER

Who is that?

PATSY

I don't know his name. Don't need to know.

SISTER

Where is he?

PATSY

He's right here.

SISTER

Here? I see no one.

PATSY

He's here. I don't need to see him. We see with the flesh.

SISTER

He is a spirit?

PATSY

You mean, like a ghost? Naw. He's no ghost. He just has never lived yet. If he never lived yet, then he never died. And if he has never died, how can he be a ghost? Simple as that.

SISTER

He has never lived?

PATSY

He will someday. Long ahead of us.

SISTER

Perhaps he is a demon?!

PATSY

[Laughing hysterically:]
I ask you; would a demon praise the Lord?

SISTER

No. I don't suppose so. Brother Elijah believes that some hear such songs from Heaven because they are pure, and other's do not hear them because they have not reached such purity. I'll be watching you, Patsy Roberts.

PATSY

Call me Patsy. I'm not their slave any more. I'm free now, right?

SISTER

Yes, you are free.

PATSY

I'm nobody's slave?

SISTER

That's correct.

PATSY

Do I still get a gold crown?

SISTER

That remains to be seen. We all do if we follow true simplicity.

PATSY

[Distracted.]

Do you hear that?

SISTER

What?

PATSY

[She hums, then stops.]

Just now. Surely you heard that.

SISTER

I don't believe I did.

PATSY

There. There it is again. I can hear him.

SISTER

The boy's voice?

PATSY

Yes. Can't you hear it? Well, you must be right then.

[SISTER smiles with pride]

The impure just can't hear it.

SISTER

[SISTER clears her throat, awaits more responses from
PATSY but nothing comes.]

Do you have any other questions?

PATSY

Yes.

SISTER

What then?

PATSY

Do you ever smile?

SISTER

I beg your pardon?

237

PATSY

If you are filled with the joy of a Shaker, don't you think you ought to smile some?

SISTER

You may go now to the quarters. Make yourself kindly welcome with us.

> [SISTER exits. PATSY takes up humming her tune once more. But she stops and we hear the tune continued by RANDY somewhere unseen, off in the distance. A distance in time. PATSY reaches for him, and touches his music. The lights dim out on her.]

Act One
Scene Two

[RANDY is reaching for the music, continuing the tune of PATSY; the lights shine on him, bringing us into the twentieth century Shaker Village, 1996. RANDY is a man dressed in Shaker attire, a reenactor, in his late forties. JEFF, an African American man in his thirties and fellow interpreter, has been offstage trying on a Shaker shirt. RANDY finishes the tune as JEFF arrives wearing the Shaker shirt.]

JEFF

I love that hymn.

RANDY

Which hymn is that?
> [He pulls out a pair of Shaker trousers from a box.]

JEFF

The one you were just humming.

RANDY

> [Of the shirt:]

How does it fit?

JEFF

Fine, I think. A little big maybe? Do you tuck it in?

238

RANDY

We just leave it out.

[Continuing to hum, he passes JEFF the trousers.]

JEFF

"Sweet Mother Home." We used to sing it in choir. It was a black woman who wrote it. She had been a slave and became a Shaker here at Shakertown.

RANDY

When was that?

JEFF

[He takes off his jeans from under the shirt and puts on the pants.]

Around the War of 1812. That's the extent of my Shaker knowledge. I didn't think they had slavery here at Shakertown.

RANDY

Once you became a Shaker, you were a free man. Or woman.

JEFF

The way they all worked here, you'd think they had their own type of slavery.

RANDY

"Hands to work and hearts to God." They had their fun times, too.

JEFF

Really? When was that?

RANDY

Every once in a while, a whole family would take a day off.

JEFF

You mean, like a vacation? It takes work to get things together for a vacation. Then you come home and have to catch up on everything, put everything back. I need a vacation after I take a vacation!

RANDY

It was called the Day of Releasement. They would enjoy picnics and harvest festivals.

JEFF

[Of the pants:]
They seem awful big.

RANDY

You adjust it in the back. Turn around.
                [He ties the back of the pants for JEFF.]
It was an interesting ritual, the Day of Releasement. I've been researching
it. It's shrouded in mystery. There was a time when it was more than just
a day off.
                [Of the pants:]
There you go.
                [Of the Day of Releasement:]
Kind of like Halloween and Christmas; holidays have strayed away from
their humble beginnings. Even the word "Easter" has nothing to do with
the Christian faith.
                [Back to the clothing:]
So, tell me what you need to get started. You have your own boots, I see.

JEFF

I think my costume is ready.

RANDY

Historic dress. We are not acting, Jeffery. We are presenting a living history
of the Shakers. The way they might have lived in the early Nineteenth
Century.

JEFF

But I can still speak to the public in modern day, right?

RANDY

You have to. They'll ask questions, and you want to be polite and hospitable.
"Make them kindly welcomed here." You've been practicing the music?

JEFF

Yes. Will we get together again to rehearse the dancing, or was yesterday it?

RANDY

Don't worry, you'll get the hang of it when we do it tomorrow. Listen, we'll
be doing it so many times that you'll be a pro before the day is out.

JEFF

I just don't want to stick out like a sore thumb. 'Let everyone know I'm the
new kid on the block.

RANDY

Trust me, you'll be fine. Don't try to be someone else. Be yourself. That's
your gift. Always be true to it.
          [RANDY hums the tune again.]
So, it's a hymn. What did you call it?

JEFF

Sweet Mother Home.

RANDY

Well, I've "been gifted with the song."
          [RANDY hands him a straw hat. JEFF puts on the hat.]
Perfect. You'll need it in the hot summer sun here in Kentucky. That's
why they left so many trees here in the village: for the shade. Most Shaker
villages disapproved of trees and shrubs for decoration. Everything had
to be utilitarian.

JEFF

Did you grow up around here, Randy?

RANDY

Oh, no. I was born in West Virginia. We came here to Kentucky when I
was a kid.

JEFF

What brought you to Shakertown?

RANDY

An advertisement in a magazine for singers here at Shaker Village. I
suddenly realized that I was tired of not doing what I really loved in life.
Singing. I'd had a career in business and that ad made me take a good look
at myself. I wasn't getting any younger and I could see myself becoming
an old businessman unhappy, unfulfilled, unsung. It happened kind of late
in life, but it took me up until that moment to have the courage to do the
thing I really wanted to do. Or to appreciate my musical roots.
          [He laughs at himself.]

241

I didn't know anything about the Shakers. I brought my own audition music with me. From show tunes!
[He sings from *My Fair Lady*:]
"I'm getting married in the morning!"
Not quite your Shaker idea.
[He laughs. And from *South Pacific*:]
"There is nothing like a dame!"
They all kid me now that I have finally repented from my worldly ways!
[He goes through a box of clothes, putting shirts on hangers.]
But when I saw this place and began to understand who the Shakers had been . . . That first day I was here, I'll never forget. It was a cold November day. Gray sky. The rolling hills. The peacefulness of the place. In the Trustees House, the servers were all dressed as Shakers and passed around the biggest relish bowl. Pickled watermelon rinds. Bowls of vegetables. And the Shaker lemon pie. And no tipping. It was like stepping back into the past. Where are you from?

JEFF

Here in Burgin.

RANDY

That's right, you told me! Forgive me, I'm "singing to the choir."

JEFF

I've always loved this place, too. The Shakers were great craftsmen. And inventors.

RANDY

You can just feel the Spirit of God here, can't you? No wonder they had such spiritual experiences.

JEFF

Yes.

RANDY

It's what made them different from the other churches. Seems the more sophisticated people got, the less spiritual they became. You've heard of Cane Ridge?

JEFF

The big log church. Outside Paris, Kentucky

242

RANDY

That's where the revivals began. Where they started out speaking in tongues, rolling on the floor. Foaming at the mouth . . . That's what interested the Shakers and brought them down here. Pretty soon that kind of ecstatic behavior was too emotional for the "higher class" people of Kentucky. They went on to putting pianos and organs in their churches. But the Shakers held true to their simplicity.

JEFF

They foamed at the mouth?

RANDY

[Laughing:]
No. But they offered the miracles and magic that the churches lost. They believed a person could be touched by Heaven. Moved from the other side. That the chasm between this life and the next could be opened. At times, anyways. By certain people.
[He goes to the window.]
Sometimes I . . . I feel their presence. Those good humbled hearted people. Of gentle words. When I sing, it's as if they are singing with me. Or I am singing with them. Just now I had that feeling about the song I was humming. Patsy. Patsy Roberts? Maybe that's who it was.

JEFF

Patsy Roberts.

RANDY

I could feel her as close to me as you are now. Sounds kind of crazy. But then the world thought the Shakers kind of crazy.

JEFF

When the town sold at auction, everybody from miles around came just to see what was hidden behind all of these doors of those crazy people.

RANDY

[Putting away the rest of the clothes.]
I think we are all set for lunch.

JEFF

Is it okay to eat in the costume? Historic dress, I mean.

243

RANDY

Listen, you'll be living in it from now on. Everything is cotton—wash and wear. Just leave your things here. They'll be safe; I'll lock the door. You go on. I'll join you in a few minutes.

> [JEFF leaves. RANDY, aware that no one is around, bursts into song:]

We got mangoes and bananas
You can pick right off a tree
We got volleyball and ping-pong
And a lot of dandy games
What ain't we got? We ain't——

> [He suddenly stops. Patsy's tune interrupts him. He resorts to humming it again.]

It is a sweet tune. Sweet as honey.

> [There is something about the tune that makes him feel no longer alone, but before an audience. An audience maybe of one. The tune brings a memory. He tries his best to remember it. Rubs the chill from his arms. Smiles. Leaves to join the others for lunch.]

END OF ACT ONE

Act Two
Scene One

The lights come up and we see the old stone Shaker Meeting House of worship, three years later, 1815. The cast represents Shakers assembled in dance. They dance a circle dance.

CIRCLE DANCE

> [At the end of the dance, the Believers exit the House leaving PATSY and EUGENE, a young African American man in his thirties, dressed of "the world" and carrying a bouquet of flowers.]

PATSY

Eugene. What are you doing here?

EUGENE

I'm a free man, Patsy. My master gave me my freedom. Look at me. A free man!

PATSY

I am so happy for you, Eugene.

EUGENE

I've come to take you as my wife. Like a promised you. I've come to take you home with me.

PATSY

That was some time ago.

EUGENE

Don't you understand? You can come live with me and you'll be free. I've saved money. I can buy your freedom, so that the two of us can leave together.

PATSY

Eugene. You are looking good. It is good to see you again. But I must go now to help with dinner.

EUGENE

I've come to take you home! To Paint Lick.

PATSY

This is my home, Eugene.

EUGENE

What? Living like half a woman?

PATSY

It was good to see you. Please give my best to your mother.
[She starts to leave.]

EUGENE

Please. Hear me out. Can we sit down? Just for a minute?

PATSY

[She leads them to a bench where they sit beneath a tree.]
What'd you think of the dance?

EUGENE

What was all that shakin' of the hands you were doing?

PATSY

Shakin' the devil out. All that's carnal. And the turning represents turning
back to God. When we finished, we were in the same place as when we
started.

EUGENE

You don't have the devil in you. I'm not sure its proper; a man should be
in a pew and listen to the Word of the Lord, not get up and jump around
like some wild animal.

PATSY

Is that what it looked like? I feel very close to God when I dance.

EUGENE

You can't be serious that you want to stay here? And not have babies?

PATSY

I like my life here.

246

EUGENE

But with me, you can be free to have your own house to clean. And a kitchen of your own to cook in. And our clothes to wash. And kids to feed and teach. A garden to hoe. And a husband to obey.

PATSY

Such freedom you offer; it's so mighty tempting!

EUGENE

There's so much more just waiting for you out there.

PATSY

These people don't believe in slavery. They don't even buy sugar.

EUGENE

Why is that?

PATSY

Surely you know that sugar is sold for slaves? We only use honey, and raise our own bees. And the sweetest of honey it is, too.

EUGENE

Having a family isn't slavery

PATSY

I love you, Eugene. I'll always love you. But sometimes the greatest generosity is being unattached.

EUGENE

I brought you these flowers.

PATSY

Thank you.

EUGENE

What? They aren't good enough for you?

PATSY

We grow them for food and medicine. Not for pleasure to cut and admire.
[She places them between them on the bench.]

247

EUGENE

Don't you think that God made beautiful things for us to admire? He made you and you're beautiful. And I've admired you from the first moment I set eyes on you.

PATSY

Eugene, I really must go.

EUGENE

Patsy, I'm not asking you again. I want you as my wife. No one will ask you again. I've come to take you home.

PATSY

My home is in heaven. Our Mother's Home, and no one will ever take it away from me.

EUGENE

And that's it? That's all you want? You've settled, Patsy. You've sold out. You're a slave done sold yourself out!

PATSY

What more could there be? Our Mother's Home is so sweet. Sweet as the smell of honey suckle. Sweet as the taste of the honey comb.

EUGENE

And reaching down for it's going to sting the fire out of you! I'm free now, Patsy. We can be married. And you can have my children.

PATSY

Dear, dear sweet Eugene. You are freed now until someone comes and captures you and takes you back to the fields. Don't you see? We will never truly be free in this life. Even if you could find us a place where we'd be safe, people would always look at me and say, "See her? That's the girl who used to be a slave!" As though I weren't a real person. Just some thing. Carrying the scares that never heal. But here . . . in this village, well, it's kind of like Heaven on earth. They don't see the color of my skin. They look at my heart. They see me as an equal. A sister.

I was cleaning an old cow bell the other day. When I was finished, you could see the brass, and what a shine it had! You'd never dreamed there could be such a shine. We're like that old bell. Deep down underneath all

248

the dirt of this world, there's a soul that shines. Perfect, Eugene; created by God in His image as perfect as He is. And His grace is totally, completely free.

EUGENE

You are howling at the moon! Patsy, you break my heart.

PATSY

I'm sorry for that. But maybe a heart is like the soil. Until its broken, it can never truly produce a hundredfold.

EUGENE
[He violently grabs PATSY by the arm.]
Patsy! You are my woman. I am your man, and I say that you are going to come with me. Now! And that's an order!

PATSY
[Without flinching]
I'm not afraid of being beaten. I've been beaten and whipped most of my life.
[She pulls away from him]
I was going to suggest that you join us here. But I don't think you'd like it. Goodbye, Eugene.

[SISTER approaches. She has been watching and comes to help.]

SISTER

Is everything all right, Patsy?

PATSY

This is an old friend of mine, Sister. Eugene. From Paint Lick. Eugene, this is Sister Hannah. Eugene was just leaving.
[EUGENE takes his flowers, rudely turns away from them, and leaves.]

SISTER

He doesn't seem very happy.

PATSY

He'll get over it. And before he knows it. Time is like that.

249

SISTER

It sure has flown by since you came here. Patsy? I wondered. Have you had any more gifts of song?

PATSY

Yes. Sometimes.

SISTER

Any dreams? Anything that might seem like a vision? I just want you to know that we are here to help, if you ever need to speak with someone about them. At any time.

PATSY

Thank you.

SISTER

Never be afraid of the unknown. Not if it is of God. If it is an "unknown tongue," then an interpreter will be sent.

PATSY

Could I ask you about something?

SISTER

May I ask you something?

PATSY

Sure you can. Anything. But can I ask you first?

SISTER

No. I meant, *May* I . . . ?

PATSY

If you insist. What do you want to know?

SISTER

Never mind. Ask me your question.

PATSY

The Day of Releasement? What do you know about it?

250

SISTER

[SISTER's expression changes. She looks away as they walk.]
Why do you ask?

PATSY

Mr. and Mrs. Roberts were talking about it the other day. Susanna heard
them.

SISTER

It's the day set aside to be off work. We had one a month ago.

PATSY

Is that all you know of it? Isn't there something else? The Roberts seem to
think so. At least, that's what they told Susanna.

SISTER

You must speak to Brother Elijah.

BROTHER

[Who has arrived and overheard them.]
Speak to Brother Elijah about what?

SISTER

Good Brother . . . Sister Patsy has a question. I thought you would be best
to discuss it with her.
[SISTER looks knowingly to him, who returns her glance.]

BROTHER

What is your question, child?

SISTER

Go ahead, Sister. Share with our good Brother your question.

PATSY

[Somewhat surprised:]
I just was asking about the Day of Releasement.

BROTHER

I see.

251

SISTER

If you would not mind, Brother? Perhaps you could explain?

BROTHER

Of course. Sister Patsy, would you take a turn with me?

SISTER

I'll leave the two of you, then.
> [SISTER nods to BROTHER and exits. BROTHER and PATSY stroll down the street of the Shaker Village.]

BROTHER

So, you want to know about The Releasement.

PATSY

I know what they say of it.

BROTHER

You are a clever girl. Gifted with the Spirit. I wondered how long it would be before you wanted to know more.

PATSY

They say it is the day off from work. A day for fun.

BROTHER

And that's what they want you to believe. That's what it has become. And there are reasons for it. But before it was safe, it was something else. You already know that, I can tell.

PATSY

But what it is, I do not know.

BROTHER

No, you wouldn't.
> [He chooses his words carefully.]
Before I came here to Pleasant Hill, I lived in Indiana with my family. My wife and child.

PATSY

You were married?

252

BROTHER

Yes. I wasn't always Brother Elijah. I was a farmer in Knox County, in the town called Busseron.

> [He takes a deep breath. He stops walking. There is a long silence. PATSY starts to feel uncomfortable. His behavior makes her uneasy. She becomes scared.]

Suppose . . .

PATSY

> [Bravely]

Suppose?

BROTHER

> [He speaks very slowly now]

Suppose I were to tell you that you could bring down someone from Heaven just for a day?

> [He looks to her for a response. She is listening.]

Just one more time? To say to them what remained unsaid. Just to see them again, hear their voice. Give them a kiss, and have one more chance to tell them that you love them. It is called The Day of Releasement.

PATSY

Sounds beautiful. And a little daft.

BROTHER

> [He laughs.]

Yes, I suppose it is. Much of what happens here is seen as daft to the outside world.

A few years back, where I lived, there was an outbreak of malaria. I lost my wife and child. So, I joined the Believers at West Union. But the village had been built on an Indian trail. The Shawnee would join us in the Feast Dance, but then they started screeching like demons and taking up clubs and hatchets. We feared their attack, so we left and came here.

I had read about The Releasement in some old papers at West Union. So, when I came here, I began to seek for it.

PATSY

It's a big secret, isn't it?

BROTHER

Not just with the Believers. I think it has existed from the beginning of time. It's just that some religious groups chose to guard it. And then those guards died. No, I really don't think it's unique to us. Not at all. We may have given it its name. But it's been around a long, long time.

PATSY

And you took The Releasement Day? And your wife and child came back to you?

BROTHER

Yes. As difficult as it may be to hear and believe. They came back for that day. That most glorious day.

> [He walks away from her and we see the expression of joy in him as he remembers. He becomes a different person as he speaks.]

I cannot begin to tell you how glorious it was. It was a Mt. Sinai experience for me!

PATSY

Maybe it was a dream? Maybe it just seemed real--

BROTHER

It was no dream. It was real. As real as you are standing before me. The veil separating this life from the next is thin. You don't believe me?

PATSY

I don't know.

BROTHER

Well, that's fair. And honest.

PATSY

You sure you hadn't been sipping the moonshine?

BROTHER

> [He laughs.]

No. I hadn't been sipping the moonshine.

PATSY

If you really did have it, then why not take it again and again . . . next year and every year!

BROTHER

No.

PATSY

No?

BROTHER

No. The funny thing is, that was all I needed. I've never wanted it again. I've never needed it since. I know that must be hard to understand.

PATSY

But if it can bring back one person, how come you got two?

BROTHER

I don't know.

PATSY

That sure is some story. Do you know of many people who have taken it?

BROTHER

A few.

PATSY

Sister Hannah?

BROTHER

I'll let her answer that. Let me ask you something, if I may? Did you know that the Roberts have left the Village?

PATSY

No. Where did they go?

BROTHER

I was about to ask you that.

PATSY

Susanna told me that they were asking about the Releasement.

255

BROTHER

Were they? What were they saying about it, if you don't mind me asking?

PATSY

I don't want to be a tattle tale.

BROTHER

No, of course you don't. I respect that.

PATSY

[Too quickly and eagerly:]
They were talking about "the book!"

BROTHER

The book? I wonder where they heard about that?

PATSY

They saw it! In a dream or a vision or something.

BROTHER

Did they say anything else?

PATSY

Susanna found it very strange. They said some other things, but it didn't make any sense to her.

BROTHER

Things about . . . the book?

PATSY

She didn't say. She didn't understand it. Just that they read about it all in some old journals they found. They read about the book, and then they saw it. It appeared to them.

BROTHER

Then, I worry for their safety.

PATSY

What's in the book?

256

BROTHER

Names and dates. Of those being released and when. It's really best not to
know too much about it. Tell me, do you have any idea where the Roberts
may have gone?

PATSY

No.

BROTHER

Of course, we are all free to leave the Village at any time. Our blessing and
curse. Let me ask you this. If the Roberts could have a day with anyone who
has passed, who do you think that might be? Let us walk back to the Office.

[They turn around and continue walking.]

PATSY

They wouldn't have time for such a thing unless they could profit from it!
[She looks for laughter, but there is only a revelation:]
Of course! They were forever taking about this money their aunt had buried
on her farm. They used to make me go there and dig.

BROTHER

Ah! That makes sense.

PATSY

If the aunt did come back to them, she could tell them where to dig . . .

BROTHER

Yes.

PATSY

They are awful people.

BROTHER

Be grateful. Be grateful you are not like that.

PATSY

Ain't that the truth! I used to have a dream I woke up in hell.

BROTHER

Goodness. How'd you know it was hell?

257

PATSY

Because I dreamed I woke up as Mrs. Roberts!

BROTHER

[He cannot stop himself from chuckling.]

And a blessing you awoke! Now, I will return you to Sister Hannah. You are free to tell her whatever you like about what we talked about.

PATSY

Thank you, Brother.

BROTHER

Thank you, Sister, for sharing so honestly. And let us keep the Roberts in our prayers.

PATSY

Lord knows they need 'em!

BROTHER

Don't we all?

PATSY

Yes.

[BROTHER leaves, as SISTER has arrived and sits at her desk inside the Office.]

SISTER

Did you have a good talk with Brother Elijah?

PATSY

Yes. I've never known such kind good people as here at Pleasant Hill.

SISTER

The good we have comes from Above. He told you?

PATSY

About the Releasement. Yes.

SISTER

And you believed him?

258

PATSY

I don't know. Did it happen to you?

SISTER

Is that what he told you?

PATSY

He wouldn't say. Did it?

SISTER

Did he ask you about the Roberts?

PATSY

Yes. I told him what Susanna had said. But they had told her not to talk about it.

SISTER

The Roberts had lots of things you weren't supposed to talk about, didn't they?

PATSY

More than I could keep up with. The Brother and I figure they went to conjure up her old aunt and find her money.

SISTER

Oh. I am sorry for them.

PATSY

Did you? Take the Releasement?
        [SISTER will not answer.]
Brother Elijah said he had learned about the Releasement at West Union.

SISTER

Yes.

PATSY

Is that where you learned of it?

SISTER

No.

PATSY

But you came from West Union, too, didn't you?

SISTER

I hadn't been there long. The Pidgeon Roost people had been killed by the Shawnee. Fever and ague were everywhere. We thought then it was the end of the world.

PATSY

That was right before I came.

SISTER

Yes. I remember you that first day. You brought such light and joy to this place.

PATSY

Did I? You didn't tell me.

SISTER

No. I didn't. I should have. I could tell you were different. I remember you singing. We told you about your gift then, as I recall. And you told me about the boy in the future. Maybe it's best we don't remember the future; the past is hard enough.

PATSY

I remember you telling me about my gift.

SISTER

Someone like you, Patsy, understands the Heavenly things. The Roberts do not. That's why I fear for them.

PATSY

So, you did take the Releasement. Please tell me.

SISTER

What else do you know about me?

PATSY

That when you smile, the world lights up around you.

Thank you for saying that. I could not smile for a long time. You helped me with that.

PATSY

I can't imagine how.

SISTER

I once was like you. But married and with children. A young wife and mother. Much like Mother Ann had been. Once.

PATSY

A Believer?

SISTER

No, not then. Not until after the earthquakes. The chimney of our house fell and killed my babies. They had been sitting before the fire. I converted afterwards, but my husband abandoned me much the way that Mother Ann's husband did her. So, I went to West Union alone.

PATSY

I am so sorry. I didn't know. I can't imagine how it would be to lose your babies. It would kill me!

SISTER

It did me.

PATSY

But you survived!

SISTER

I existed.

PATSY

You are a woman of courage and faith! "The Lord be my strength and shield; my heart trust in him, and he help me. My heart leap for joy, and with my song I praise him." So, it was Brother Elijah told you about The Releasement?

SISTER

No. It was Sister Matilda.

261

PATSY

Sister Matilda? You mean our Sister Matilda? Here? That old thing? Forgive me, Sister. I mean, I just never thought that—

SISTER

That there was anything special about old Sister Matilda? No, you wouldn't to look at her, would you? It just goes to show that you can't tell a true person by their outside. The Lord looks on the heart. Sister Matilda is the oldest of our village and closest to Mother Ann. She felt sorry for me. She thought it would help me. Naïve and still so full of grieve, I asked for the Releasement. In secret, of course.
[Bitterly:]
It must always be in secret. And it came.

PATSY

And it was glorious?!

[Like the beat of a drum, a silence sounds.]

SISTER

It was horrible!
[SISTER begins to weep and continues her story behind a veil of tears and emotion.]
It made it so much worse! Yes, it was glorious at first! Straight from heaven! But then the day ended. And they left me. Again. And this second time was so much worse than the first.
[PATSY goes to her and cradles her with affection.]
You sweet, sweet child.
[SISTER dries her tears.]
Some things are not meant for us. That's why it's been forgotten. That's why it needs to be forgotten! We are not strong enough for it. That's why from early on the Israelites believed the name of Jehovah was too great to speak and that if you spoke it, it would kill you. So it is with The Day of Releasement. You want to take it, don't you? Even in spite of what I've told you?

PATSY

Yes.

SISTER

[Shaking her head.]

262

You don't know what you're asking.

PATSY

I know who I'd like to see. To spend the day with. How do I go about it?

SISTER

Sister Matilda has visions of a book and the names are written in it. Only she can tell you if your mother's name is there.

PATSY

My mother?

SISTER

The one you wish to see.

PATSY

But I am not thinking of my mother.

SISTER

No? Are you sure? I thought--
         [SISTER looks at her and knows without PATSY telling her.]
It's the one you sing to, in your songs, isn't it? The one that connects with you. That boy. The one from the future. But he hasn't died. He hasn't even been born.

PATSY

With God all things are possible.

SISTER

         [SISTER thinks about it, looks at PATSY with compassion.]
I must take it to Sister Matilda. She will give us clarity on the matter. Come back tomorrow. I will have an answer for you then.

PATSY

         [Standing]
Thank you, Sister.

SISTER

I wish I could persuade you against this.

263

PATSY

But Brother Elijah had a glorious experience. He told me so himself. Maybe it will be the same for me?

SISTER

I hope it will be.
                    [She smiles.]

PATSY

There it is. You are awful pretty when you smile.
                    [SISTER blushes and smiles again; she tosses her head and
                    proudly walks away. PATSY is left in a pool of light, greeted
                    once again with emotion as she becomes an instrument of
                    the music. She sings:]
                         Oh, my . . .
                    [She hums the rest]
                         Oh, my pretty Mother's home,
                    [She hums the rest]
                         Oh, my pretty Mother's home,
                         Sweeter than the honey in the comb.

                    [The lights fade out on her as they fade up on RANDY
                    singing the end of the hymn. 1999.]

Act Two
Scene Two

The lights have faded up on RANDY, connected once again to PATSY but through her music. It is 1999, three years later.

RANDY

            [Singing:]
                 Oh, my pretty Mother's home,
                 sweeter than the honey in the comb.

            [We hear applause from a crowd of tourists in the Meeting
            House at Shaker Village. The lights come up to reveal the
            reenactment of a Shaker funeral drama performed by actors
            and singers. At Center stage is set a simple wooden coffin.]

JEFF

Today we bury our good Sister Martha. She lived but a simple life. A free life. By turning from the ways of the world, she now is in the valley of love.

RANDY

[Sings:]

Lay me now, lay me low,
Lay me low, low,
Where Mother can find me,
Where Mother can own me
Where Mother can bless me.

JEFF

[Reads from a Bible:]

From the Apostle Paul to the Church in Corinth we read, "Therefore if any man be in Christ, he is a new creature: old things are passed away; behold, all things are become new." And from the Book of Revelation, "And God shall wipe away all tears from their eyes; and there shall be no more death, neither sorrow, nor crying, neither shall there be any more pain: for the former things are passed away."

RANDY

[Sings from *The Humble Heart*:]

Tall cedars fall before the wind
The tempest breaks the oak.
While slender vines will bow and bend
And rise beneath the stroke.
I've chosen me one pleasant grove
And set my lovely vine.
Here in my vineyard I will rove
The humble heart is mine.

SHAKER ONE

In my Father's house are many mansions.

SHAKER TWO

Although we grieve the loss of our dear sister, Martha, we are comforted knowing that she is safe in the arms of Mother Ann.

SHAKER THREE

[Ecstatically, pointing to the sky.]

I see Sister. I see her there above us!

SHAKER ONE

I see her too!

SHAKER TWO

We will miss you, Sister!

SHAKER THREE

Remember us, Sister! God bless you! We love you!

[The others shout above their salutations of love and respect to an ascending Sister Martha that we cannot see.]

RANDY

[Sings:]
Love is Little, Love is Low
Love will make your Spirit grow
[He speaks:]
For love is little,
love is low,
love will make your Spirit grow.
Grow in Peace, Grow in Light
Love will do the thing that's right.
For love is little,
love is low,
love will make your Spirit grow.

[The crowd applauds and disperses. RANDY and JEFF nod and thank them as they leave.]

RANDY

For a funeral reenactment, I thought the kids in there today were well behaved.

JEFF

Not always.
[They laugh.]

RANDY

No, not always. Sometimes I forget that children lived here, too.

266

JEFF

There must have been lots of orphans.

RANDY

Yes, after the wars and the cholera.

JEFF

Can you image had the children stayed? The Village might never have died.
But once they were given a choice, they were out of here.

RANDY

Their generosity was the cause of their own demise. During the Civil War,
the Shakers fed every troop that came through, Union and Confederate.
They saw all people as children of God.
      [He sings to himself. JEFF joins in harmony at the end:]
        Come little children, come and go
        In the pretty valley that is down low
        There I can find you, there I can help you,
        In the pretty valley that is down low.
Do you think you'll get married? Have children?

JEFF

No, thank you. I'm got nephews and nieces enough. Dad used to bring us
here when we were their age. He would tell us about when he was a kid
and how there was an old woman still living in one of the houses. He said
she was the oldest Shaker living at the time.

RANDY

He must remember this place before the restoration.

JEFF

She lived in one room with a tv set. A Shaker with a television set. How
progressive is that?!
      [He moves into the center of the street.]
He said his parents used to drive through here every time they went to
Lexington. Get gas. Stop at the store. It was just a regular little pit stop.
Except the old buildings were all boarded up. One day, the Trustees' House
was open and he and my aunt went exploring. There were big rolls of carpet
stacked inside. And in the basement, there were chains on the walls. For
them it was a dungeon where they kept prisoners! Something about tying
up basil and yarrow they just didn't find too exciting.

267

[Noticing the quietness of RANDY:]
Are you okay?

RANDY

Sure.

JEFF

I noticed you during the concert. You seemed so far away.

RANDY

Did I? I think I recognized an old friend in the audience. It made me think about Mother Ann losing her children and becoming bitter. I was fortunate to come from a loving family, who wanted the very best for me. And introduced me to a loving God. A God of forgiveness and acceptance. A God bigger than time itself. As a kid every Sunday I listened to the Scriptures telling how God is the same yesterday, today, and tomorrow. That those who live in faith on this side will live on the next . . . Like Sister Martha in our funeral reenactment.

JEFF

Your church experience growing up was a good one?

RANDY

Yes. I was there every time the doors opened. That's where I learned my love for music: in the church choir. My dad was the minister.

JEFF

Ah! A preacher's kid!

RANDY

Guilty. A "PK."

JEFF

Yet, you turned out quite well.

RANDY

Do you think?
        [He contorts into a freakish shape. They laugh.]
I think the Shakers got Galatians right: In Christ Jesus we are neither slave nor free, male or female, ... White or black. Young or old. Rich or poor. Gay or straight.

268

JEFF

Me thinkest you be might generous with the Scripture there.

RANDY

The Scripture teaches generosity. You don't think you'll ever get married?

JEFF

If the right person came along.

RANDY

And how do you find that?

JEFF

The right person? I don't know. Hasn't happened yet. I've found many of the wrong ones.

> [JOHN, a friend of Randy's, enters: a man in his forties, dressed in summer shorts wearing sunglasses and a straw hat, holding a program.]

JOHN

Randy!

RANDY

John?
> [JOHN and RANDY embrace.]

JOHN

It's so good to see you again, old buddy!

RANDY

John, you will remember Jeff from the Funeral Reenactment; Jeff, this is an old friend of mine, John, whom I haven't seen in years--

JOHN

It's been a while. You sounded great in there. As always.
[To JEFF:]
All of you. It really was beautiful.

JEFF

Thank you.

JOHN

The echo in that building is amazing.

JEFF

It's the construction. No posts in the room--the support of the roof is all in the attic. Hey, let me let you two catch up. Good to meet you, John. Randy, I'll see you later.
                    [He goes about his business and exits.]

JOHN

Don't let me rush you off!

RANDY

He has a tour he has to give. How did you know I was here?

JOHN

We didn't. We're here with a conference.

RANDY

Oh.

JOHN

Randy, I want you to meet my wife. Sharon.
                    [SHARON joins him, a pretty woman in her forties. He pulls
                    her close with his arm around her.]
Sharon, this is Randy.

SHARON

                    [She eyes RANDY carefully. Her words are carefully chosen
                    and stilted.]
Not the infamous Randy that we've heard so much about!

RANDY

Nice to meet you. So, . . . you got married. It has been a while.
                    [RANDY stands awkwardly not knowing at first how to
                    respond. He quickly puts his feelings aside, laughs, and
                    embraces SHARON. He heartily shakes JOHN's hand. It
                    breaks the ice. A little.]
Congratulations! And best wishes!

Thank you.

[There is a moment of difficult silence. To her husband:]
I want to stop by the gift shop, if you don't mind—before it gets crowded.

JOHN

Yes, good idea. Before it gets crowded.

SHARON

Will you excuse me? Randy, it is so good to finally meet you.

[SHARON kisses her husband.]
I'm sure you boys have a lot to catch up on. Why don't I just meet you at
the Dining Hall? Randy, can you join us?

RANDY

They ask us not to eat with the guests, but thank you.

SHARON

Come visit us then sometime, we'd love to have you.

[She leaves.]

RANDY

Well . . .

JOHN

I'm sorry, I should have written to you. Life gets so busy and flies by ...

RANDY

Yes, it does. It can get hard to keep in touch. Thank God for email!

JOHN

I'm an idiot when it comes to the computer. You should have come to the
wedding!

RANDY

I would have loved to; had I been invited.

JOHN

I'm sorry.

RANDY

She is lovely.

JOHN

She is, isn't she? And a saint to put up with me.

RANDY

No doubt. So, you've seen the Village? I'm just headed down the street.

JOHN

I'll walk with you. If that's all right?

RANDY

What about your wife?

JOHN

Are you kidding? She's shopping. She'll be busy for hours.

RANDY

It's not that big a shop.
          [They walk.]
Is this your first time here?

JOHN

Yes, it's beautiful.

RANDY

The same architect who restored Colonial Williamsburg did this place as well.

JOHN

Really? It's so peaceful. The landscape around really makes it look like you are going back in time.

RANDY

The foundation that bought the place had the foresight to buy up as much land as they could. Shame they couldn't have bought more: that factory in the distance kind of kills the ambiance.

JOHN

And your outfit! Look at you.

RANDY

The lady who made it was very true to the period.

JOHN

You look like you stepped out of the pages of history.

RANDY

[Of seeing JOHN again:]
We can't seem to leave the past behind.
[Another grim silence.]

JOHN

So, you are still singing.

RANDY

I had no idea you got married. I bet it was a beautiful wedding.

JOHN

We were so busy. And we only invited close friends.
[JOHN is oblivious to how that sounds.]
You need a wife.

RANDY

Do I?

JOHN

Don't tell me you've gotten too wrapped up in this Shaker thing? Living in the past. You need a good woman. Settle down.

RANDY

I'm settled.

JOHN

Someone to whip you in shape. Keep you from being lonely.

RANDY

I'm not lonely.

JOHN

Pick out your clothes. Keep you out of her kitchen. Wake you up at the crack of dawn--

RANDY

I like to cook. And the rooster gets me up.

JOHN

You don't know what you're missing. Honey-do lists. Keeping the yard cut, the car working, fixing the plumbing and electricity. Cleaning out the gutters. Bring home the bacon. Pay her credit cards. Take her to the movies. Buy her expensive clothes and jewelry. Make you a better man.
[He stops and looks ahead]
Where does the road lead?

RANDY

[With a double meaning:]
To the cemetery.

JOHN

Ah, yes. I see. So, the Shakers didn't have tombstones? Just a little rock to show where they were buried. Poor things.

RANDY

And true simplicity.
[JOHN is quickly distracted by his friends coming down the street.]

JOHN

[Whispering intensely:]
Good God, there they are! Don't look!
[JOHN turns away, but RANDY's instant reaction is to look.]
I said don't look!
[He turns RANDY around away from the couple who is approaching.]
I was hoping to lose them for a bit. We'll be having lunch with them in a while.

RANDY

They were at the service.

JOHN

We brought them.

RANDY

They are guests of yours?

JOHN

Guests from hell.

RANDY

Why'd you bring them?

JOHN

We met them on a cruise. Somehow, they took a liking to us, and Sharon—bless her heart—happened to invite them to come see us sometime in Kentucky. We never dreamed they would take us up on it. And low and behold, the other day, guess who landed at our doorstep!

RANDY

[Unable to refrain from looking over his shoulder, JOHN turns him again.]

They are waving at us.

JOHN

Are they?

[JOHN turns around; pretending he has just spotted them, he waves back.]

Terrible troublemakers. Every night at dinner they would insult one of the guests. By the last night of the cruise, it was just them and us. They ran off every neighbor where they lived.

RANDY

How do you know?

JOHN

They told us! They bragged about it. They have no friends. They moved to be next to their children. Their children moved away. I was enjoying that funeral reenactment so much! I had forgotten that Simon Legree and Cruella de Vil were watching it beside us. I was the first one out—I couldn't stand to hear their criticism of it. Because it was religious, I knew they would tear it apart--

RANDY

They have no faith affiliation?

275

I'm sure they did. Once. But God moved away. Haven't you noticed? As they pass each tree ahead, the birds flee for their lives.

RANDY

[Laughing.]
They can't be all that bad.

JOHN

Worse, I tell you. They're coming this way.

[BERNIE and GWYNETH approach: an older couple, British. In tweeds and caps and walking canes.]

BERNIE and GWYNETH

Hello! Who is your friend?

JOHN

Uh, Bernie and Gwen, this is Randy. An old friend of mine. But he has to be going--

BERNIE

Weren't you in the funeral we just saw?

JOHN

Funeral? What funeral? Were you?

GWYNETH

Yes, Bernie dear, I think he was—

JOHN

No, uh, Randy and I used to be . . . a—roommates—

BERNIE

Yes, I think you were in the funeral. And didn't you sing?

JOHN

You know, we've got reservations for lunch, and we don't want to be late—

GWYNETH

Yes, he did—

JOHN

Randy, it was so good running into you. We better get—

GWYNETH

I want to tell you what I thought of it—

BERNIE

I want to weigh in on it, too—

JOHN

Oh, God—

GWYNETH
[GWYNETH goes up to RANDY in tears.]
It was the most beautiful thing I have every experienced.
[BERNIE hands her a handkerchief. She weeps into it.]
I was so moved.

RANDY

Thank you.

JOHN
[Relieved.]
Well.

BERNIE

Let's get to the Greasy Spoon before the crowd gets there.

RANDY

The Trustees' House.

BERNIE

I hope they'll let us eat there. Of course, there is no other choice.

RANDY

I mean, that's its name. The Trustee's House.

BERNIE

Why don't you come join us? John's paying.

277

JOHN

Randy's not allowed to eat with the guests in costume.

GWYNETH

You can take it off, we don't stand on ceremony.

RANDY

Thank you, anyway.

BERNIE

[To his wife as they exit:]

See, what did I tell you? The food probably stinks. And my bowels haven't moved since we got here--

[BERNIE and GWYNETH are gone.]

JOHN

They liked the service. Miracles never cease!

RANDY

The Shakers specialized in miracles.

JOHN

Well, "once more unto the breeches!" Great to see you again, Randy.

RANDY

Same here. And again, congratulations. Sharon is a lucky girl.

[JOHN exits]

Would you have married, Patsy? Were you happy here? You were free here. You were an equal. Did you find it here? Did you reach it?

[He sings from *Simple Gifts*:]

When true simplicity is gained,
To bow and to bend we shan't be ashamed.
To turn, turn, will be our delight
'til by turning, turning we come round right.

Act Three
Scene One

Outside at the field of Mt. Sinai, near Pleasant Hill. A week later, 1999.

JEFF

So, tell me again, what took place out here?

RANDY

This is where Mother's Work was done. During the "Era of Manifestations." They kept the public away.

JEFF

I was expecting a High Place when you said they called it Mt. Sinai. It's just a lowly cow pasture.

RANDY

You have to use your imagination, it's all they had. The Era of Manifestations, went on up into the 1850s. It spread down from Massachusetts, from New York. With messages from Mother Ann herself. Children traveled off to the Spirit Land. Artists were inspired to paint--like the Tree of Life. You've seen it. The big tree with branches--

JEFF

The tree with the big balls?

RANDY

Those are fruits.

JEFF

Yeah. Big balls.

RANDY

Fruits. It was a "Gift Drawing," from an artist up in Massachusetts. In the 1850s. She was an instrument of art like Patsy was of music. The artist was told by Mother Ann that the tree grew in the Spirit Land and its name was, The Tree of Life.

JEFF

Mother Ann was long dead by then.

RANDY

That's right.

JEFF

So how did Mother Ann speak to the artist?

279

RANDY

By a medium.

JEFF

A fortune teller?

RANDY

No. I don't think the Shakers called it that. There were old members here at Pleasant Hill acquainted with the Spirit Land during Patsy's time. Anyway, this field was assigned as their playground. This is where the Shakers received all kinds of visions from God. Patsy was older and wrote many of her hymns during those years. Here the past touched the future. And the future touched the past. And Heaven and Earth met.

JEFF

It must have been a heavenly hoe down.

RANDY

Jeff, why is it so easy to remember the past?

JEFF

Is it? It's always censored to someone's frame of reference. What was it with Lincoln's assassination? I think like a hundred people witnessed the shooting at Ford's Theater and they all had a hundred different tales to tell. Not one was the same. Seems like I read where one woman swore up and down that a rope came from nowhere and pulled Booth off the stage.

RANDY

Why can't we remember the future? If we can remember the past.

JEFF

The future hasn't happened yet.

RANDY

How do we know?

JEFF

We just do.

RANDY

We always think of time as linear. Maybe it's not like that. Maybe it's like a deck of cards, stacked on top of one another and not spread out.

JEFF

Well, there's your answer. The Shakers didn't believe in card playing. Or drinking. Or sex.

RANDY

The hundreds who came here to this field—I don't know, maybe thousands--had visions from the Spirit Land. Is Heaven confined to past? Or future, or time itself? The young ones found it exciting and believed. The older ones became afraid of it and got disenchanted.

When you hear Christmas music, what does it make you think of?

JEFF

Christmases in the past, of course. The best time machine is a song.

RANDY

It never makes you think of Christmas Yet to Come?

JEFF

In the future?

RANDY

When you hear the Star-Spangled Banner, do you think only of the War of 1812, or does it give you an exalted spirit of patriotism for years ahead as well?

JEFF

You're getting way too cosmic for me.

RANDY

[Changing the subject:]

I wonder if when Patsy sang her songs, she thought of us now singing them. Or maybe she is singing them now. At the same time that we sing them. Maybe there is only one time.

JEFF

Until Daylight Savings!

RANDY

[His eyes closed, his hands to the heavens, he takes a deep
breath, sings From *Gentle Words*:]

What the dew is to the flowers gentle words are to the soul
And a blessing to the giver and so dear
To the receiver we should never withhold.
Gentle Words kindly spoken often soothe the troubled mind
While links of love are broken by words that are unkind.
Then O Thou gentle spirit, my constant guardian be,
"Do to others," be my motto, "as I'd have them do to me."

[He lays down in the grass and looks up at the sky.]
We spend so much time looking ahead or behind us. Horizontally. Never
vertically. Have you noticed? And all the time it's right there above us.
[He motions for him to lie down in the grass, too.]

Come on.

[JEFF, reluctantly, joins him but only sits.]

JEFF

Let's hope there's not a bull around. Or a copperhead.

RANDY

All the people who had known Mother Ann had died off, you see, so this
was how the young people came to connect with her. Channeling her spirit.
Bringing her back. The young women at North Union wrote about traveling
to the "City of Delight" in the Spirit World; there they saw slave masters
serving their former slaves. Do you think that kind of heavenly thing is
over, or can it happen today just like it did then? Bringing someone down
from Heaven and spending the day with them. "Releasement." If you could
do that, for a day, who would it be? If you could bring down anybody?

JEFF

Anybody?

RANDY

Anybody. But just for a day.

JEFF

Jimi Hendrix?

282

RANDY

Makes you wonder, doesn't it? Do you think there is such a thing as reincarnation?

JEFF

I don't know.

RANDY

There's a lot of things we don't know, isn't there? Jesus said that John the Baptist was Elijah reincarnated.

JEFF

But then Elijah never died, he was taken up into heaven . . . right?

RANDY

Maybe all of this was just a once in a lifetime thing.

JEFF

This Field of Dreams. Shaker Woodstock.

RANDY

Maybe God answers the gentle heart.

JEFF

If so, it would sure be you.

RANDY

Not me.

JEFF

You are the kindest and most gentle person I know.

RANDY

Thanks. I'm far from perfect.

JEFF

I never said you were perfect . . .

> [RANDY hauls off and lands him with a playful punch. JEFF pretends to cringe. RANDY lies in the grass and takes a deep breath.]

RANDY

The Day of Releasement.
> [He stops there. JEFF waits for more. Nothing.]

Can you work for me on Friday?

JEFF

No problem.

RANDY

You won't forget?

JEFF

No, I'll remember.

RANDY

Thanks.

JEFF

You going somewhere?
> [RANDY, eyes closed, is so comfortable in the grass, he does
> not answer.]

I never asked you; did you join your friend for lunch last week?

RANDY

He's married.

JEFF

I bet you enjoyed seeing him again.

RANDY

He said I needed a good woman.

JEFF

He didn't know that you already had one.

RANDY

Who is that, pray tell?

JEFF

Patsy, of course. She's your honey.

RANDY

Patsy Roberts?

JEFF

Who else?

RANDY

Why do you say that?

JEFF

Because you never stop talking about her. Because you light up when you talk about her.

RANDY

I feel a connection with her.

JEFF

Through her music?

RANDY

Music transports us. Like a fragrance, it holds a memory

JEFF

Music changes. Like this "rap music." Is it the same as "hip hop?" I was just getting used to rock.

RANDY

There was this young guy I met once. A wild thing. I wanted to share my faith with him. I knew we had nothing in common and there was no way I could ever relate to him. But I learned I was wrong. I noticed he was wearing a rock t-shirt.

JEFF

Heavy metal?

RANDY

Yeah.

JEFF

Yeah, I'd say you didn't have much in common.

285

RANDY

So I thought. But we did: *music.* We had music in common. Don't you see? Maybe his was not my kind of music, but it was music, just the same. Right when I thought we were on opposite sides, we had a connection. Because all music is spiritual.

JEFF

And you and Patsy have a connection?

RANDY

You disapprove, don't you?

JEFF

Your friend said you needed a good woman. I don't think he meant a colored woman.

RANDY

I'd of thought you to be more concerned about our time difference!

JEFF

That too. You're too old for her.
                [They laugh.]

RANDY

Just a few hundred years.

JEFF

You or she?

RANDY

It depends upon which direction you face.

JEFF

You are so funny.

RANDY

Not any funnier than us dressed in her time period trying to resurrect the spirit of that age. Eating their food. Singing their songs. Dancing their dances. What if Patsy lived today? What if Patsy was a man? What if she *was* older than I? Richer or poorer than I? Would it make any difference? She would still be who she is.

JEFF

Who she *was*.

RANDY

Who she *is*.

JEFF

I'm worried about you.

RANDY

My friend was, too. But all I needed was a good woman.

JEFF

And you have one.

RANDY

I discovered in the records that the Roberts family left the village.

JEFF

Lot of them got dissatisfied. You think they took her with them?

RANDY

Why would you say that?

JEFF

She was their property.

RANDY

I never thought of that.

JEFF

Can you image having freedom here just to have it taken away? It must have been heartbreaking for her.

RANDY
[He suddenly sits up:]

I've got to warn her.

JEFF

Just go up to the cemetery—

287

RANDY

You haven't heard a word I've said.

JEFF

It doesn't make sense--

RANDY

I want to warn her!
[He stands and paces.]

JEFF

Okay. And how do you propose to do that?

RANDY

I don't know. I don't know. The day is set. It can't be changed.

JEFF

What are you talking about? What day?

RANDY

My heart breaks at the thought of her heart breaking.

JEFF

Well, when you love someone, that's the way it works. Love is bound to
make you miserable. It sure did me. There's your proof: you are in love
with the little slave girl.
[RANDY falls back into the grass, sitting.]
Maybe that's why Mother Ann was so opposed to love and marriage. Her
children all got sick and died from it, and her heart was left broken. Her
husband abandoned her. She wanted to spare the world that pain.

RANDY

I've never been in love before. This is all new for me. I always thought it
had to be with a little house with a picket fence and hollyhocks growing in
the front yard. Never like this.

JEFF

I must say, you picked a strange one.

RANDY

Do you really think we pick it? Or is it thrust upon us?

288

JEFF

That's a good question.

RANDY

I don't even think I'm talking about romantic love. Maybe it's the kind of love that the Shakers were seeking. I just know . . .
[He is up again.]
I want to jump up and down all the time. The world has never been so beautiful! Or tasted so sweet.

JEFF

Sweet as honey.

RANDY

Yes. Sweet as honey.

JEFF

I can tell you about romantic love. The feeling takes you to such heights. And the higher you go, the farther the drop.

RANDY

I want to shout it out loud. From the mountain tops, to the valleys. The fields. To the bees!

JEFF

To the bees?

RANDY

Surely, you've heard of that? People talking to the bees? Keeping them updated? Oh, yes. People used to talk to the bees, as far back as the Celts.
[JEFF laughs.]
No, seriously. Whenever someone died in the family, or a baby was born, you had to tell the bees. If you didn't, it caused the bees to leave or make less honey. People actually believed that bees were the link between our physical world and the spirit world. The Shakers raised bees. Think about it. So much of our crops in the world depend upon bees for pollination.

JEFF

You just don't see as many bees as you once did. Because of pesticides, I bet.
[He stands up.]

I think you've gotten too deep in this Shaker-spirit-thing. Like they did. But. I'm glad for you. However it works out, I'm glad for you. Everyone should be in love at least once in their lives.

RANDY

If only I could warn her.

JEFF

[Sarcastically:]
Tell it to the bees. I've got to get to the broom house. I've got to make brooms for the afternoon. Time to come back to the present, Randy. Or the present past.
[He starts to leave.]
You going to be all right?

RANDY

I think so.
[JEFF leaves and goes back to the Village. RANDY is left with his music; he sings]
Oh, my pretty Mother's home,
sweeter than the honey in the comb.
Oh my pretty Mother's home,
sweeter than the honey in the comb.

Come, come pretty love, come come come
Come, come pretty love, I want some.

[RANDY fades away from the future Shaker Village as PATSY appears from its past, joining in the song.]

Act Three
Scene Two

[PATSY appears singing her hymn. A week later in her time. The field of Mt. Sinai.]

PATSY

Come, come pretty love, come come come
Come, come pretty love, I want some.
Oh, my pretty Mother's home,

sweeter than the honey in the comb.
Oh my pretty Mother's home,
sweeter than the honey in the comb.

[PATSY lies down in the grass. SISTER has been looking for her. SISTER walks up to PATSY and sits with her in the grass.]

SISTER

There you are. I've been looking for you. What are you doing out here?

PATSY

One of the cows got out. They got her back in.

SISTER

That's good.

PATSY

I feel him here.

SISTER

The cow?

PATSY

No.

SISTER

Ah. Your friend. You feel his presence out here in the field.

PATSY

Yes.

SISTER

I can see why. It is so beautiful out here.

PATSY

Like heaven.

SISTER

I have your answer from Sister Matilda.

PATSY

She had a vision? Of the Book? What'd she say?

SISTER

Let's walk back and I'll tell you.
                [PATSY hops up but the SISTER has to have a hand to help
                her up.]
You'll find as you get older, it's easy to get down. But not so easy, to get up.

Sister Matilda said that the date is there, set for day after tomorrow. Friday.
And the recipient's Day is the same. The day after tomorrow.

PATSY

That makes sense, don't it?

SISTER

But your young man's name is not listed on that day.

PATSY

But you said the recipient's name is there. That's him.

SISTER

No, that's you.

PATSY

I don't understand.

SISTER

He can't be the recipient. He's not dead.

PATSY

That's right.

SISTER

He has to be a spirit to call him back.

PATSY

And he's alive. In his time. He's very much alive there, just like me, here.

SISTER

Sister Matilda said the same. And if he is not of the deceased—

PATSY

I know he's not. I feel his presence now when I sing.

SISTER

Then the only way for a Releasement is for him to call down . . . you.

PATSY

Me. Yes! He must call *me* down. In his time, I am dead.

SISTER

She said the same. And she said that he is planning to take Releasement day after tomorrow. I don't know how he knows to do this—I did not understand this part—but he is planning it.

PATSY

Maybe . . . if two hearts beat as one, the other knows these things.

SISTER

Does he know that you are a colored woman?

PATSY

Such a thing would never matter to him. If he is a white man, it wouldn't matter to me.

SISTER

There are two problems. Sister Matilda says that his name is not written because—no, first let me ask you this. Do you know that the Roberts have returned? And they are leaving the village for good?

PATSY

What?

SISTER

Yes, today.

PATSY

They went looking for that money like I said, didn't they? And they found it?

SISTER

Yes.

PATSY

That means they found out about the Releasement.

SISTER

Yes. In some old books. Then they visited Sister Matilda.

PATSY

And they called down the aunt? The one that buried the money. And now that they got money, they're leaving.

SISTER

Some people do not adjust well with our way of living. One is always free to come or go.

PATSY

The Believers were fine for them while they were poor and hungry but now that they got money, it doesn't suit them. Well, if that don't raise the pole on the polecat!

SISTER

They are taking their children with them. Not the older sisters.

PATSY

No, they wouldn't, would they? Because they can't get no husbands. Sister, you've been so good to them. They would have had no place to go had you not taken them in here. It is just ungrateful. That's all it is. Ungrateful on their part.

SISTER

We are not to judge, Sister.

PATSY

You take the orphans in and when they're of age, they leave and go back to the world. I've seen it happen over and over now. They are just as ungrateful!

SISTER

Not all of them.

PATSY

Most of them!

SISTER

[Quietly:]
Yes, most of them.

PATSY

It ain't right. It's just ain't right, I tell you! What do you think Mother Ann
would have to say about it?! She wouldn't like it one darn bit. Lawsy, no!

SISTER

[SISTER looks at the sky.]
It looks like it may rain. We best hurry back.
[They continue walking.]
When Mother Ann secured passage to America, on the ship Mariah, she
had with her but a small number of nine Believers. They said the Mariah
would sink but she said, "God will not condemn it when we are in it." As
they sailed for the new world, the Brothers and Sisters sang and danced
with such Spirit that the captain threatened to throw them overboard.
Mother Ann told them, "It is better to listen to God than to man."

PATSY

What happened?

SISTER

A storm arose and loosened a board in the ship. They could not pump out
the water fast enough. The Mariah began to sink.

PATSY

Just the way they had been warned.

SISTER

Ah, but Mother Ann had seen a vision. She saw two bright angels standing
by the mast of the ship who promised their safety. She told the captain and
all his crew to trust in God. They laughed at her. She and her companions
just joined the crew in pumping out the water. Then, a terrible wave came
and shook the ship. *It closed the board.* The Mariah sailed safely to New
York. It took them eleven weeks, but that captain allowed them to worship
as they felt led. We must trust in God.

PATSY

I trust in God. I'd just rather not have the wave.

SISTER

[Laughs:]
You are a joy to me. I'm glad you and your sisters will be staying.

PATSY

This is my home. I will never leave. This is Mother's home to me.

SISTER

Sweeter than the honey in the comb?

PATSY

Sweeter than the honey in the comb!

SISTER

[SISTER takes her hands.]
Bless you. Bless you, dear Child. You bring the light of Heaven to every
room you enter. You have lightened my way since you have been with us.
Like a big *terrible* wave!

[They laugh and arrive back at the room in the Office.
NAMON and JINNY Roberts are waiting for them.]

JINNY

Well, we can't wait all day!

SISTER

You wish to see me?

NAMON

We are ready to leave now.

SISTER

I understood that you had already left.

JINNY

[To NAMON:]
Excuse me! I'll handle this. You go back into the carriage. See that the
horse is watered before we go.

NAMON

But I—

296

JINNY

Go!

[NAMON leaves. To the SISTER:]

We are leaving your Village, Sister, for good! I cannot say that our stay has been enjoyable. It has been work. We have contributed our share to building your Village. Maybe in some strange way, we are better for our stay, time will tell. I wish you, Godspeed, Sister.

SISTER

I am sorry that our ways have not pleased you.

JINNY

It's more like a prison. Another form of slavery. And too much fried catfish breakfast for me.

SISTER

True simplicity takes a lifetime. Did you forget something?

JINNY

I say I did! Patsy, come. We are leaving. When we get to our new home, you can fix us all a good cup of tea with sugar, not honey!

SISTER

I understood that you were leaving your daughters—your older daughters behind.

JINNY

I am. But Patsy is our slave. Patsy, go get our luggage.

SISTER

There is no luggage. When you surrendered worldly goods, we gave your things to the poor. Sister Patsy has decided to stay here at the Village with us. She has been the receiver of gift songs. Divinely touched. An *instrument*.

JINNY

You're the one touched! Patsy is a slave, and we are taking her with us. She will walk behind the carriage.

SISTER

To Pennsylvania?

JINNY

Yes, to Pennsylvania. Patsy, go outside, now!

SISTER

Patsy is not going with you.

JINNY

Oh, yes, she is!

SISTER

She is not.

JINNY

I'll remind you that she is our property.

SISTER

You swore off all property to the Society of Believers when you came here.

JINNY

And we will take back what is ours!

SISTER

You gave it freely.

JINNY

We had no choice when we did, now we do. And we choose to take what is rightfully ours with us! Patsy, I said, go!

PATSY

No.

      [Like the end of the dance, the room stops in silence.]

JINNY

What did you say?

PATSY

I said, "No."

JINNY

Well! What would your Mother Ann say about that!

PATSY

Mother Ann Lee says that in the afterlife, I'll wear a golden crown, and you'll be the slave!

JINNY

Slavery is in the Bible! Tell her, Sister.

SISTER

Yes, because they had no means to stop it then. It says to treat your slaves "justly and fairly, realizing that you too have a Master in heaven." Did you treat Patsy justly and fairly?

JINNY

That is none of your affair!

PATSY

You treated me bad, Jinny Roberts. The Believers here took us in and showed us kindness, and now you turn your back on them. You are not a good person. You are selfish and self-centered.

JINNY

[JINNY goes to PATSY and slaps her across the face. NAMON reenters.]
You ungrateful niggra!

SISTER

Stop it! Apologize to Sister Patsy, this minute.

JINNY

[She laughs in her face:]
Sister Patsy! My ass!

NAMON

We have money enough now. We don't need her. Let her stay, Jinny--

SISTER

Is that all you want? Money?
[SISTER throws a bag of money on the table.]
Let us buy her freedom. This is what you paid for her. And more.

NAMON

Take the money.
>[JINNY moves towards the money. SISTER blocks her path.]

SISTER

First . . . tell her the truth.
>[There is a silence. JINNY moves towards the money, but
>SISTER moves towards JINNY.]

You owe it to her, don't you think?

PATSY

What truth?

JINNY

I don't know what you mean——

SISTER

Shall you tell her, or shall I?
>[JINNY is frozen.]

Patsy, this is your mother.

>[Silence.]

NAMON

Jinny's not her mother.

JINNY

>[To SISTER:]

I'm not the same as I was. The Releasement changed me.

SISTER

Seeing your aunt again?

NAMON

Finding that money changed her.

JINNY

>[To NAMON:]

Don't you see? Patsy is a twin.

NAMON

What?

JINNY

A twin to Susanna. I lied to you. The Sister is telling the truth.
[To SISTER:]
Oh, Sister, I've carried this guilt for too long. *Please.* I don't want to go to Hell!

NAMON

You mean to say, . . . Patsy and Susanna are sisters?

JINNY

Did you never suspect? They have the same birthday. The same year. The same day—

NAMON

But that would make Patsy our daughter. And that can't be. Patsy's a darkee.

JINNY

You stupid, stupid man! Don't you see? Yes, Patsy is a negro. Susanna is not! I gave birth to both of them. I am Patsy's mother, for God's sake!

NAMON

But Susanna ain't no darkee.

JINNY

[To SISTER for some sort of empathy:]
Do you see why I wanted to come here?

NAMON

Patsy looks nothing like me.

JINNY

Exactly. That's because you are not her father!

NAMON

I'd have to be if they are twins.

JINNY

No . . . you do not . . .

NAMON

This is all a bunch of nonsense—

JINNY

Would you just please go wait in the carriage.

NAMON

Well, take the money--

JINNY

Go! Please. I'll explain later.
        [NAMON puts on his hat; he grabs the money and leaves.
        JINNY turns to PATSY.]
What Sister has said is true. I am your mother.

PATSY

My mother?

JINNY

I couldn't have told the truth. They would have killed us both. To keep you as a slave was the only way. The only way.

SISTER

And Patsy's father?

JINNY

You know. Why do you make me tell it! Yes! The foreman on our farm. I gave him money to get away. And I gave you away to a wet nurse and she raised you.

PATSY

Aunt Sadie.

SISTER

And the father?

302

JINNY

They hanged him. His name was Williamson. I had no choice, don't you
see? I had to save her life.

PATSY

Williamson?

SISTER

"Had to save *her* life?"

JINNY

Yes. Forgive me.

SISTER

I am not the one from whom you need forgiveness.

JINNY
[She falls to her knees.]
God forgive me! Mother Ann, help me! I don't want to go to hell! Save me!

SISTER

It is not God from whom you need forgiveness. God has always forgiven you.
[She nods to PATSY.]

JINNY
[She struggles to get up. PATSY goes to her and helps her up.]
Forgive me, Patsy. Forgive me for not being the mother that you deserved.
You have been a faithful slave.

PATSY

Daughter. I will go with you!

JINNY

No.

PATSY

You said I was to go--
[She moves towards JINNY for some sort of maternal
affection; but JINNY, defensively, backs away weeping.]

303

JINNY

No! **No**, I can't!
>   [She runs from the room weeping.]

SISTER

She did it to save your life.

PATSY

She did it to save her own life. She's just a bad potato.

SISTER

An undone potato.
>   [PATSY laughs. SISTER joins her in the laugh. But it dies
>   quickly.]

PATSY

Susannah is my sister. I've always loved her like a sister.

SISTER

I am so sorry.

PATSY

For what?

SISTER

For your loss.

PATSY

Can't lose something I never had.

SISTER

Mother Ann's love is love enough for the both of us.

PATSY

I must repay you for that money.

SISTER

Our Lord has paid the debt for all of us, Patsy.

PATSY

Patsy *Williamson*.

SISTER

Patsy Williamson.

[She looks lovingly at PATSY.]

Now then. I must tell you all that Sister Matilda instructed.

PATSY

There is more?

SISTER

The reason that your friend's name was not in the book. Your Releasement is the same for him as for you. The day after tomorrow. The second day of July.

PATSY

Yes.

SISTER

The reason his name was not in the book is that he will not be there on that day.

PATSY

Where will he be?

SISTER

This is not easy for me. Sister Matilda said that there will be an accident. Tomorrow. The first day of July. Not here but *there*.

[She corrects herself, trying herself to understand this.]

Not now, but then. He will be living in servanthood to others, as we do here, when it happens. Afterwards, there will be a great . . . wave of sadness that will shroud those who know and love him. And his music will be silenced.

PATSY

What does that mean? That he . . . he's going . . . to die? He's going to be killed? Is that what it means?

[PATSY is silent. She goes to the window and looks out.]

SISTER

Sister Matilda shared this in the greatest of confidence. I trust you will tell no one.

PATSY

I must go to her.

SISTER

No.

PATSY

I must!

SISTER

No! The old sister is not well. She cannot see anyone.

PATSY

The book! She must write his name in the book!

SISTER

Now I wish I had never told you. See, this is why the Releasement is dangerous.

        [She breathes a heavy sigh, fighting hard to put her own
        memories and feelings aside for PATSY's sake.]

I speak the truth. I confess that I do not understand it. Any of it. But I know it is the truth. Patsy, there are some mysteries that we are not meant to understand.

PATSY

I must warn him. I must warn him if he is in danger!

SISTER

        [She goes to PATSY at the window.]

But how?

PATSY

        [PATSY weeps. SISTER holds her lovingly like a mother.]

It hurts so bad.

SISTER

Simplicity is not unlike a willow tree. It may make us bow and bend, but we will not break. Sometimes a great wave is the thing that saves us.

PATSY

How can I save *him*?!

SISTER

There is but one Savior. This person whose love is dear to you, you must remember that God created him. God loves him and knows him best of all. He is in God's hands.

PATSY

[PATSY, with tears in her eyes, can only nod her head. They
sit on a bench.]
There must be something I can do.

SISTER

You once said that he was here.

PATSY

Yes.
[The future puts them at a loss as they sit.]

SISTER

When my babies were killed, an Elder from the church came to pray with us. But he said nothing. I found it so strange. He just stood there. And cried with us.
[With a moment of enlightenment.]
When I first went to West Union, there was an old woman there. Good and holy. I used to nurse her in her last days. I found that I couldn't lengthen her days. And I couldn't stop Death from coming to her door, no matter how hard I wanted to bolt it. I learned, and it was a hard lesson, I learned that there was one thing that I could do.

PATSY

What was that?

SISTER

Be there for her. Like that Elder had been for us. Be there with her as she left this life and traveled to the next. I couldn't go with her. I couldn't stop her from going. But I could hold her hand and simply be there for her. Like the angel that stood at your side when you were the child with fever. Do you remember?

PATSY

But I can't hold his hand. How can I be there for him?

307

SISTER

Love finds its way. I look at you and I see a different person. Not the frightened little girl who came here three years ago. But a woman who has rewritten her childhood. Free and untouched by her past. Surely this has been your releasement.

       [SISTER smiles at her, kisses PATSY on the forehead and leaves PATSY to herself.]

PATSY

[PATSY goes to the window. She hesitates. She sings:]

Oh, my pretty Mother's home,
sweeter than the honey in the comb.
Oh my pretty Mother's home,
sweeter than the honey in the comb.

Come, come pretty love, come come come
Come, come pretty love, I want some.

[We hear the voice of RANDY singing with her. Surpassing race and social status. Surpassing the flesh, and everything of this earthly realm; of time itself:]

PATSY and RANDY
Oh, my pretty Mother's home,
sweeter than the honey in the comb.
Oh my pretty Mother's home,
sweeter than the honey in the comb.

CURTAIN

Postscript

Mother Ann Lee

Ann Lee was born February 29, 1736 into a Quaker blacksmith's family in Manchester, England. Unable to go to a school and be educated, she worked the Manchester cotton mills. From an early age, she believed the prophets from the Bible sent spiritual messages telling her that sexual relations between men and women was sinful. Forced to marry blacksmith Abraham Stanley when she was twenty-six years of age, she gave birth to four children who died in infancy. She blamed their deaths

Figure 13
Mother Ann Lee. February 29, 1736—September 8, 1784.

on the depraved side of her human nature. In 1758, after joining a small sect of "Shaking Quakers" formed by James and Jane Wardley and dissenters of the Anglican, Methodist, and Quaker churches, she began to believe that perfect holiness was attainable through celibacy. The Wardleys taught her that the shaking and trembling in dance was caused by the Holy Spirit purging sin from the body. While in prison for disrupting an Anglican worship service in 1770, she experienced a vision of Christ who told her that she was the fulfillment of His second coming.[34]

The Shaker belief in the duality that God, the omniscient, omnipotent, omnipresent, has the attributes of both maleness and femaleness. Mother Ann Lee, was not Christ, nor did she claim to be. She is simply the helpmate, the bride of Christ, testifying both to the indwelling of Christ and her subservience to Him. "I have been walking with Christ in heavenly union. Christ is ever with me, both in sitting down and in rising up; in going out and in coming in. If I walk in groves and valleys, there He is with me and I

---

[34] Thomas Parrish, *Restoring Shakertown*, The University Press of Kentucky, Lexington, KY, 2005, pp. 5-6; Thomas D. Clark, F. Gerald Ham, *Pleasant Hill and Its Shakers* (Harrodsburg, KY: Pleasant Hill Press, 1968), pp. 4-6.

converse with Him as one friend converses with another, face to face . . .The second appearing of Christ is in His Church."[35]

Receiving a revelation to come to America, Ann Lee and eight followers boarded the *Maria* on the nineteenth of May, 1774. They arrived safely in New York on the sixth of August. John Hocknell, one of their immigrants, purchased property at Niskayuna, New York (later Watervliet), and in what was little more than a wilderness, their unique Shaker life in community flourished. After much hardship and persecution, Shaker societies were set up in nine states: New York, Massachusetts, Connecticut, Maine, New Hampshire, Ohio, Indiana, Pennsylvania, and Kentucky.[36]

Figure 14
The Sacred Dance, *Gleanings from Old Shaker Journals*, Compiled by Clara Endicott Sears, 1916.

Mother Ann Lee and her converts maintained neutrality during the American Revolution. Ann Lee and her followers were pacifists and did not side with the British nor the colonists. The public continued to criticize them over the years as they refused to celebrate the Fourth of July, it being a holiday of war.[37]

The violent hardships of attacks, imprisonments and poverty lead to the failing health and the death of Mother Ann at Watervliet, age forty-eight,

---

[35] Sabbath Day Lake Shaker Village, established 1783, "Principals and Beliefs," www.maineshakers.com.
[36] Sister R. Mildred Barker, *The Sabbathday Lake Shakers: An Introduction to The Shaker Heritage* (Sabbathday Lake, Maine: The Shaker Press, 1985), pp. 2-3.
[37] Joseph Manca, *Journal of the American Revolution*, "The Shakers and the American Revolution," August 12, 2015, (https://allthingsliberty.com/author/joseph-manca/), p. 1, 9.

on the 8th of September 1784, ten years after landing in New York.[38] She is buried in the Shaker cemetery near the Watervliet Shaker Historic District.

A time of mystical visions and revelations began in 1837 with the Shakers in New Lebanon. This mystical ten-year period became known as the Era of Manifestations and "Mother Ann's Work." Many of the Shakers saw visions and dreamed of deceased Shakers along with historical figures such as George Washington who became a frequent visionary spirit.[39]

Orphans left from the wars and epidemics, seemed the future for the Shaker villages. At the Shaker Village, Canterbury, New Hampshire, boys helped on the farm for four months of summer and girls went to school. They were taught to be farmers, artisans, and housekeepers. Unfortunately, most of them when of age went back to "the world." But they took with them lasting gifts of the peaceful communities: love, kindness, industry, and simplicity.[40]

Shaker Village of Pleasant Hill

The late eighteenth century saw the beginning of "The Second Great Awakening" of religion in America that continued into the early nineteenth century. At large outdoor camp meetings, clergy from Protestant groups preached for days accompanied by music and dancing that added to create an emotional revival. Thousands of settlers in the Ohio Valley of Kentucky were attracted to these ecumenical religious gatherings. Here people who had been scattered in isolation found for the first time a community on the frontier.

This spiritual awakening caught the attention of the Shakers who felt compelled to expand their ministry into the ripe harvest of Kentucky. The leader of the Shaker Ministry at New Lebanon, New York, Lucy Wright, decided to send missionaries to help convert the west. On the first of the new year, 1805, John Meacham, Benjamin Seth Youngs, and Issachar

---

[38] Thomas Parrish, *Restoring Shakertown*, The University Press of Kentucky, Lexington, KY, 2005, p. 8.

[39] Joseph Manca, *Journal of the American Revolution*, "The Shakers and the American Revolution," August 12, 2015, (https://allthingsliberty.com/author/joseph-manca/), p 9.

[40] Flo Morse and Vincent Newton, *The Shakers' Guide to Good Manners* (New York, NY: The Countryman Press, 1998, 2017, pp. 9, 24.

Bates, set out to bring the Shaker beliefs to the wilderness of Kentucky. By this time, eleven Shaker communities had been established in New York and New England.[41]

Pleasant Hill was founded in 1806 and grew to 500 residents, 250 buildings, and 4000 acres of land for farming. In 1807, South Union village was established with 350 workers and 6000 acres of land. These Shakers experimented with silk worms and produced garden seeds in packages that were widely sold across the nation.[42] In the middle of the Pleasant Hill village, a stone meeting house of worship was built in 1810; damaged by the New Madrid earthquake, it was rebuilt in 1820, as a wooden frame meetinghouse 60 by 44 feet.[43]

Figure 15
Shaker Village of Pleasant Hill

At Shaker Village, a destitute family could be fed and housed. Enslaved persons were free and viewed as a brother or sister. It was a community of gender and diversity equality. Immigrants from other countries, Germany, Italy, etc. brought their traditions and languages. Occasionally, someone from "the world" would come after having "mard themselves in the world in some way or other," while others might come in honorable standing in the world. William S. Byrd approached the village free from economic deprivation whose father, an attorney, was an influential political figure in the Ohio Valley.[44]

---

[41] Stephen J. Paterwic, *Historical Dictionary of the Shakers* (Lanham, Md.: Scarecrow Press, 2008).

[42] Lowell H. Harrison and James C. Klotter, *A New History of Kentucky* (Lexington, KY: The University Press of Kentucky, 1982), pp. 135, 155.

[43] Julia Neal, *The Kentucky Shakers* (Lexington, KY: The University Press of Kentucky, 1982), pp. 15, 16.

[44] Stephen J. Stein, *Letters from a Kyoung Shaker, William S. Byrd at Pleasant Hill* (Lexington, KY: The University Press of Kentucky, 1985), pp. 1, 8.

Their simple lifestyle was different from the beauty, architecture, and icons of Catholic and Protestant churches. Ecclesiastical aesthetics was found within. "Hands to work and hearts to God."

The last living Shakers of Pleasant Hill deeded their 1,800 acres in 1910, to George Bohon of Harrodsburg. He agreed to care for them until their deaths. Under the leadership of Earl D. Wallace, a crusade began to restore the Village as a monument to its religious and social past as a viable rural community. James Lowry Cogar, native of Woodford County and first curator of Colonial Williamsburg, Virginia, supervised the restoration.[45]

The serenity of Shaker life caught the attention of world renown author and monk Thomas Merton who was pleased at the efforts to restore the Shaker Village of Pleasant Hill. "The Shakers and their spirituality seem to me to be extremely significant, as an authentic American form of the Monastic Life, with a Utopian and eschatological cast. The superb and simple products of their craftsmanship are not only eloquent in themselves, but they also speak for the genuine spiritual vitality of the Shakers, and testify to the validity of their ideal, . . ."[46]

Patsy Roberts Williamson

Patsy Roberts Williamson, an African American woman, was among the earliest converts to the Shaker faith in central Kentucky. Born in North Carolina in January 7, 1791, she was living in nearby Madison County in 1809 when Shaker records indicate she "believed." The year before, Betsy Roberts, the eldest Roberts' sibling joined Shaker Village. Susannah, Caucasian twin to Patsy, joined January 1809. Namon Roberts and Jinny Roberts joined in 1812, with Patsy. When the Roberts left the society in 1815, the Shakers purchased Patsy's freedom. The Shakers "purchased her that she might remain with them." Patsy signed the first Church covenant of 1814 with her mark. Patsy lived in the East Family until her death

---

[45] Thomas D. Clark, F. Gerald Ham, *Pleasant Hill and Its Shakers* (Harrodsburg, KY: Pleasant Hill Press, 1968) pp. 94-5.

[46] Thomas Merton to Ralph McCallister, October 29, 1961. Paul M. Pearson and the Merton Legacy Trust, *Thomas Merton Seeking Paradise, The Spirit of the Shakers* (Maryknoll, NY: Orbis Books, 2003), pp. 118-9.

in 1860, where "she continued zealous in the cause, according to her understanding."[47]

Besides a few hymns written by Patsy, little is recorded of her special duties and activities during her long years at Pleasant Hill. It is certain that she and her Shaker sisters were busy with textile production, cooking, cleaning, preserving, and laundry.

Although all official Pleasant Hill documents – roll book, biographical register, covenants, U. S. censuses – record the name Patsy Williamson, the following entry on the occasion of her decease attaches the name of her former owners:

August 28, 1860. Patsy (Williamson) Roberts deceased at the East House after an illness of four or five years. She was colored and had been a slave. She believed in the year 1809. Her owners having believed and again turned away, they offered her for sale and Believers purchased her that she might remain with them which she did and continued zealous into the cause, according to her understanding till death.[48]

Patsy Roberts composed many Shaker hymns including *Mother's Good Drink, Pretty Mother's Home,* and *Come, Pretty Love.*

From the beginning of Shaker Village in 1806 until the 1880s, there were counted nineteen freed enslaved persons as members in the village among the some 500 inhabitants.[49]

Quakers, Camisards, and Shakers believed in the possibility of unmediated manifestations of the spirit. These perennial modes of religious experience and expression characterized the worship of the original eight Shakers

---

[47] Holly Wood, Music Program Specialist, Shaker Village of Pleasant Hill; *Village@ Work, Inspiring Tomorrow's Trailblazers,* "African American Experiences at Pleasant Hill: Patsy Roberts (Williamson)" (Harrodsburg, Kentucky: blog.shakervillageky.org, March 11, 2021); Christian Goodwillie and Carol Medlicott, *This Chosen, Pleasant Hill: Shakers of the Kentucky Bluegrass,* Shakertown and Pleasant Hill, Kentucky, Inc.: Straggling Tembler Press, 2022.
[48] Jacob A. Glover, Director of Public Programs and Education, Shaker Village of Pleasant Hill, November 9, 2020, email to playwright.
[49] Vickie Cimprich, "Free and Freed Shakers and Affiliates of African Descent at Pleasant Hill," *Kentucky Register of the Kentucky Historical Society,* Volume 111, Number 4, Autumn 2013, pp. 489-523 (Article) Published by Kentucky Historical Society.

who migrated from Manchester to New York in 1774. This kind of prayer, song, and body movement may or may not have been among the features of Shaker life that attracted early converts of African descent. Such converts included Prime, Hannah, Betsy, and Phebe Lane at the early Shaker village in Watervliet near Albany, New York.[50]

Because little has been recorded about the life of Patsy Roberts Williamson, the playwright has used liberties. Things that may have been but are not factual through proof. We do know that she was a twin; her sister was accepted as Caucasian while she was considered African.[51] But we do not know if she was the child of the Roberts family. The spiritual connection between a man in the twentieth century and a woman in the nineteenth century has been created for drama as has the secret tradition of the "Day of Releasement."

Randy Folger

Randy Folger is the inspiration of the character "RANDY" in this play. This is not a play about Mr. Folger. His music has been an inspiration for many including the playwright, and the playwright created this character only to honor Mr. Folger's memory.

Born June 13, 1952 in Fort Lewis West Virginia Son of the Rev. Richard K. and Elaine D. Lamb Folger of Mansfield Ohio. Originally from Olympia, WA., his father was a Baptist minister

Randy Folger

Figure 16
Randy Folger "Gentle Words, Shaker Music," 1993.

---

[50] The Shaker Collection of the Western Reserve Historical Society in Cleveland, Ohio membership card file abstracted by Wallace Cathcart, reel 123, index of proper names, 11-17. This card file provides sketchy but useful information about Shakers of African descent at the founding villages in New York and Massachusetts. An 1860s photo of Sister Phebe (or Phoebe) Lane appears in SCWRHS, reel 89. See also "African American Shakers: In the Berkshires and Beyond," http://www.hancockshakervillage.org (accessed April 2, 2012).

[51] Archives, Shaker Village at Pleasant Hill, Harrodsburg, Kentucky.

and Randy grew up singing in the church. The Folger family moved to Kentucky in 1958. Randy attended Bob Jones University and Western Kentucky University.

He was an actor in Ragged Edge Community Theater of Harrodsburg and performed in *The Fantasticks* and *Shenandoah*. He served the Kentucky National Guard and was a member of Oak Hill Baptist Church.

Randy came to Shaker Village of Pleasant Hill in 1990, as the Music and Special Programs manager. April through October, Randy performed weekends four concerts a day. He researched Shaker journals and hymns, recorded three music albums of Shaker music, and transcribed a Pleasant Hill hymnal into modern notation. A speaker on Shaker music, history, and theology, he lectured at Elder Hostels and schools. Randy wrote and performed an original theater piece in 1998 with the South Bend Symphonic Choir of South Bend Indiana

Randy Folger died Thursday July 1, 1999 at Chinn Lane in a car accident, while delivering a pizza to a friend who was in the process of moving.[52]

---

[52] "Killed in Accident off US 68," July 1999.

Bibliography

"African American Shakers: In the Berkshires and Beyond." http://www.hancockshakervillage.org, April 2, 2012.

Barker, Sister R. Mildred. *The Sabbathday Lake Shakers: An Introduction to The Shaker Heritage.* Sabbathday Lake, Maine: The Shaker Press, 1985.

Cathcart, Wallace. The Shaker Collection of the Western Reserve Historical Society in Cleveland, Ohio.

Cimprich, Vickie. "Free and Freed Shakers and Affiliates of African Descent at Pleasant Hill," *Kentucky Register of the Kentucky Historical Society,* Volume 111, Number 4, Autumn 2013. (Article) Published by Kentucky Historical Society.

Clark, Thomas D., Ham, F. Gerald. *Pleasant Hill and Its Shakers.* Harrodsburg, KY: Pleasant Hill Press, 1968.

Glover, Jacob A. Director of Public Programs and Education, Shaker Village of Pleasant Hill, November 9, 2020, email to playwright.

Goodwillie, Christian and Medlicott, Carol. *This Chosen, Pleasant Hill: Shakers of the Kentucky Bluegrass.* Shakertown and Pleasant Hill, Kentucky, Inc.: Straggling Tembler Press, 2022.

Harrison, Lowell H. and Klotter, James C. *A New History of Kentucky.* Lexington, KY: The University Press of Kentucky, 1982.

Manca, Joseph. *Journal of the American Revolution,* "The Shakers and the American Revolution," August 12, 2015. https://allthingsliberty.com/author/joseph-manca/.

Merton, Thomas to McCallister, Ralph, October 29, 1961. Paul M. Pearson and the Merton Legacy Trust, *Thomas Merton Seeking Paradise, The Spirit of the Shakers* Maryknoll, NY: Orbis Books, 2003.

Morse, Flo and Newton, Vincent. *The Shakers' Guide to Good Manners.* New York, NY: The Countryman Press, 1998, 2017.

Neal, Julia. *The Kentucky Shakers*. Lexington, KY: The University Press of Kentucky, 1982.

Parrish, Thomas. *Restoring Shakertown*. The University Press of Kentucky, Lexington, KY, 2005.

Paterwic, Stephen J. *Historical Dictionary of the Shakers*. Lanham, Md.: Scarecrow Press, 2008.

Sabbath Day Lake Shaker Village, established 1783, "Principals and Beliefs," www.maineshakers.com.

Stein, Stephen J. *Letters from a Young Shaker, William S. Byrd at Pleasant Hill*. Lexington, KY: The University Press of Kentucky, 1985.

Wood, Holly Music Program Specialist, Shaker Village of Pleasant Hill. *Village@Work, Inspiring Tomorrow's Trailblazers*, "African American Experiences at Pleasant Hill: Patsy Roberts (Williamson)." Harrodsburg, Kentucky: blog.shakervillageky.org, March 11, 2021. Conversations with Holy Wood, the author.

Pioneer Christmas in Kentucky

Introduction

MILFORD

The Virginia General Assembly authorized formation of Madison County on 15 December 1785 without designating a town to serve as the county seat. The Governor of Virginia, Patrick Henry, picked a compromise site as the county seat. At that time, it was designated only as "Madison Court House". A temporary courthouse was sufficiently completed on 22 May 1787.

The Virginia General Assembly passed an act formalizing a town at this site in December 1789 and designated nine men to serve as its trustees. The name "Milford" was chosen, possibly to honor John Kinkaid's slave, whom he later freed.

Milford's location was topographically challenging with a questionable water supply, and it lacked political support. In February 1798, after prominent local citizens petitioned the Kentucky Legislature, the county seat was moved to Richmond.

MADISON COUNTY HISTORICAL SOCIETY

The Madison County Historical Society was formed in 1891 after the Madison County Court of Claims formed a committee of 10 prominent citizens, whose purpose was to locate and preserve "relics of the Pioneer Days of Madison County as can be brought together within the bounds of the county, and for the erection of proper memorials to mark important historical events and places in such a manner as to perpetuate and preserve them." These artifacts were going to be displayed in a cabinet in the courthouse.

For more information about the Madison County Historical Society, visit the website at www.madisoncountykyhistory.org or on Facebook at http// facebook.com/madisoncountyhs

Sharon Graves
President, Madison County Historical Society
2024

Pioneer Christmas in Kentucky

CHARACTERS

SUSANNAH Nobel widow tavern owner

John OAKLEY carpenter and Grog owner

ABIGAIL Phelps wife to John Phelps tavern owner

SALLIE Logan wife to Sam Logan the tanner

TIMMY Logan son of Sam and Sallie

MINERVA town prophetess from western Virginia

ANNA MAE the untamed frontier gal of Milford

BOYS the noisy boys of Milford

GIRLS the sweet young girls of Milford

Preacher Griffin POND traveling minister to the Meeting House

CHLOE Flinn orphaned ward to Daniel and Rebecca Boone

SUE Moran wife to Green Moran, Poosey Ridge

BETSY Logwood wife to Joe and keeper of the General Store

ISABEL Barnes wife of James Barnes, owner of the Mill

REBECCA Boone first white lady of the Kentucky River, wife to Daniel

Joe KENNEDY husband to Margaret and Sheriff of Milford

Daniel BOONE the Scout and Surveyor of Kentucky

Tom CROW first resident of Milford, built the jail under the Courthouse.

Joe LOGWOOD main General Store owner, "Special Bail" for Green Moran

PAUL Campbell son of large land owner on Poosey Ridge

MARGARET Kennedy wife to Joe Kennedy the Sheriff

John MILLER Revolutionary War veteran and Magistrate

Green CLAY State representative, Court designated deputy surveyor, inspector.

Will IRVINE County recording clerk

INDIAN "Blue Jacket" Shawnee Chief

Green MORAN husband to Sue; small land owner on Poosey Ridge

Act One

The guests are seated at their tables in the Old Meetinghouse on the road to Milford. SETTLERS, dressed in late 18th Century apparel, serve hot spiced apple cider. It is December 1788. The room is darkened. We hear the sounds of the wilderness, leaves, and birds, etc. Joe LOGWOOD appears old and ragged. Around him in the shadows we hear the soloist sing *"A Song for Milford:"*

SOLOIST

Sing a song for Milford, sing a song tonight
While the skies are empty and the moon is bright;
Though it's long forgotten and nothing there remains
Just a song for Milford that we sing again.

Candles in the windows, melt away like snow
Even all the windows vanished long ago.
So, bring back an ember and kindle the lights,
While we remember Milford, sing a song tonight.

TOWNSFOLK

Some say, "The good old times weren't so good sometimes,"
And how we glamorize the past from present crimes.
But in that life, my dream was fair;
For every time I closed my eyes, I saw you there.

SOLOIST

Why do we remember all the hate we've known?
And the good surrender, when we need it so?
So, bring back an ember and kindle the lights.
While we remember Milford, sing a song tonight.

TOWNSFOLK

All is well at Milford. Sing a song tonight.

[Joe LOGWOOD is gone. Lights reveal the Old Log Meetinghouse in Madison County, Virginia, a December evening of 1788. It is a gathering of the town folk of Milford for the Christmas dinner. SUSANNAH Nobel acts as hostess and looks over the crowd to count the number to be fed; but she is also looking for something else. The word has gone out that the secret papers of "Black Bob Morgan's Gang" have been hidden in the lockbox in the Milford Courthouse in hopes of luring the murderers to their town. As the doors are open and welcoming to all, guest have wandered in to join a festive Christmas Dinner,

[John OAKLEY enters.]

SUSANNAH
John Oakley,
[Whispering with intense suspense]
have you heard anything?

OAKLEY
Not tonight. How could you over this crowd! More and more people are coming West every day.

SUSANNAH
[To the crowd:]
Good evening and welcome to Milford!
[There are "Welcomes!" from the room. She speaks to the audience.]
Our people have moved away from the Fort and cut a clearing of our own and built houses that are forts within themselves. And so, we have our little town: Milford. It gets its name from Taylor Fork crossing to Haines Mill. A ford: shallow enough to wade through. "Mill ford."

[ABIGAIL enters. OAKLEY beats SUSANNAH to it:]

OAKLEY
Evening, Abigail and Sallie.

[Every time the question arises it is with the same trepidation:]
Have you heard anything?

ABIGAIL
Not tonight.
[To the present travelers]
Tonight it's Christmas at Milford! Once a year we get everyone together for our annual Christmas feast here in the Meeting House.

SALLIE

A Christmas tradition. Lot's of people. Everyone from the county comes out for this special night. Even Daniel Boone from his winter hunt.

OAKLEY

[He lifts his glass for a toast]
To Daniel Boone!

SUSANNAH

Not, yet, John! We've all got to wait.

OAKLEY

What are we waiting for?

SUSANNAH

Grace, for one thing.

ABIGAIL

And Christmas is about waiting, isn't it? But it's hard with such good cooks here in Milford.

OAKLEY

And it's hard to wait when a fella's stomach's a growlin'!

SUSANNAH

Was that your stomach, John Oakley? I thought you were singing!

SALLIE

Our ladies of Milford have been cooking all week for tonight. We've got bear meat and buffalo tongue and venison, squirrel, and rabbit and chicken . . . Corn, pumpkin soup, and Mammy Lou's famous corn pone!

[MINERVA enters. The old wise woman of the town, smoking her pipe]

ABIGAIL and SALLIE

Evening, Minerva. *Have you heard anything?*

MINERVA

Not tonight. But *I dreamed last night a dream* . . .

327

SALLIE

A Christmas dream! Of candies and savory pies?

SUSANNAH

Sugar plums and syllabub?

ABIGAIL

Of oranges and sweet meats?

MINERVA

. . . of hedge apples . . .

SUSANNAH

Hedge apples?

MINERVA

It was hedge apples . . .

ABIGAIL

You can't cook hedge apples.

SALLIE

Our cow tried to swallow a hedge apple whole. It killed her!

MINERVA

It was hedge apples . . .

SALLIE
[Rethinking this]
Well, . . . they are a pretty color green . . .

ABIGAIL

And they have a lovely smell.

SALLIE

It must be a sign of peace! "The wolf shall dwell with the lamb . . .

ABIGAIL

"and the leopard shall lie down with the kid!"

SALLIE and ABIGAIL

And a little child will lead them!

MINERVA

DEATH!

[Simply and calmly, she walks to the side and sits.]

SALLIE

I think I've lost my appetite.

BOY

Not me. I could eat a bear!

[ANNA MAE, a young woman dirty and in hunting clothes, and the young man TIMOTHY enter.]

ANNA MAE

Well, you'd have to know how to shoot one first before yous can eat him! AND NO, don't ask me, because I haven't heard a thing out there tonight.

[They all try and quiet her, looking around to see who heard]

SALLIE

Anna Mae, this is the Christmas dinner. When everyone gets all dressed up and all . . .

ANNA MAE

That's why I put on my best!
[She spits into a nearby bucket]

MINERVA

What about you, Timothy? *Have you heard anything?*

TIMOTHY

Just the growl of my stomach!

SALLIE

We have to wait for Grace.

TIMOTHY

Where is she?

SALLIE

We have to wait until Grace is spoken.

TIMOTHY

Who's she spoken for?

[Preacher POND appears.]

SUSANNAH

Preacher Pond can say the Grace.

TIMOTHY

Preacher Pond, *Have you heard anything?*

POND

Not tonight.

SUSANNAH

Will you say Grace, Preacher Pond?

[POND removes his hat, about to pray but BETSY arrives:]

SUSANNAH, OAKLEY, ABIGAIL,
SALLIE, MINERVA, TIMOTHY:

Evening, Betsy! *Have you heard anything?*

BETSY

Not tonight. It couldn't happen tonight, do you suppose?

EVERYONE

Shh—

[The room gets quiet.]

SUSANNAH

[Explaining to any guest who might have overheard]
Christmas is full of secrets.

ABIGAIL

St. Nicholas! He was a Christmas secret. He knew a family of daughters
that needed help.

[The little child CHLOE enters carrying a hedge apple.
POND walks away.]

St. Nicholas secretly left the little girls sacks of gold like the gifts the wise men brought the Christ Child. It saved the children and they never knew who had given them the money. He's the spirit of giving at Christmastime.

SALLIE

This is your last stop on the road to town. So, settle back and expect to enjoy yourself tonight. For that's the way the Lord would want it. That's the way it is in Milford.

SUSANNAH

Those old fashioned days are back to remember. We make you kindly welcome here at our "pioneer Christmas!"
[SETTLERS sing "Pioneer Christmas."]

CHORUS:
I love a Pioneer Christmas in Kentucky
Where the simple ways of doing things are dear.
I love a Pioneer Christmas in Kentucky
Where the olden days bring happiness and cheer.

And when the snow falls softly on the Meadow
And the trees are trimmed in mistletoe
We'll keep a home fire burning for you brightly
Invite you in and keep you from the cold.

CHORUS

The Lord our God was born on Christmas morning
In a stable far way in Bethlehem
But we'll make room for Him in old Kentucky
With featherbed, cornbread, and country ham.

CHORUS

We're breaking ground on trials and temptations
And trying things we've never tried before
So, hitch your wagon, be a pioneer
Refuse to be a "settler" anymore.

331

CHORUS

Great Meadow, Land of Tomorrow,
Oh, Great Spirit, come smiling down
On your Great Meadow, Land of Tomorrow,
On your handmade Happy Hunting Ground.

The years are passing by us in a moment
And it won't be long before our time is gone
It is my prayer for those of you who hear this to
To raise your voice and carry on this song

CHORUS

Great Meadow, Land of Tomorrow,
Oh, Great Spirit, come smiling down
On your Great Meadow, Land of Tomorrow,
On your handmade Happy Hunting Ground.

[SUE enters]

BETSY
Evening, Sue! *Have you heard anything?*

SUE
Not tonight.

SUSANNAH
[To the crowd]
That's Sue Moran from out Poosey Ridge. She stays to herself out on their farm.

ABIGAIL
[Whispering]
It's her husband's been feudin' with the Campbells.

SALLIE
[Whispering]
I thought the Campbells went South--

332

ABIGAIL

Their son's back. Her husband stole fifty of their acres while's they was gone. Just put a fence up around it pretending it was his all along.

SALLIE

No . . . .!

ANNA MAE

I'd a shoot him!

SUSANNAH

Shh——

> [BETSY has picked out some men at a table and has been talking with them]

BETSY

Susannah, we have some men here headed to town tonight after the dinner. Maybe we should tell them how to get there so they don't get lost.

SALLIE

What do they look like?

ABIGAIL

Have you seen them before?

ANNA MAE

Sounds suspicious . . .

SUSANNAH

It's not as if they were going to the courthouse——

BETSY
[From talking with the men]
They're going to the courthouse . . .

ABIGAIL
[To SALLIE]
Where's the signal?

333

SALLIE

[To ABIGAIL]
I sure never heard it.

ANNA MAE

Well, it can't be them.

[They breathe a sigh of relief]

ABIGAIL

It can't be them if there was no signal.

SALLIE

[To ABIGAIL]
My goodness, you are so suspicious!

SUSANNAH

[To the men]
The town and courthouse is just down the hill. About a mile.

ABIGAIL

Not to the bottom of the hill; you just go over the creek and then up the
hill– Just follow along the creek. It bears off to the right, but you go straight.
Not to the right, but straight over the creek. Just follow the road. It bears
off to the left, but you go straight up the hill.

ANNA MAE

Just follow the short cut by Sam Estill's place! Now, there's a three way fork
and you can go right or left, but you go straight. Not right or left.

SALLIE

Not to the shortcut. Sam Estill's place isn't a mile, it's just a mile to Milford
from here. Of course, it *will* take you longer that way: Sam's going to want
to show you his dogs. And then you'll have to have a drink with him–And
his wife will want to visit with you too and she talks forever. You'll be
lucky if you get away from her before the sun goes down . . .Just follow
straight up the hill, as you were. Then around that oak tree–not the little
one but the big one.

ABIGAIL

Oh, they cut that down to size. It's little now, and the little one has grown big.

SALLIE

I meant the big little one and the little big one.

BETSY

The big little one and the little big one. You'll pass two houses . . . how far from Silver Creek would you say those houses are, Susanna?

SUSANNAH

About a mile.

ABIGAIL

Not to those houses. Not if you pass Ben Holladay's white cow that grazes by the sycamore tree. There's a path there off down Silver Creek where Nicholas Hawkins has his grist mill–it kind of curves left and then right and then left again? Not the one that goes over the creek, the bridge there is mighty rickety--

SALLIE

By the old sycamore tree, not the straight one but the bent one. Where John Pitman's spotted cow grazes.

BETSY

Where John Pitman's spotted cow grazes. Where the road forks, there's a chestnut tree there. How far from here?

SUSANNAH

About a mile–

ABIGAIL

You know where the road forks? To the left?

SALLIE

Right.

ABIGAIL

Not right. Left.

SALLIE

Right. The tree burned, just an old stump left there now. That's all that's left.

ABIGAIL

You know that old stump that's left there on the right? Well, just forget it–don't even go *there*–put it out of your mind–it's sure to confuse you--

SALLIE

That's not the right way, where the stump is left. You want to go right, where it's left. Pass John Wright's barn. Or what's left of *it*.

ABIGAIL

Anyways, once you're up on the ridge, you want to stay straight. Now, you know where that big rock is, the one that looks like Estella Estill?

SALLIE

She's thin as a bone since the diphtheria. Take the fourth turn near the third hackberry tree and you'll see a road sign: be sure to ignore that altogether. Then up the ridge and you're there. You think you can find it now? It's just over yonder.

ABIGAIL and SALLIE

Over yonder . . .

BETSY

Just over yonder . . .

ANNA MAE

Over yonder!

SUSANNAH

About a mile.

BETSY
[To the men]
You won't have any problems.

SALLIE
[To ABIGAIL and SUSANNA]
The problem with men is they **just won't ask for directions!**

SUSANNAH
[To Everyone:]

Anyways, that'll be Milford. Our county seat. Boonesborough wanted it. We had to raise such a howl for it that Governor Patrick Henry gave in and made Milford our county seat and not Boonesborough.

SALLIE

Here in Milford we have a nice big courthouse, Blacksmith shops, a hatmaker and a rope maker, Joe Logwood's General Store, my husband Sam Logan our Tanner, and of course our church, school, and meeting house where we are tonight for our dinner . . . . If you need a place to stay, Susannah Nobel owns one of the licensed taverns in town. We call them "ordinaries."

ANNA MAE

Come to think of it, "Ordinary" is a funny name for a tavern.

ABIGAIL

There's about a dozen or so ordinaries in Milford for ordinary folks like you and me. And some folk like *Daniel Boone*, not so ordinary. Daniel Boone has a habit this time of year to dig for "Sang."

ANNA MAE

Customarily.

ABIGAIL

He took a keelboat up the Ohio to sell it up in Maryland–where they ship it off to *China*--

ANNA MAE

Mercenarily.

ABIGAIL
[Annoyed at ANNA MAE's interruptions]

But the boat about sank and all the ginseng root got wet and just about ruined--

ANNA MAE

Despairingly.

ABIGAIL

They spent some days with his old friend John Vanbibber trying to dry it out--

ANNA MAE

Momentarily.

ABIGAIL

He lost a lot of money on the Sang--

ANNA MAE

Involuntarily.

ABIGAIL

Daniel Boone is a familiar figure in these here parts--

ANNA MAE

Legendarily.

ABIGAIL

He and Rebecca always stay at Nobel's Tavern where there's always an extra bed and plate.

[ABIGAIL and SALLIE look to AMMA MAE for a response. Finally:]

ANNA MAE

Ordinarily.
          [She walks off]

SUE

Susanna Nobel's the first woman in Kentucky to run her own **ordinary**. Many of our people were taken captive by the Shawnee four years ago—Mr. Nobel with them. Last year, Daniel Boone negotiated with the Shawnee on getting many of our people back. But they never found Mr. Nobel—considered him dead. A lot that were released were children like this little girl here. This is Chloe Flinn, Daniel and Rebecca haven't been able to find her parents so they've taken her in. They live over at Boone Station.

[REBECCA enters. CHLOE runs to her.]

REBECCA

Daniel couldn't convince the Shawnee to free little Chloe, so when they weren't looking, he just snuck into the Indian camp and rescued her himself. He never made a sound.

338

ANNA MAE

Hey, Timmy, how many ears does Daniel Boone have?

TIMOTHY

I don't know, Anna Mae, how many ears does Daniel Boone have?

ANNA MAE

Why, three of course.

TIMOTHY

Three?

ANNA MAE

Yeap! A left ear, a right ear, and a wild fronti-EAR!

[They laugh]
I bet ya he's out there right now a huntin' a bear.

BOY

Hunting for bears!?

REBECCA

Hunting for sang.

SUE

Aren't you boys scared of bears?

BOYS

Are you kidding? We're not scared of anything--

GIRLS

Hi, boys!

BOYS

Ahh! Girls!
[BOYS run off terrified]

SUSANNAH

They're just full of excitement. After all it is Christmas!

339

OAKLEY

To Christmas!
> [He starts to toast]

SUSANNAH

Not yet, John!

ANNA MAE
> [To REBECCA]

That's John Oakley, he's a builder and he owns his own Grog Shop.

SUSANNAH

He supplies most of our taverns.

REBECCA

I've been looking for a good Christmas gift for Daniel. What kind of grog?

SUSANNAH

What kind of spirits you got, John?

OAKLEY

What kind you want?

> [Everyone laughs]

I make the *water of life* . . . from anything that can ferment!

SUSANNAH

John Oakley makes sorghum molasses punch, juniper berry tea, apple jack, and white lighting from red pepper, and potato beer . . .

ABIGAIL

And he makes wine from grapes, and elder berries, rhubarb, and of course his famous "cherry bounce!"

POND

Cherry *Bounce*? That's a funny name.

SUSANNAH

You drink some of Oakley's brew and your cherries'll be bouncin'!

[PAUL Campbell, a young man, enters]

SUE

Evening, Paul Campbell. *Have you heard anything?*

PAUL

Not tonight.

SALLIE

[To ANNA MAE]

Now there's a nice looking fella. Just come back into town—his family owns a lot of land out Poosey Ridge . . .

ABIGAIL

Single, too. Would make a nice husband

[to ANNA MAE]

for the right gal . . .

ANNA MAE

If I see the right gal, I'll be sure to tell her. Now, I might not mind having a husband that could cook, and clean, and sew. . .I think I might just get me a couple dozen of 'em.

OAKLEY

Who are those men in the back? I'm a bit suspicious of 'em!

SALLIE

I told you!

ABIGAIL

What makes you suspicious, John?

OAKLEY

They brought their own jug!

SALLIE

So?

OAKLEY

Not from my still. That's bad stuff in that jug.

341

SUSANNAH

I don't think I've ever seen them around these parts before–

ABIGAIL

Tell them we are out of food--

SALLIE

How many are there?

BETSY

Four of them.

SUE

If it's the four of them, they're all right. Uncle Albert and Aunt Anna sent them over from Fort Boone.

SUSANNAH

Al and Anna, sent them?

ABIGAIL

If Al and Anna send them, then we've got plenty of food for all four of them; and besides, they brought their own jug with them.

OAKLEY

Not from my still. That's bad stuff.

[SUSANNAH sighs]

ABIGAIL

That's a heavy sigh there, Susannah.

SUSANNAH

How can you be sure they're not - - - "*you know who?*"

ABIGAIL and SALLIE:

You mean?–

EVERYONE

Shh—

[All are silent.]

SUSANNAH

That's a secret. Christmas is full of secrets.

ABIGAIL

Here in the Meeting House?--

SALLIE

Sitting at our tables and drinking John Oakley's grog?--

OAKLEY

Not mine! Bad jug. Bad jug.

[SUSANNAH sighs again]

ABIGAIL

Oh, Susannah, don't you sigh for me.

SALLIE

Four have come from Al and Anna.

[Pause]

OAKLEY

With a bad jug on their knee.
                    [ANNA MAE rim shots a pan]
That grog must be made from hedge apples.

ABIGAIL

I don't know of anything you can do with hedge apples but look at them!

[She takes the hedge apple from CHLOE, smells it.]

It does have a lovely smell.

REBECCA

They keep bugs away–

SALLIE

Not in Milford!

SUSANNAH

There are no bugs.

REBECCA

No bugs? Why is that?

EVERYONE

Because it's Milford!

ABIGAIL

That's right.

REBECCA

What do your frogs and snakes eat?

SALLIE

No snakes in Milford.

REBECCA

Why are there no snakes?

EVERYONE

Because it's Milford!

SUSANNAH

'Cause if you had snakes, you might get bit!

SALLIE

No one ever gets sick—

ABIGAIL

Or hurt in Milford.

REBECCA

How is that?

[As if that's the dumbest question of all:]

SUSANNAH, SALLIE, ABIGAIL

There's not a doctor in Milford!

344

[ANNA MAE rim shots the pan again]

SALLIE
Milford is a safe place. No one ever locks their doors in Milford. Why, even the jail doesn't have a lock!

ABIGAIL
Just a latch. Any fool could take a stick and lift it up through the crack.

OAKLEY
I took a stick and lifted that latch right up through that crack!

SUSANNAH
[Of OAKLEY, good naturedly]
Like she said, "Any *fool* could take a stick. . ."

CROW
The fool doth think he is wise, but the wise man knows himself to be a fool!

REBECCA
How do you keep your prisoners?

SALLIE
We don't have any prisoners in Milford.

REBECCA
How is it that you never have a prisoner in your jail?

ABIGAIL
They take a stick and lift that latch up through the crack.

Sheriff Joe Kennedy has to scour the country to fetch them back. Like when Slaughter McAllister—he borrowed his neighbor's ax without askin'.

PAUL
[To KENNEDY]
Evenin' Sherriff! *Have you heard anything?*

KENNEDY
Not tonight.

REBECCA

Wouldn't it be easier to buy a lock for the door?

ABIGAIL

No locks in Milford . . . Everyone gets along at Milford.

SALLIE

Oh, there was that time when John Caperton bit off part of Bill Young's right ear—

ABIGAIL

Was a nuisance, always a getting in the way of his rifle--he's a better aim now.

SUSANNAH

You'd have to travel the world to find a place like Milford. We in Milford come from all around the world. Why, you just as soon buy some hay from a Swiss, and some kraut from a German, share a cup of tea with an Englishman, but you best camp so as not to be too near the Irish Presbyterians--they can be a bit contentious.

ABIGAIL

Christmas traditions come from all around the world, too. In Swedish the young girls dress as Santa Lucia to bring fresh coffee and hot sweet rolls to everyone in the house.

SALLIE

Milford is like George Adam's old country, Ireland. Why, that's how Milford got it's name, you know: Adams came from a small village in Ireland called, "Milford." But there ain't no leprechauns doin' mischief in Milford.

SUSANNAH
[Of someone sitting at a table]
Now, there is another one. Have you ever seen him before?

ABIGAIL

How do you know it's not —*you know who?*

SALLIE

Looks suspicious--

ANNA MAE

I say a shoot 'em!

SUE

It can't be *you know who*. We didn't get the signal.

ABIGAIL

When the signal comes, we'll know if it's *you know who*.

SALLIE

That's right.
            [She breathes a sigh of relief]
You all are so suspicious!

REBECCA

Who's "you know who?"

EVERYONE

Shh!

ABIGAIL

We are bound to show hospitality. It's a great old legend that at Christmastime
the Christ Child has been known to wander the earth as a stranger, hoping
to be invited in as a Christmas Guest.

ANNA MAE

Well, then, it's bound to be this here fellow! He's the nearest thing to a Baby
Jesus; he smells as if his swandlin' cloth aint been changed!

SUSANNAH

            [To OAKLEY]
You taking the night shift, John?

OAKLEY

Yeap. I'll relieve the Walker boys.

ABIGAIL

            [Of the stranger]
In countries like Italy they tell an old story about a woman named Befana
who was too busy cleaning her house when the shepherds came looking
for the Christ Child. They went on without her, and ever since she has been

looking for the Christ Child and bringing gifts to every child in hopes that it might be him. You know the message of that story!

ANNA MAE

Sure do. Don't do house cleaning!

SALLIE

No. The message of that story is *to be prepared*. All of us. At every moment.

[Tom CROW enters. An older fellow, hard of hearing]

KENNEDY

Tom Crow, *Have you heard anything?*

CROW

What?

KENNEDY

I said, HAVE YOU HEARD ANYTHING?

CROW

I'LL ASK AND SEE.
    [To SUSANNAH]
Heard anything?

SUSANNAH

Not tonight, Tom.

[To the seated guests]
That's what we're always asking come night fall, "Have you heard anything tonight?"

CROW

That's what I asked you. Well, have you?

SALLIE

She said, Not tonight, Tom.

CROW

What?!

SUSANNAH, ABIGAIL, SALLIE
NOT TONIGHT, TOM!

CROW

Shhh!

[To KENNEDY as he walks away]
Women. That's what they're always saying come night fall. "Not tonight, Tom!"

ABIGAIL

Poor Tom, I'm afraid he won't hear the signal when it does come.

CROW

What's that?

SALLIE

Be careful to listen for the signal, Tom!

CROW

Probably won't hear the signal——I'm almost deaf.

SUSANNAH

Lot of things not worth hearing, Tom. Consider yourself blessed. Milford is a blessed place

CROW

What's that?

SUSANNAH

YOU'RE BLESSED!

CROW

I'm blessed! Let's eat!

SUSANNAH

Brother Pond, perhaps you should give the Blessing.
[POND removes his hat again, ready to pray, but Joe LOGWOOD enters:]

349

CROW

Evening, Joe Logwood! *Heard anything?*

LOGWOOD

Not tonight. But it is a pretty night.

ABIGAIL

There's a secret in the weather here at Milford.

SALLIE

[To Everyone:]
The weather's always pretty in Milford.

REBECCA

Well, surely it rains.

ABIGAIL

It sort of sprinkles sometimes . . . at night. Stops before sunrise. We call it dew.

SUSANNAH

Sometimes it just comes up from the ground: like in the Bible.

CROW

Doubt that the sun doth move, doubt truth to be a liar, but never doubt I love!

[POND replaces his hat and leaves.]

ABIGAIL

[To Everyone:]
We built up here on the ridge: they call it a "hogback" cause it's pointed like the back of a hog. Milford is full of hard working people. Why, that's how Milford got its name, you know: George Adam's hardest working slave is named Milford. He used to haul the water up from the creek. Then we women had to haul it in buckets from the town spring.

SALLIE

We refused to do it anymore. Now there ain't no more slaves in Milford.

LOGWOOD

So, our jailer Jesse Moore built a clever slide that hauled water in barrels from Silver Creek.

SUE

Then we made the men dig cisterns, and caught the rain in the gutters on the courthouse roof. 'Cause we needed water. To drink, to bathe, to wash our clothes, . . .

ABIGAIL

AND to put out the fires in the jail!

REBECCA

The jail burned down?

SALLIE

Good heavens, no.

ABIGAIL

No buildings ever catch fire in Milford.

REBECCA

But you said there were fires--

SALLIE

In the prisoners

ABIGAIL

In the jail

SALLIE

In their stomachs.

ABIGAIL

from too much cherry bounce!

> [MARGARET enters. A stylishly dressed woman in powdered wig.]

BETSY

They needed water to settle their stomachs: they sure didn't use it to bathe!

SALLIE

Why else do you think they were in jail?

MARGARET

[To ANNA MAE]

It wouldn't hurt you to take a bath.

ANNA MAE

[Shoving her jug at MARGARET]

You need a drink.

[MARGARET takes one look at the jug and winches]

Don't mind that: just a little spittin' tobacco.

[MARGARET, disgusted, turns her nose up and leaves.]

ABIGAIL

You see, in Milford, you can drink all you want.

SALLIE

Just so long as you stay sober--

ABIGAIL

Or you go to jail. Drunkenness is a sin in the Bible.

SALLIE

And you got to pay the Sheriff the tax levy. No "illegal liquor." Adam Starnes refused to pay it—

KENNEDY

But I knew he was a hiding it—in clever clay bottles inside his huntin' boots. My deputies and I picked him up, turned him upside down, and shook him real hard.

LOGWOOD

Terrible thing it was—

SUSANNAH

Disgraceful--

352

SALLIE

Disarming—

ABIGAIL

Disastrous—

OAKLEY

Yeahup! Wasted good shine. Bottles broke in the dirt and all spilled out.

[Men and ANNA MAE agree]

SALLIE

Adam Starnes went to jail for ninety days and was forced to dig our roads. They called him a "boot-legger" and we've been calling it that ever since.

ABIGAIL

The first record of such a one in America!

SALLIE

We are mighty proud of that here in Milford.

CROW

Uneasy lies the head that wears a crown.

BETSY

[Of Tom CROW]
A wagon of traveling players came to town—Tom Crow never has been the same. He dreams of being a great actor on the stage like David Garrick.

SUSANNAH

Tom Crow dug the jail for us. Underneath the courthouse. Isn't that right, Tom!

CROW

What's that?

ABIGAIL

We were just a saying that you was the one who dug our jail!

CROW

And my back's still a killing me. *To be, or not to be--*

SUSANNAH

Tom, you're blessed. Don't you see, you got to be grateful you got a back.

CROW

Well, no, I can't see. I'm pertin near blind in this eye!

ABIGAIL

Tom, you're blessed. At least you got another good eye.

CROW

And I have such rheumatism in my leg.

SALLIE

Tom, you're blessed. At least you have the other leg.

CROW

And it's wooden!

SUSANNAH

Tom—

CROW

I know, I know. I'm blessed!

[Whispers]
Until the termites set in!

SALLIE and ABIGAIL

Aint no termites in Milford.

CROW

OH!!!!!!!!!!

SALLIE

We are all blessed tonight. Count your blessings. Preacher Pond says he has a special blessing for tonight.

TIMOTHY

So, where's Grace you were talking about?

SUSANNAH

[Calling silence]
Preacher Pond is going to have our blessing!

[POND comes forward, removes his hat again, ready to pray:]

SUSANNAH

Where's Daniel Boone?

REBECCA

He promised to get back in time for dessert.

PAUL

[To SUE]
Good evenin.'

SUE

'Evenin.'

[It is clear that the two young people are smitten with each
other from first sight.]

PAUL

You must . . . uh, live around here?

SUE

Yes, down Poosey Ridge.

PAUL

Really?

SUE

Do you know it?

PAUL

I know it well. My father has a farm down Poosey.

SUE

Really?

Where down Poosey?

SUE

Just West.

PAUL

Really? I'm just East. Imagine that.

SUE

Yes. Imagine that.

PAUL

We must be neighbors. You West Poosey and Me East Poosey. Neighbors should get to know each other. I mean, don't you think? --to be good neighbors?

SUE

It's very important to be neighborly.

PAUL

I'm Paul Campbell.

SUE

I'm Sue Moran.

PAUL

Just the prettiest name in the world!
    [Thinks]
Moran? You're not related to . . . *Green* Moran?

SUE

I should think I am. He's my husband.

PAUL

Green Moran!?
    [His temper suddenly flared]
He stole fifty acres from my father's farm. Two full years we grubbed up cane and brush before we could plant our fields.

SUE

But your father abandoned the land . . .

PAUL

My father bought that land from the Transylvania Company. Daniel Boone himself sold it to him.

SUE

[Now she is angry]
Virginia denied the right to sell it.

PAUL

Richard Henderson had bought it from the Indians down in Carolina.

SUE

The Indians never claimed they owned it! Your parents should have bought it from Virginia like everyone else!

PAUL

What? Buy it a second time?

SUE

Well, everybody else did. Are the Campbell's any different?

PAUL

My father wasn't about to buy the land all over again. That's why Father moved us all to Texas.

SUE

Why'd you come back?

PAUL

To redeem the land, but part of it is missing.

SUE

Well, perhaps if you had kept better track of it—

PAUL

Your husband stole fifty acres of our land!

SUE

He says it was a mistake.

PAUL

He signed a Court paper at the Court House. How could it be a mistake?

SUE

You have so much land . . . and he has so little . . . He says it was a mistake.

PAUL

[He calms down]
'You believe him?

SUE

[She calms down]
He's my husband.

PAUL

But do you believe him?

MINERVA

I dreamed last night a dream. Of two hillsides. One East and one West. And two families. Yes, two families. One Camp——camp——

SUE

Could it be Campbell?

MINERVA

Don't tell me. Camp——Campbell, yes, that was the name. And the other, a color, what is it. Do I remember . . .

SUE

Green?

MINERVA

Shh. You'll break my concentration——ah, yes, I remember. **Green.** Yes. Campbell and Green. No line fence atop of the ridge between them. A well-worn path slanting up the hill a full mile to the top and down again on the other side, a friendship tie between the two families.

SUE

[To PAUL]

You see?

MINERVA

But the whole ridge was a tangle of forest trees, grape vines and cane brake, vipers and wolves! One grabbing the other by the throat like a dog shakes a rat. Lies and corruption! Death! And . . . HEDGEAPPLES!

[Softly and innocently]

So, I dreamed last night.

POND

It's a wonder you slept at all.

PAUL

[To SUE:]

Green Moran is going to pay my father and mother and my brothers for all the labor we put in that land or I'll break his neck.

SALLIE

Nonsense, that kind of thing never happens in Milford.

[Laughs]

Not in Milford.

PAUL

It will when I get my hands on him.

ANNA MAE

Just shoot him and get it over with . . .

BETSY

But the law--

CROW

The first thing we do, let's kill the lawyers!

[Everyone cheers.]

SALLIE

No, no, no. . . . Forgiveness is divine.

359

PAUL

If he robbed my family, he robbed your family, too. Why, Eb Campbell is your great Aunt Lela's nephew on his mother's side twice removed. That makes us practically cousins!

SALLIE

Cousins?
[Change of attitude]
There Green Moran is right now!

[MORAN appears, PAUL runs after him, and gets him by the neck. KENNEDY intervenes.]

KENNEDY

Are you daft! Where are your manners! 'Here at this dinner and Christmastime and all!

SALLIE
[To KENNEDY]
He stole fifty acres from Eb Campbell—and we're practically cousins, so you know what that makes you: a second cousin twice removed by marriage--that's family!

[KENNEDY starts chocking MORAN. The other's stop him.]

SUSANNAH
[Calming himself]
Preacher Pond, I think maybe you'd better pray.

POND
[Removing his hat, ready]
I have a special Prayer for tonight—

[MORAN flees.]

PAUL
[To MORAN]
You better start praying, Moran!
[To KENNEDY]
Sherriff, arrest that man! He stole fifty acres from my father's land and he ought to be in jail—

KENNEDY

Now, . . . his friend Joe Logwood has set himself up as "Special bail."

PAUL

What? You mean to say if Moran runs . . .

KENNEDY

That's right. If Moran runs then Joe Logwood here serves the time for him in jail.

PAUL

[To LOGWOOD]

Are you out of your mind, Logwood? You set yourself as Special Bail for this scoundrel?!

LOGWOOD

Green is my friend.

PAUL

He'll run out on you! Mind my word!

MINERVA

I dreamed last night a dream. Of a "special bail," it rang and rang, up one side of Poosey and down the other it rang . . .

[EVERYONE looks at her]

Sorry . . . wrong kind of "bell."

LOGWOOD

Paul, you're wrong about Green Moran. He's my friend—

MINERVA

[Remembering her dream]

Two friends!

LOGWOOD

I'd trust Green with my life. We've known each other since childhood.

MINERVA

Childhood playmates, yes—

361

LOGWOOD

He'll pay you back, Paul. Give him time—

MINERVA

Time, yes . . . don't tell me, you'll disturb my concentration. Yes, . . . and a cherry tree.

[EVERYONE looks to her bewildered again]

—but they all turned to hedge apples. And the hedge apples were stolen away . . . into a cellar, and they smelled . . . they smelled . . .

ABIGAIL

Hedge apples have such a lovely smell--

MINERVA

Like rot! They stank like rot . . .like sulphur, pole cat, the outhouse, like Tom Crow's BREATH!

[Simply, calmly as she walks away:]
So, I dreamed last night.

CROW

What's that?!
　　　　　[Grabs his gun]

SUSANNAH, ABIGAIL, SALLIE
NOT TONIGHT, TOM!

REBECCA
　　　　[To SUE]
You have some mighty interesting folk here in Milford . . .

SUE

They tell me that you were the first white woman to stand on the banks of the Kentucky River.

REBECCA

My daughter Jemima and I. That was back when Daniel came here with the Long Hunters.

SUE

The Long Hunters. They called them that because they hunted with their
long rifles?

REBECCA

I think because they took so LONG scouting out this place.
[They laugh]
The Indian was the first to come here and he loved this land. It was full of
game, the rivers full of fish, the air fresh and clear. Daniel always said that
there was lots of "elbow room" in Kentucky.

SUE

What was it like when you first met Daniel Boone? Was it love at first sight?

REBECCA

[Nodding]
He tried to shoot me.

SUE

Tried to *shoot you*?

REBECCA

[Laughs]
It was night. Daniel had gone 'firehunting' along the creek with a torch. I
was herding cows that had strayed until past nightfall and I got lost. I saw
his torch; Daniel saw its reflection in my eyes and leveled his rifle right at
me! He thought I was a deer.

SUE

It's a miracle you weren't killed!

REBECCA

He gave up "firehunting" after that night.

SUE

Tell me about your first date. Was it romantic?

REBECCA

[Nodding]
He tried to stab me.

SUE

Stab you?

REBECCA

It was at a "cherry picking" with several of our friends, lots of young people. Daniel and I sat upon a ridge of green turf under the cherry trees. He in his hunting shirt, and I in my white cambric apron. He took out his hunting knife and began dropping it--cutting and stabbing holes up one corner of my apron. I didn't say a word. Nowadays he always tells that he was trying my temper. When I didn't fly into a passion, he knew that I was the woman for him!

ANNA MAE

If only I had a feller that was a flirtin with me, and a snugglin up real close like, to go a sparkin under the moonlight, holdin my hand and all . . .
      [She thinks better of it.]
I'd 'a shoot him!
      [She exits]

SUE

It's hard to be a frontier wife, isn't it? With the men out hunting and gone so much.

REBECCA

Once Daniel went as far off as Florida. I told him that he could go, but he had to be home for Christmas dinner.

SUE

Did he make it back?

REBECCA

At twelve o'clock on the dot he walked into the house, took his seat at the table, and commenced to say Grace.

SUE

      [Laughing]
Had he washed his hands?

REBECCA

This year I made him a dried cherry pie. He promised to be home in time for dessert.

SUE

You always trusted him to keep his word?

REBECCA

If you can't trust your husband, you can't have much of a husband to trust.

SUE
                    [Sadly]
True.

REBECCA

Folks ought always to keep their things and houses in good order.

OAKLEY

Christmas wouldn't be Christmas without cherries. Cherry bounce, that is!
                    [He raises his glass]
To Cherry Bounce–

SUSANNAH, ABIGAIL, SALLIE:

Not yet, John!

MILLER

Evening, Mrs. Kennedy. Heard anything?

MARGARET

Not tonight.

REBECCA

What is it you are waiting to hear?

MARGARET

The fox horns of course.

              [ABIGAIL and SALLIE interrupt]

REBECCA

Fox horns?

MARGARET
              [Catching herself]
We do a lot of *fox hunting* these days. Christmas and all.

365

[The others look bewildered at her.]

REBECCA

In the dark?

MARGARET

Sure!
[Desperate to make up a story:]
It makes it harder for the fox to hide . . .

[The others groan.]

REBECCA

I thought maybe you were going to say it was a signal or something for Black Bob Morgan's Gang.

[She has everyone's attention.]

We've all heard that those papers are hidden in the courthouse—don't you think they'll come back for them? Perhaps the Sherriff should do something about that.

MARGARET

I'm sure he has thought of it already.

REBECCA

But are you sure?

MARGARET

I should say I am!

REBECCA

Who is the Sherriff here anyway?

MARGARET

[Getting hot]
The Sherriff here is none other than Joseph Kennedy. Do have a problem with that?

REBECCA

No, I was just saying that I thought the Sherriff should have a plan in case--

MARGARET

Don't you worry, dearie. Joseph Kennedy, Sherriff of Milford, County seat of Madison County, Virginia has it UNDER CONTROL. You people of Boonesborough are still just mad that Patrick Henry granted us the county seat.

REBECCA

The county seat should have gone to Boonesborough. It is the oldest settlement.

MARGARET

Get over it!

REBECCA

Up on the ridge, you're just asking for a tornado.

MARGARET

And down by the river, you're just asking for it to flood. Again!

REBECCA

At least we have a water source--

KENNEDY

Ladies, please.

REBECCA

I'm just saying that those cutthroats will come as soon as they hear about those papers. They're probably on their way right now. At Boonesborough my husband would have a plan.

MARGARET

Well, at Milford my husband, Joseph Kennedy, Sherriff of Milford, County seat of Madison County, Virginia, has a plan, believe you me--

REBECCA

At Boonesborough my husband would have a *signal* though. Like . . . those fox horns. They could be a signal. Daniel would plan something like that—

MARGARET

Your husband, Daniel Boone of Boonesborough, is a little too late for the likes of my husband Joe Kennedy, Sherriff of Milford, County seat of

Madison County, Virginia because Joe has beat him to it! That **is** Joe's plan all right! And when the fox horns sound, we'll all be down at the courthouse, loaded, aimed and ready to blast the heads off those Black Bob Morgan villains!

KENNEDY

Now you've a done it woman!

MARGARET

Me? Why, everybody knows that the patrol will sound the fox horns and then we are all to circle the courthouse--

KENNEDY

They do now.

MARGARET

Well . . . well . . . . Oh! Well, the harm's done.
[To REBECCA]
Don't you blame yourself now, Rebecca. We all know how hard it is to keep a secret—But I wouldn't worry about it. There's not a poor sinner here looks dangerous to me, much less have a lick of common sense. So, tell them what we're talking about.

ABIGAIL

First you have to understand that there is a room in our courthouse that never gets used. And it has a good sheet iron lined vault. It belongs to Will Irvine, the county recording clerk.

SALLIE

He's got five thousand acres of land over there along Tate's creek and he can't leave it to come do his work in Milford. He keeps the strong box in his house and expects all and sundry to go to his farm if you need to have business with the county clerk.

MINERVA

He lives over on "Dreaming Creek."

REBECCA

Daniel Boone named that creek.

MINERVA

He fell asleep beside that creek and dreamed . . . sweet, sweet dreams . . .
[She sighs, then:]
. . . of Indians. An attack! Blood, Death!
[Calmly:]
So, he dreamed that night.

REBECCA

The dream warmed him. They soon fell upon him but he was prepared.

ABIGAIL

John Miller is our appointed magistrate; was a Colonel in the Revolutionary War. He protects us from the Indian attacks. Governor Shelby named him lieutenant colonel. John Miller was the one placed the levy on the liquor.

ISABEL

You see, we believe in peace, but peace with justice.

BETSY

Lieutenant Colonel John Miller convinced the Virginia Legislature to make Milford our county seat. Even though Boonesborough made a big fuss over it.

MARGARET
[To KENNEDY]
Tell them about Black Bob Morgan's gang!

KENNEDY

I was going to.--

ISABEL

You see, it was late August afternoon, and the noisy boys were swimming in the deep hole in the creek below the Court House. Jailer Jesse Moore was asleep--

MARGARET

No! No! You've got it all wrong. That's not what happened at all.

It was late August afternoon, the noisy boys were swimming in the deep hole in the creek below the Court House, Jailer Jesse Moore was asleep in the Court room, and Sheriff Joe Kennedy was leaned back against the

Court House wall in his sleeves, and unarmed. When suddenly three highwaymen dressed in loggers clothes walked briskly up the hill. One of them—short and stubby and built like a bear, pulled out a hunting knife, another a pistol, and the third a long rifle!

ISABEL

"You be Joe Kennedy, sheriff of this here county?" He says to Joe. "You got a prisoner in yon jail house we want. Git him out peaceable; otherwise and certain you get killed."

MARGARET

Just a week before he put a ragged, dirty, shifty eyed stranger in jail for lounging around the town and wouldn't give account of himself. Strangers in these parts are suspicious characters until they prove themselves otherwise.

ISABEL

Joe found him wandering around Oakley's Grog shop. He was glib of tongue-- didn't speak no English. Had a big wad of money. Finally, Joe got his name out of him. What was it, it was hard to understand, the way he talked. Some foreign name. Oh, yes. Said his name was *"Benjamin Franklin"* and he hailed from *Philadelphia.*

MARGARET

He hadn't never heard that name before and he don't know where Philadelphia is. Tell him where Philadelphia be, John Oakley.

OAKLEY

Uh . . . I think, . . . Philadelphy, did you say?

LOGWOOD

[Laughs.]
Tell em, John.

OAKLEY

You tell 'm, Joe!

LOGWOOD

Uh, . . . Preacher Pond?

POND

Uh, now, it's in the Bible. Revelation.

KENNEDY

Can't be far . . .

SUSANNAH

About a mile?

MARGARET

Never mind! Get back to the story, Joe!

KENNEDY

Well,--

ISABEL

These three highwaymen come asking for him. "Now, fellers," said Joe, "I ain't much concerned about this prisoner you talking about, but we're law abiding folks here. He's my prisoner. What for you want him out?"

MARGARET

No, no, no! You've got it all wrong!

These three highwaymen come asking for him. "Now, fellers," said Joe, "I ain't much concerned about this prisoner you talking about, but we're law abiding folks here. He's my prisoner. What for you want him out?" "Stop the talk and open the jail door!" yelled the feller with the long rifle. Now mind you, Joe has a long rifle, one of the few in the community, and don't think he don't know how to use it!

KENNEDY

I wasn't afraid of 'em and I told them to go to––

[EVERYONE stops him!]
. . .well, . . . I told 'em *where they could go*, let's just say.

ANNA MAE

He told 'em they could go ***straight to hell.*** Which weren't too smart, 'cause it set 'em off!

ISABEL

Then Joe called for Jesse, the Jailer.

371

MARGARET

Jesse was a nappin in the jail, but he up and plunged out the door in one moment. Came a runnin when he heard you a cussin!

LOGWOOD

They fired the rifle at Joe but it hit poor jailer Jesse Moore between the eyes as he came out the door, and Jesse fell to the ground *dead*.

ANNA MAE

The pistol got Joe in the right leg. Those murderers carted off Benjamin Franklin in a canoe down mouth of Silver Creek to finish him off with the knife. It was all planned.

ABIGAIL

People in the town were running around in wild excitement. The women rang the Court House bell to summon help, cleaned out the wound in Joe's leg. Nothing like this had happened since the last big Indian raid four years ago.

SALLIE

Now the jail was dug under the floor of the courthouse and was walled in with huge stones and had two small windows high up that only a cat or groundhog could crawl through. In one of these windows the prisoner had stuffed a roll of papers.

MARGARET

No, no, no! Who is tellin' this story!
            [Calmly]
Go ahead, Joe.

KENNEDY

These papers—

MARGARET

These papers told of the names and plans of the Black Bob Morgan's Gang who made a business of robbing people along the Natchez Trace way down in Tennessee and down the Mississippi river.

CROW

The world is grown so bad, that wrens make prey where eagles dare not perch!

ANNA MAE

These papers named their soon-to-be victims and maps of their hideouts along the river forts from Pittsburgh all the way to New Orleans.

KENNEDY

And we locked the papers away in the strongbox. In the courthouse. Here at Milford where they will be safe.

[Others start to chime in–]

I said, *where they will be safe* AND WE NEED NOT SAY NOTHING MORE.

[Others start to chime in–]

Nothing.

[Others start to chime in–]
More.

So, that's how it all began. With those three shifty eyed scoundrels who rode up to the courthouse door at Milford.

[Sadly, with guilt]
I was the cause of Jesse's end.

MARGARET

Now, Joe . . .

KENNEDY

If only I hadn't called his name. **If only** I'd gone and opened the jail door as they told me to. **If only** I hadn't let the bandits have their way--

MARGARET

If only you'd get your foot off my skirt—

KENNEDY

Oh, sorry.
[He quickly moves his foot.]

MINERVA

I dreamed last night a dream. It was the ghost of *Jesse Moore.*

SUSANNAH

Really?

[EVERYONE responds, interested.]

SUSANNAH

How'd he look?

ABIGAIL

How'd he look?

SALLIE

Was he happy?

ISABEL

I hope he's put on some weight.

MINERVA

He looked . . . *dead.* But happy. Yes, I remember now. He was smiling.

[Everyone is relieved to hear this.]

He has a beard now—I almost didn't recognize him . . .

[Everyone laughs, pleased to hear about Jesse]

And he spoke to me . . .

KENNEDY

What did he say? He said he forgives me?

MINERVA

He said . . . MURDER! DEATH! BLOOD! Hedge apple in the snow. Blood
in the snow! Weeping and gnashing of teeth! . . .
    [She calms herself]
That's what I dreamed last night.

ANNA MAE

I'd a shoot him.

BETSY

You can't shoot a ghost.

REBECCA

You don't have ghosts in Milford.

SUSANNAH

No, but we have a ghost story. It happened right here in this very Meeting House. Tell it, Abigail.

[Everyone gathers around ABIGAIL to hear the story.]

ABIGAIL

It was a winter's night like this, too, just before Christmas. John Phelps and Joe Deatherage went courting us gals. They were heading back to town and had to stop inside this meetinghouse here because it was lightening and thundering so bad.

SALLIE

'Like we said, at Milford we always leave our doors unlocked . . .

REBECCA

I know: because there aren't any *locks* in Milford. We have locks at Boonesborough—

[Everyone "shhhes" her]

It was right before Christmas and the doors to the Meetinghouse were unlocked–in fact, the wind had blown them open. Poor Phelps and Deatherage came inside for shelter. Well, . . . they saw this big . . .dark . . . "apparition" up here laying on the floor and it went "aaaaahhhhh!." It like 'scared the men to death. But they were brave fellows and made themselves walk up closer to see what it was. Closer . . . and closer. Only when the lightning flashed could they get another glimpse of it. What was it? The lightening flashed and the thunder roared and the "thing" went "AAAAhhhh!" Even louder. They crouched closer and closer. "AAAAHHHHH!" Finally . . .they came right up on it, and . . . . .and, . . .the lightning flashed and . . .

375

SUE
. . . And?

PAUL
And?

REBECCA
And?

ABIGAIL
AND . . .the *old black cow* stood up and went "MOOOOOOO!"

[Everyone laughs]

The cow had come in to weather the storm, too, and fallen asleep up here and was snoring! They took the reins from their horses and led it outside once the storm let up.

SUSANNAH
Everything needs shelter from the storms. Sometimes finding shelter in the winter has not been so easy. Like that Hard Winter of '79.

REBECCA
We ran out of food at the fort. The river froze to the bottoms, and turkeys froze in the trees. Lots of animals couldn't find shelter and froze.

SALLIE
Many people starved to death.

SUSANNAH
Even Christmas can be a hard time for folks. That first Christmas in Bethlehem wasn't easy for the Holy Family. The poor Christ Child was born there in a manger, in a stable, in that simple little town. To bring hope to all people of all times.

MINERVA
I dreamed last night a dream. "We all growl like bears, we moan like doves . . ."

POND
"We look for justice, but there is none; For salvation, but it is far from us"

CROW

Cowards die many times before their deaths; the valiant never taste of death but once!

SUSANNAH

Preacher Pond, isn't it time for that prayer? There's not a soul in here that's harmful.

[POND removes his hat: a BEAR runs in. Everyone screams. They shoot unsuccessfully at the bear. The bear leaves.]

ANNA MAE

I could of shot him had you men not been in the way!

REBECCA

Looks like Milford isn't as safe as you tell. That bear could have killed somebody.

SALLIE

That bear didn't come in here to hurt nobody. It came in here so as we could shoot it for supper.

SUSANNAH

And here's supper now!

[The food is brought in and placed on the tables. IMMEDIATELY the signal is heard. Foxhorns. Everyone freezes. Someone drops a tray—but no one moves for a long moment. Then, as if coming alive at one moment, everyone grabs a gun and rushes out the door. Tom CROW looks around confused.]

ANNA MAE

NOW, Tom!

CROW

A horse! A horse! My kingdom for a horse!

[He runs out. The room is silent. Food on the table. POND rushes in, takes off his hat, and hurriedly prays:]

377

POND

For-these-gifts-we-are-about-to-receive-may-the-Lord-make-us-truly-grateful!

[He rushes out. He rushes back in.]

Amen!

[He disappears]

Act Two

Everyone returns in great commotion and joy! Hoopin' and a hollerin'!

MARGARET

Let Joe tell it! After all, it was his plan!

[The crowd calms down.]

KENNEDY

Well, I had come in contact with Morgan's Gang of thieves last year when I trailed Zeke Baber to Memphis and brought him back dead. I learned the ways of those highway men. So I laid a trap.

MARGARET

Joe set out the word that all the plans of Black Bob Morgan's Gang were kept in the strongbox at Milford.

ISABEL

He made a copy of it all and sent the originals to the United States Marshal in Pittsburgh.

MARGARET

Although he don't know where that is either.

SUSANNAH

Then he built a bomb—

ABIGAIL

--Made out of powder and lead—

SALLIE

--And placed it in the county clerk's vault in a box—

MARGARET

That's not right! Hey, who's telling this story anyways!

SUSANNAH and ABIGAIL

Sorry . . .

MARGARET

Go ahead, Joe.

[KENNEDY starts to speak--]

Joe built a bomb made out of powder and lead and placed it in the county clerk's vault in a box with the papers he had copied labeled plain so everybody could see.

ANNA MAE
[Whispering]
See, *they didn't know that Will Irvine kept the strong box at his farm*--

MARGARET
[To SALLIE]
Do you mind! That's not right! You have it all wrong!
[To the crowd]
You see, . . . *they didn't know that Will Irvine kept the strong box at his farm*. It takes a full day to ride to Milford to do business and get home by sun down—so, if you have business with the county clerk, he wants you to go to his house and see about it there.

CROW

It took a few months but those highwaymen heard about it and headed this way. Around Halloween, the lure brought the game. First, they sent a scout—

ANNA MAE

Said he was on his way from Tennessee to Fort Boone to pass his last declining days with his son—

KENNEDY

There was no son. He was a spy, the liar.

SALLIE

So, we've been preparing ever since then. Knives and pistols were placed at convenient points along the ridge.

TIMMY

We boys have been patrolling the river banks up and down for twenty miles from the mouth of Silver Creek. Joe brought out three big extra-long fox horns that could be heard five miles away.

ABIGAIL

They practiced the call signals. With twelve of our finest riflemen.

ANNA MAE

And women!

ISABEL

Our men have tramped up and down along the foot of the hogback every night for a full week now. There were ten of the Morgan highwaymen. They were after the papers to deliver them to Black Bob Morgan himself. They went straight into the courthouse . . . broke open the vault and there was the strongbox.

KENNEDY

I had thrown the key into the cistern so as nobody accidentally could open it. Cause I hadn't told no one about the bomb!

SUSANNAH

You sure are good at keeping a secret!

CROW

[With two mugs]
How about a toast, John Oakley!

REBECCA

Daniel can never keep a secret from me.

MARGARET

Are you kiddin? I knew about it all the time. Why sure!
[She takes a mug from CROW]
No, you can't keep a thing from me! Anyways, . . .they forced open the strongbox and . . .

[She pauses dramatically, leisurely taking a slow drink from her mug. Pause. Her head smokes!]

OAKLEY

Must be the cherry bounce.

ANNA MAE

Or the white lightning. Little Chloe mixed the two—

ABIGAIL

Chloe, shame on you!

KENNEDY

Give her some air!
[MARGARET stiff as a board falls backward to the floor.]
She'll sleep it off—won't remember a thing by mornin'. She never does.

SALLIE

Anyway, that strongbox exploded and killed two of them, the rest of them rushed out the door of the clerk's office–

KENNEDY

And we riddled them with our long rifles and pistol balls!

[Everyone cheers. John MILLER enters. A very dignified man, well dressed in velvet, wearing a stylish powdered wig.]

MILLER

Sounds like quite a victory!

SUSANNAH

Why, its John Miller. Evenin', John!

[Everyone cheers a welcome to MILLER.]

MILLER

You got them all?

KENNEDY

Yeaup! We got 'em all!

[Everyone cheers.]

OAKLEY

All but one!

ANNA MAE

What? NO!!

SUSANNAH

One?

ABIGAIL

One of them got away?

SALLIE

We let one go?

OAKLEY

One of 'em got away, all right. I saw him running. *But not before* he was hit in the head by a big old **hedge apple**. About knocked 'em dead. Then he was off down Silver Creek.

ANNA MAE

A hedge apple? But we was all with our rifles. Who was it—

OAKLEY

Who else? Who didn't have a rifle?

[There is a moment of silence as they think and then consider:]

EVERYONE

Chloe???

[Everyone cheers CHLOE.]

CROW

Be not afraid of greatness; some are born great, some achieve greatness, and some have greatness THRUST upon them!

LOGWOOD

We buried those outlaws in the upper end of the ridge–each with a cross, with an inscription to all would-be evil doers of these words:

KENNEDY

"This to robbers."

SUSANNAH

It was the fox horns that called all the people together around the courthouse.

[Everyone applauds and go back to their places for the dinner.]

There have been many nights to remember. But the greatest of all . . . took place on a night in Bethlehem. Who will tell *the Christmas story?*

ABIGAIL

You told it last year, Sallie. It's my turn this year—

SALLIE

No, it isn't. It's my turn, you told it last year—

ABIGAIL

Did I? Well, you tell it, then--

SALLIE

Oh, I don't mind, really. You tell it this year. Maybe it was me that told it last year—

ABIGAIL

Come to think of it, I'm pretty sure it was me that told it last year. You tell it--

ANNA MAE

Well, somebody tell it before the kid grows up and can't fit in the manger!

SUSANNAH

The Christmas story should be told by the woman of strength and dignity
[Looking to REBECCA]
One who "opens her mouth with wisdom, and the teaching of kindness is on her tongue . ."

ANNA MAE

Well, if you insist! Gather round, children. I'm to tell the story of the first Christmas. You see, it was like this. There was this gal named "Mary." God chose her to be the mother of the Christ Child. She was spoken for by Joseph. But she was in "the family way," and she and Joseph weren't yet married.

[She scratches her head]

Come to think of it, is this a fittin' story to tell these kids?

MINERVA

Joseph had a dream. To take the poor young Mary as his wife--

ANNA MAE

That's right. And so, they got hitched and went to Bethlehem--which was a little town where Joseph's kinfolks were from. It must have been somewhat like Milford, very crowded with folks traveling. So crowded in fact, that there was no place for Mary and Joseph to stay. That ol Inn Keeper, well, he should of taken him out and shot him! But he didn't.

So they stayed in a stable with the critters, the cows and horses, and chickens . . . and . . . a duck. And the poor Christ Child was born in the cold stable, and they laid the young'un on the hay. The cows just ate around him.

A great star appeared in the sky. People came from miles around to him. Shepherds and farmers and hunters and Kings who were dark skinned and very different from Mary and Joseph. They brought him gold, and frank . . . frank . . . just a lot of pretty little things.

[The INDIAN approaches]

The shepherds and the Kings came to worship the Christ Child because they knew that God loved everyone no matter how different they might seem.

Heaven had named him many names: Wonderful Counselor, Mighty God, Everlasting Father, Prince of Peace. But his Pa, Joseph, named him "Jesus." Because he came to save us from our sins.

BOONE

[Disguised under his cloak]

Kind of like a "Special Bail" for all us humans, wouldn't you say? I wonder . . .what were their names?

KENNEDY

Who?

BOONE

[Still cloaked]

The highwaymen. What were their names? Whose lives you so eagerly killed?

KENNEDY

What do you mean? We didn't ask them their names.

[Everyone cheers.]

BOONE

[Unrecognizable under his cloak]

Then how did you know they were from Morgan's Gang? They could have been anyone, seeking those papers. Not unlike the wise men that came searching.

KENNEDY

There's no comparison! These men we buried, were pure evil!

BOONE

So you presumed. And wasn't King Herod pure evil who sent the Wise Men to Bethlehem?

[He takes off his cloak, hands off his rifle. Now he is recognized.]

CROW

Why, its Daniel Boone!

MILLER

Daniel Boone!

[As the others chime in, MILLER welcomes BOONE with a handshake]

385

BOONE

I heard the rumor of the papers in the courthouse. Had I been a few minutes earlier, you might have buried me with them.

MILLER

Perhaps Boone is right. Even if they were Morgan's Men-- Is it right to take justice in our own hands?

KENNEDY

Had we not fought off the Indian raids, we wouldn't have our fort to this day!

[Everyone chimes in the celebration of their victory]

I remember when Colonel Campbell and the two boys, Sanders and M'Quinney, went across the river from the fort--it was Christmas time--and they found that McQuinney boy scalped! And that Sanders boy no doubt shared the same. The hunters were sent out to get the Indians: paid five pounds for every Indian scalp they should produce. But they came back with none. Why Daniel's daughter, Jemima, and the Calaway girls were kidnapped from their canoe and would have been scalped, hadn't Daniel shot those Indians while they were cooking breakfast.

MILLER

This taking one life for another doesn't even out the score. Henderson got us all started seeking revenge on each other. One redman for a whiteman, one whiteman for a red man. It's got to stop. And it's got to stop here and now.

Not long from now, whether we like it or not, we are going to have to become our own state. And it's going to have to be united we stand divided we fall.

POND

Our friends light candles tonight to celebrate Hannukah. They protected their Temple much as we have our courthouse. In its history, it is full of bloodshed, taking one life for the other. And yet no matter how much they killed, no matter how hard they fought and burned and ravaged, they could not make the lamps of the temple come back to life. God had to do that. And the oil was supplied not through murder but through miracle. We are always at the mercy of God. Colonel Miller, introduce your friend.

386

MILLER
[Of the INDIAN:]
This is our friend "Blue Jacket." He's the one who saved our people at
Limestone! His birth name was Marmaduke Van Sweringen. He was
captured by the Shawnee when he was young and they named him "Blue
Jacket" because he wore a blue linsey shirt. Last year he was captured by
our white settlers.

BOONE
You'd a think they would be mighty glad to have him back safe and sound
after all those years! But no, they tried to kill him. They wouldn't believe
he was one of their own.

CROW
How sharper than a serpent's tooth it is to have a thankless child!

BOONE
The mob wouldn't listen to reason, brought him to me, and to appease
them, I tied him and locked him up in his cabin. But Blue Jacket cut the
ropes and escaped.

CROW
How'd he do that?

REBECCA
[As BOONE looks away in guilt]
A *knife just so happened to be sticking in the logs near him!* Good to have
you home, Daniel! What took you so darn long!

BOONE
My little girl, I told you I'd be home in time for Christmas dinner!

OAKLEY
Wait a minute. A knife *just happened to be sticking out of a log*? Just how
is it they didn't catch sight of him escaping?

BOONE
I served them all some of your Cherry Bounce!

[Everyone laughs]

387

KENNEDY

Our own state, you say? It'll need a good name. A name of integrity and valor. I know! ***Kennedy State***!

MARGARET

I married a crazy man! Where do you get to thinking like that? You'll have to excuse him, Colonel Daniel. Colonel Miller. "Kennedy" State! Ha! He means . . . MARGARET KENNEDY STATE!

[Everyone starts arguing and promoting their own names for the state]

MILLER

Calm down. It will be the state of *Kentucky*. And we won't have to ride to Virginia for our assemblies.

BOONE

It's an Iroquois name. Kanta-ke.

KENNEDY

But how many of us speak Iroquois?!

[Everyone chimes in agreement.]

BOONE

It means "Great Meadow." Used to be you would not have walked out in any direction for more than a mile without shooting a buck or a bear. There were thousands of buffalo on the hills of Kentucky; the land looked as if it never would become poor. To hunt in those days was a pleasure indeed. It was a land of cane and clover, "the Land of Tomorrow." A land of peace. A heaven of a place.

MILLER

A heaven of a place has got to have peace makers. Isn't that right, Rev. Pond? And to be peacemakers in this wild town of yours, there will have to be some changes made.

KENNEDY

What kind of changes?

388

MILLER

Well, for one thing, we have to grow. You want to grow, don't you? There isn't any water source up here.

MARGARET

We should move our county seat to Silver Creek? It's too far.

MILLER

I was thinking Dreaming Creek.

MARGARET

Of course. Gee, I wish we knew someone who lived down at Dreaming Creek. Who could sell their land and make a big profit for it. Oh, that's right! You, Colonel Miller, YOU live down at Dreaming Creek!

[There is an uproar.]

KENNEDY

You take the seat from us, over my dead body!

MILLER

You can't stop progress. Besides, I have a brick factory.

MARGARET

What are we going to do?

KENNEDY

I'll tell you what we are going to do. Rev. Pond, what are we going to do?

POND

We will ride down and take it back.

KENNEDY

Yeah! That's what we'll do. We'll ride down and take it back!

POND

All of our men on horseback!

KENNEDY

Yeah! All of our men on horseback!

POND

All 300 of them!

KENNEDY

Yeah! All 300 hundred of them!
    [Pause]
Three hundred?

POND

Like the Battle of Thermopylae. The Persian invasion of Greece. 480 BC. Three hundred Spartans charged the Persians on horseback and took back their land.

KENNEDY

Yeah. Just like the Battle of Therm—Just like Rev. Pond said. You move the seat to your farm, John Miller, and we will all ride down and take it back with 300 men on horseback!

MARGARET
    [Whispering to her husband]
Where you going to get three hundred men at Milford?

KENNEDY

Well. I'll tell you where we're going to get 300 men on horseback! Rev. Pond, where we going to get 300 men on horseback?

POND

Of course, the Spartans were joined by 700 Thespians, 900 Heltons and 400 Thebans . . .

MILLER

You all have just got to stop taking the law into your own hands! Once we become a state, that's going to stop.

TIMMY

Hey! Green Moran slipped aboard the largest raft at the mouth of Silver Creek—

LOGWOOD

What?!

MILLER

With the loggers. On their way to New Orleans.

KENNEDY

No, come to think of it . . . he wasn't at his post at the Courthouse—

[BETSY screams.]

LOGWOOD

No! It can't be--

KENNEDY

He was out on bail. Special bail.
[He gets out his handcuffs.]

BETSY

My dear good husband, Joe! What a faithful true friend he is! To go to
prison for his friend. YOU IDIOT!
[She starts hitting him]
You've ruined us!
[As they go off with Sheriff KENNEDY]
We will lose the store! And everything.

[SUE stands by herself. PAUL goes to her.]

PAUL

Your husband has fled and left his friend to serve his time in jail.

SUE

He'll be back once he gets unloaded at New Orleans. Won't he?

MINERVA

Last night I had a dream about New Orleans.
[She waits]
Then I woke up.

POND

That woman must have slept a long time last night . . .

MINERVA

Didn't get a wink! But there was . . . a family there--

391

PAUL

In New Orleans?

MINERVA

No, in western Virginia. The name . . . the name . . . FLINN! Two girls and a boy. The father and mother killed. . . . Little girl named . . .

SUE

Chloe?

MINERVA

Shh! Something like . . . Chloe!

PAUL

Amazing. You dreamed that last night?

MINERVA

No, we lived next door. It must be her family; I can take you to them.

REBECCA

You hear that, Chloe? We just may have found your family.

BOONE

Only one way to find out. We'll head back to Virginia and see if we can't find them for you! This might just be a merry Christmas after all.

[SUE goes to MILLER]

SUE

Is it true? That my husband ran off free and clear . . .

MILLER

Free, yes. Clear, not quite: he got a good pounding on the head from Chloe's hedge apple!

[PAUL goes to SUE]

PAUL

I'm sorry.

SUE

You were right about him.

PAUL

If you need help . . . I mean, I'm just over the ridge. On the East side.

SUE

Yes. And I on the West.

PAUL

Neighbors ought to be neighborly.

[ANNA MAE appears, beautiful, wearing a wedding dress]

BOONE

Why look at that? Can it be . . .

EVERYONE

Anna Mae?!

ANNA MAE

You laugh, and I'll shoot ya! I figure, its high time I get a husband. If you can't beat, em, join us. Who wants to get hitched?

SUZANNAH

Anna Mae . . . don't be so eager.

ABIGAIL

You got to let them come to you.

SALLY

And then you got to make them wait.

SUZANNAH

Find out what his interests are. And put your own aside.

ANNA MAE

Hey, Timmy. How about us goin bear huntin now that the woods is safe again?

[The women groan and walk away.]

TIMMY

Well, I'd love to, but you see, I'm kind of spoken for.

ANNA MAE

Spoken for? By who?

BOY

[With a pretty girl]

By Grace!

[They exit]

CROWE

Anna Mae, you sure clean up good!

ANNA MAE

Forget it, Tom. Oh, you can out-chase a cougar better'in any frontier man here in Milford and there weren't never a braver and stronger man around. You're my best friend. But it wouldn't work. Not at your age.

CROWE

I'm not as old as you think. I make everyone think that just so they'll leave me alone.

ANNA MAE

You're the "oldest man in Milford."

CROWE

Oh, that! You heared wrong. I'm the "Goldest Man in Milford." I've got more gold and land than I can shake a stick at. Ah, the course of true love never did run smooth!

ANNA MAE

No kiddin? I don't see no problem in that! **Not tonight, Tom!**

[She grabs him and they are off.]

OAKLEY

Looks like a romantic Christmas! Susannah, what do you say we get hitched!

SUSANNAH

Why John Oakley, why'd you want to marry me?

OAKLEY

Because I love you. And besides, . . .it'd be good for business!

> [The following characters walk down into the light at the edge of the stage.]

SUSANNAH

Joe Logwood served the two months in jail; afterwards, he begged Joe Kennedy to make him a deputy so he could hunt down Green Moran. He left Milford.

MILLER

In the meantime, John Miller and Green Clay persuaded the Kentucky Legislature to move the county seat. And early one March morning, the court papers were stolen away to Miller's barn where the court held session. Legend has it that 300 men on horseback rode up to protest, and Joe Kennedy's brother David fought the black smith in the stray pen–

SALLIE

Even bit off his finger in the fight.

ABIGAIL

But Kennedy lost the fight.

MILLER

It was the first rebellion against the laws and constitutional authority of the Commonwealth of Kentucky. The town of Richmond was born. Named after the capital of Virginia–John Miller's home town.

SALLIE

By the spring of 1799, the court ordered the closing of the road to Milford, leaving the log meeting house sitting here on this hill.

REBECCA

Daniel and Rebecca Boone discovered Chloe Flinn's family in western Virginia and returned her safely to them.

SUE

And what became of Green Moran? Joe Logwood went to New Orleans . . . but Green Moran wasn't in the city. He went to Texas and North Carolina . . . but he wasn't there either.

Seven years passed. Sue Moran got a divorce from Green Moran--without a word from him he was considered legally dead. She married Paul Campbell and they joined their properties together and there was peace on Poosey . . . or until all those little Campbells started running around!
> [LOGWOOD, old and ragged, enters and looks around as if scouting the hillside. We hear the leaves and birds, etc. once again.]

SUSANNAH

They say that Joe Logwood traveled all over America looking for Green Moran, filled with vengeance. But Green Moran was never heard of again.

ABIGAIL

After *sixteen years*, Joe Logwood came back home to Kentucky. He hobbled up the knob of the hill. He looked around. But Milford was gone.

SALLIE

His store was gone. His wife and kids were gone.

ABIGAIL

All was gone.

SALLIE

Not a sight or sound of anyone . . . All Logwood could say, was simply:

LOGWOOD

"Oh, hell!"
> [He leaves]

ABIGAIL

And he went to Lexington and joined the Kentucky Volunteers in the War of 1812.

SUSANNAH

Milford, like Christmas, has a lesson for us to learn.

396

ABIGAIL

Year after year.

SALLIE

We go searching after things we think are so important, when sometimes the things we need are right here all around us.

ABIGAIL

We think we can always come back to them, but we can't. We think they are all going to stay the same and last forever, but they don't. They never did. They never will. All we really ever have is . . .*now.*

CROW

Now is the winter of our discontent made glorious summer!

SALLIE

So, say a prayer tonight before you drift off to sleep, and remember all the brave men and women who have made today possible for you . . .

ABIGAIL

And whatever happens, wherever you go . . . try not to wander away from God's love, but if you do . . . turn around. You'll always find it right there.

SUSANNAH

This year, have a merry Christmas . . .

MINERVA

. . .and may peace be in your dreams.

SUSANNAH

And **now**, Preacher Pond. How about ending us with a prayer?

[POND removes his hat, ready, but is immediately interrupted:]

SETTLERS sing:

The years are passing by us in a moment
And it won't be long before our time is gone,
It is my prayer for those of you who hear this
To raise your voice and carry on this song:

I love a pioneer Christmas in Kentucky
Where the simple ways of doing things are dear,
I love a pioneer Christmas in Kentucky
Where the olden days bring happiness and cheer.

Great Meadow, Land of Tomorrow,
O Great Spirit, come smiling down
On your great meadow, land of tomorrow,
On your Handmade happy hunting ground.

All is well at Milford, sing a song tonight!

CURTAIN

Postscript

Milford was established as the county seat of Madison in 1785, by Virginia Governor Patrick Henry, on land given by George Adams, and it went into effect a few months later in 1786. Green Clay, grandson to Cassius Marcellus Clay, wrote that Madison County of 1786 "ran along the winding Kentucky River from the three forks westwardly about fifty miles, and then south at both sides at a zigzag fashion all the way to the Tennessee line. A vast acreage of mountains and valleys, giant poplars, oak, walnut, pine, and a dozen other trees, large and small streams, underbrush and cane, all of it infested by bears, wolves, wild cats, poisonous snakes and deadly Indians wandering about hunting wild turkeys, fur bearing animals, and white men."[53] In 1776, Kentucky was one county of Virginia. In 1780, it was divided into Jefferson, Fayette, and Lincoln counties. In 1784, Nelson County was formed, and in 1785 Mercer and Madison counties. Madison County then was a large piece of land that today is sixteen counties.

Figure 17
Poosey Ridge Sunset. McCalla Rogers and Matthew Walker as Sue Moran and Paul Campbell. 2009.

---

[53] Green Clay, "County Seat of Madison Established at Milford on Silver Creek, 1786," *The Daily Register*, March 9, 1946.

The streets of Milford had tree stumps that were dodged by the narrow and short winter oxen or horse drawn sleds. There were in the town, four major streets, the Courthouse with basement jail, the stocks, a tannery, two or three blacksmith shops, hatmaker and ropemaker, and two log stores. John Oakly's carpenter shop was located across from the courthouse and in the back of it was his "Grog" Shop where he made "the water of life from anything that would ferment."

Oakly made corn juice, juniper berry tea, sorghum rum punch, apple jack, white lighting from red pepper, potato beer, and wine from grapes, elderberries, rhubarb, and cherries. There were a dozen or so houses that kept licensed taverns or "ordinaries" where travelers could find accommodations for the night. Such taverns in town were owned by Sam Shackelford, John Phelps, Samuel Estill and Ben Holiday, and the widow Susannah Nobel who was the first female tavern owner.[54]

Dinner at the taverns was one shilling, three pence; breakfast, one shilling; pasturage, hay or fodder for a horse, twenty-four hours, six pence. Whiskey per cup, ten cents; rum punch per cup, fifteen cents. The Court fixed a law to punish drunkenness: "It was drink all you want, but stay sober." A levy was placed upon the sale of alcohol. Adams Starnes refused to pay the tax and hid the white lightning in his hunting boots in cleverly made clay bottles until Sheriff Joseph Kennedy and his deputies turned him upside down--Starnes became the very first recorded "boot legger." Starnes was sent to jail for ninety days and was forced to build the Milford roads.[55]

It was Joe Kennedy who had come across a "shifty eyed stranger" in Oakley's Grog Shop on a hot summer day in August of 1788. Although he did not speak English, when asked his name he swore to be "Benjamin Franklin" from Philadelphia. Kennedy put him in jail, not knowing at the time that he was hiding very important documents hidden in the lining of his coat, the names of soon to be victims and the secret hideouts of "The Black Bob Morgan's Gang," a band of thieves who robbed and murdered along the Natchez Trace from Tennessee to the Mississippi River.

---

[54] Ibid.
[55] Green Clay, "County Seat of Madison Established at Milford on Silver Creek, 1786," *The Daily Register*, March 9, 1946.

A week later, three highway men carrying a hunting knife, a pistol, and long rifle, rode up to the Courthouse and demanded from Kennedy his prisoner. Kennedy spoke peacefully to them and called for the jailer. Inside the jail, Franklin overhearing the goings on, cut the secret papers from his coat and hid them in the windowsill. Outside, the strangers

Figure 18
Cast 2009.

impatiently ordered Joe Kennedy to open the jail door. "Go to plumb hell," was Kennedy's response, at which time the long rifle was raised to the Sheriff's head and fired. Joe ducked in time, but jailer Jesse Moore coming through the door met the bullet between the eyes and fell dead. A shot from the pistol caught the Sheriff in the leg and the bandits broke into the Courthouse, kidnapped Franklin from the cellar, and disappeared down Silver Creek.

The women and children came running to bandage Kennedy's leg, and the Courthouse bell was rung, calling the men in from the fields. It was only after a new jailer had been appointed that the discovery was made of Franklin's papers. When the mail carrier passed through Milford on his way to Boonesborough and Maysville, Kennedy secretly gave him the papers to be sent to the United States Marshall in Pittsburg. A month later another suspicious character appeared in town claiming to be on his way to Boonesborough to see his son, but was asking strange questions about Franklin. Kennedy sent him on his way to spread the tail that Franklin's papers where locked safely in the strongbox in the vault at the Milford Courthouse.

The plan was to coax the highwaymen back into town and avenge the death of jailer Jesse Moore. Boys were placed on patrol at the riverbanks for twenty miles; fire arms and knives were hidden at strategic points. Joe secured three long fox horns that could be heard five miles away and he practiced their secret sounds with twelve of the finest riflemen. What he did not tell them was that he had built a bomb of powder and lead and placed it in the county clerk's vault in the strongbox. What strangers to Milford did not know was that William Irvine, the county recording clerk, kept all the county papers in a strong box at his home, refusing to spend his time in the "bur-tailed town of Milford."

Figure 19
Margarette Kennedy and Rebecca Boone

Two Walker brothers from Paint Lick had been trudging up and down the river banks for weeks when during a night before Christmas they sounded the fox horn. The river patrol and the hollow patrols on both sides of the town crept uphill to take their places. A dangerous looking gang was heavily armed and headed for the papers locked in the strongbox in the vault of the Milford Courthouse.

The invaders got into the county clerk's office and the vault, broke open the strongbox and Joe Kennedy's bomb exploded killing two of them while the others ran for their lives out of the Courthouse only to be met by the men and women of Milford who had surrounded the building. "Long rifles and pistol balls riddled each body as it appeared in sight." No prisoners were taken that night.

A great ceremony commenced with all the nearby settlers burying the outlaws on the ridge. Over each grave they placed a cross with the words carved from hunting knives: "This to robbers."

After Kentucky became its own state in 1792, plans in Madison County began to change. In March of 1798, Magistrate Col. John Miller convinced the Kentucky Legislature to move the county seat to his barn on "Dreaming Creek." The people of Milford revolted with some 300 men on horseback. To appease the town, a fighting contest was held between Miller's strongest man, blacksmith William Kerley and the strongest man of Milford, Sheriff Joe Kennedy's brother David. Milford lost, but only after Kennedy chewed off Kerley's finger. It was the first rebellion against the laws and constitutional authority of the Commonwealth of Kentucky.[56] John Miller was born 1750, in Albemarle County, Virginia. He served George Washington's army at the siege of Yorktown, and was commissioned a colonel in the regular army. He came to the Kentucky territory in 1784, purchasing several hundred acres of land in Madison County at $1.25 an acre, which he named "Richmond." He first built a log house on Collins Street. A few years later he built his home and tavern on the corner of Main and First Street. John Miller donated two acres of his land for the building of a Court House and jail, and records for the new county seat were temporarily housed in his barn. Later, a two-story log house was built with seven rooms and a brick underground vault, until the present Court House was built in 1847.[57]

Figure 20
Cast 2008.

Mammy Lou Miller was the cook at Miller's Tavern who created a far-reaching reputation of good food for the town. She was particularly known for her corn breads and pudding, which she cooked and sold at the merchant

---

[56] William E. Ellis, H. E. Everman, and Richard D. Sears, *Madison County: 200 Years in Retrospect*, The Madison County Historical Society, 1985, pp. 49-50. John T. Sullivan, *Madison County Past and Present, Madison County Homecoming 1965*, "Milford," Radio Station WEKY, Richmond, Kentucky, July 1965, p. 14.

[57] Green Clay, "Madison County Court House Has Served Century of Use," "Fought with Washington," "Miller Presented Offer," *The Richmond Register*, Richmond, Madison County, Kentucky, November 19, 1949.

stalls erected in the town square. From the profits of her cornbread sales, she purchased her freedom and that of her two children and moved to Lexington.[58]

The roads to Milford were ordered closed and the town began to die out. Only the foundations of the building are left buried in the ground there today. Joe Kennedy's brother, John Jr., had blazed the Wilderness Road with Daniel Boone in 1775.

Figure 21
Sheriff Joe Kennedy [Kenn Riley], Minerva [Miriam Rozeman], Daniel Boone [Gordon Edwards], Col. John Miller [Larry Bobbert].

Their other brother, Thomas Kennedy, representing Madison County, was chairman of the committee that chose Frankfort as capital when Kentucky became a state in 1792, and his son went on to be portrayed by Harriet Beecher Stowe as Mr. Shelby in *Uncle Tom's Cabin*.

Milford was the first town in Kentucky to be named after an African slave "Milford," by Captain John Kincaid from Ireland, and that man Milford was one of the first slaves to be freed in Kentucky. Susanna Nobel is recorded as one of the first women in Kentucky to own and run her own business. The term "boot-legger" is thought to have originated from an event in Milford. And the battle to keep the county seat from the move to Richmond in 1798, was the first rebellion against the laws and constitutional authority of the Commonwealth of Kentucky.

---

[58] Green Clay, "Mammy Lou Bought Freedom with Profits from Corn Meal Products Sold at Market," *The Richmond Register*, 137th Year, No. 295, Richmond, Madison County Kentucky, Saturday June 9, 1945.

Pioneer Christmas in Kentucky began in the winter of 1992, in the corner

blockhouse of Fort Boonesborough in Richmond, Kentucky. It commemorated the 200th birthday of the state. It was the first time since the Fort had been built that a winter program took place and the first time—so I was told—that the fireplaces had been used. A unique partnership with Church and State, the script was historically accurate, footnoted, and approved by The Society

Figure 22

Pioneer Christmas in Kentucky at Fort Boonesborough. Jerry Perry as Daniel Boone

of Boonesborough; no modern music was used. The choir of White Oak Pond Church sang the songs that I wrote with Bill McKenney doing the arrangements, Bill Tomlinson played the keyboard disguised as a harpsicord, and a full meal was catered. The script was set in the Hard Winter of 1779, with Daniel Boone and his Native American friends coming to the rescue of hungry settlers. The second year we moved down the Fort to the museum blockhouse where we would perform for the following nine years until a fire broke out one summer in the opposite blockhouse giftshop and delayed our return. For several years we took a hiatus while the church building itself expanded its Education Wing.

It was suggested to me that we return to the "Pioneer Christmas" program but that I rewrite it set at Milford, the first county seat assigned the very year the Old Log Meeting House was built, 1785. The Meeting House would later in 1790 take the name from its pastor, Griffin Pond, as White Oak Pond Church. Nancy Long suggested we do it in our church sanctuary that had been rebuilt in 1869. So, we built a huge paper mâché stone fireplace, covered the walls with log painted canvases, replaced the pews with gingham covered tables, and lit the room with candles. The old Pond Church Ghost Story was resurrected and used. Milford was created. Although the town was just over the hill, "a ways."

The years that followed recreated the zany but enduring characters of Milford. We added the Virginia Reel. We entered the Richmond Christmas

Parade with smoking chimney and carrying firearms through Main Street and won first prize. Many of the actors have now gone on to join the characters they portrayed. The town folk of Milford once forgotten but for a brief shining moment remembered. Our loved ones lost but for a little while.

Bibliography

Clay, Green. "County Seat of Madison Established at Milford on Silver Creek, 1786." *The Daily Register*, March 9, 1946.

Clay, Green. "Madison County Court House Has Served Century of Use," "Fought with Washington," "Miller Presented Offer." *The Richmond Register*. Richmond, Madison County, Kentucky, November 19, 1949.

Clay, Green. "Mammy Lou Bought Freedom with Profits from Corn Meal Products Sold at Market." *The Richmond Register*, 137th Year, No. 295, Richmond, Madison County Kentucky, Saturday June 9, 1945.

Ellis, William E.; Everman, H. E.; Sears, Richard D. *Madison County: 200 Years in Retrospect*. The Madison County Historical Society, 1985.

Faracher, John Mack, Daniel Boone. *The Life and Legend of an American Pioneer*. New York, New York: Henry Holt and Company, Inc., 1992.

Madison County Past and Present, Madison County Homecoming 1965. John T. Sullivan, "Milford," Radio Station WEKY, Richmond, Kentucky, July 1965.

Moon Above
Benson Valley

Introduction

Welcome to Buffalo Trace Distillery, the World's Most Award-Winning Distillery.

Nestled along the Kentucky River in Frankfort, the Distillery has been making fine bourbon whiskey for more than 200 years. Buffalo Trace Distillery is home to many iconic brands such as Blanton's, Eagle Rare, Weller, Elmer T. Lee, E.H. Taylor, Jr. and more.

Awarded Whisky Magazine's "Icons of Whisky" 2024 Visitor Attraction of the Year, Buffalo Trace Distillery offers complimentary tours and tastings 7 days a week. During a tour, guests will go behind the scenes of the Distillery stepping into iconic landmarks such as Warehouse C, which dates back to 1885.

When visiting Buffalo Trace Distillery, you will walk amidst the path of rolling bourbon barrels and be captivated by the alluring smell bourbon sleeping inside the aging warehouses. The Distillery's engaging tour guides can teach guests of all levels about the bourbon making process and through storytelling will bring the history of Buffalo Trace to life.

Plan your visit today! If you are interested in scheduling a tour, visit reservations.buffalotracedistillery.com.

Cory McCauley
Associate PR Manager
Buffalo Trace
Frankfort, Kentucky

Moon Above Benson Valley

We see the moon on a night in early May 1923. "Hare Moon," named for the rabbits and flowers of springtime. From the dark, a piano plays *Some Sunny Day*, and we hear the following:

VOICE ONE

It's the police! Everybody!
    [The piano music stops.]
Clear the bar! Act natural. Remember, this aint Crawfish Bottom!

> [Lights come up on ALENA, a girl ten years of age, hiding in the bushes nearby, timid and frightened. She attempts to reveal herself but loses courage. We see the front porch of Sundown Inn, Bald Knob, Frankfort, Kentucky. Double screen doors, smooth columns with Tuscan capitals. White clapboard, green trim. Green shutters at the windows. Wooden steps newly painted.

> [BILL Vest steps out from the screen doors of the Inn to greet the SHERIFF, who comes up the steps. BILL is a man in his early thirties; he wears a white shirt, sleeves rolled to the elbows, tie, and a clean bib apron. He carries a cup in one hand, a towel in the other. SHERIFF is in uniform.]

BILL

'Evening, Sheriff!

SHERIFF

'Evening, Bill.

BILL

What brings you up here on the Knob?

SHERIFF

Looking for Charlie. The Italian. Have you seen him?

BILL

He was up here earlier. We had a skuttle. He left.

SHERIFF

He went down to Fallis' place. Got into a fight.

BILL

Always a fight going on down in the Craw.

SHERIFF

Usually, John Fallis makes my job easier down there. No one messes with him. He keeps his own order.

BILL

With his guns and knives.

SHERIFF

With that group you have to.

BILL

That's why they call him the King of Craw.

SHERIFF

Something not right about a man like Charlie drinkin himself to death. With a beautiful wife and three kids.

BILL

He's a mean drunk. I told him not to come back. I'm not doing him any good giving him drinks.

SHERIFF

I just was by the house. He's not there. Do you know where he could have gone?

BILL

Maybe he went back down to the Craw?

SHERIFF

I doubt it. I can't imagine. Charlie's awful sick, Bill.

BILL

I know something's wrong.

SHERIFF

As I was pulling him off the fight—right around his waist, there was a big sore. I mean, huge. It stunk so bad . . . Like his inside were rottin out.

BILL

Really?

SHERIFF

He must be in a lot of pain.

BILL

He's been self-medicating, you think? I know he's been out of work. Work right now is hard to find--

Pour you a drink? Straight up or on the rocks?
        [He offers him the cup]

SHERIFF

Damnit, Bill. Can you be a bit more discreet?

BILL

What? It's *coffee*.

SHERIFF

Okay. *Black*. Straight up. You ought to thank Fallis. He usually keeps all the attention down his way so it don't come up here.

BILL

Keeps some of my best customers, too.

SHERIFF

You don't want up here what they have down there. You run a clean respectable business. Square dancing on weekends. No whores. No gamblin'.

BILL

No cheatin', anyway.

415

SHERIFF

You have a store just as nice as Fallis——

BILL

We sell groceries, eggs, and bacon, and fresh vegetables. He has a still in
his back room.

SHERIFF

And supplies you.

BILL

Yeah, But I don't brew it——

SHERIFF

But he supplies you——

BILL

But I don't brew it.

SHERIFF

So, it's okay to buy it from him, just not to make it? 'Least you know what
you're getting.

BILL

And your point? We all agree that Prohibition is stupid. But so is breaking
the law. John Fallis has broken as many laws as jaws, arms, legs . . . He gets
away with it. You can't catch him. Just try and he'll fake his own death!
Blew up his boat, only found his hat floating in the river. Then he shows
up one day all surprised! Don't you remember that?

SHERIFF

Remember? I went to his funeral.

BILL

His boy was caught at the circus peekin' in the tent of the girlie show. You
all grabbed him and Fallis came shootin' with both hands loaded. Took out
half of the police force. Did he serve time? He was supposed to. All the other
police officers hate him. I don't know why you want to take his side.

SHERIFF

You ever been down to the Craw?

My grandmother didn't raise me to be seen down there. I ain't no Crawbat, never will be.

SHERIFF

At least you had a grandmother to raise you. John Fallis grew up from dirt, his mother a prostitute, his Daddy a drunk who left them. You know why they call it "Craw" don't you? From the crawfish when the river floods. It's the only land the poor freed slaves could afford. It was "the bottom," but it gave them a home when no one else would. And he made something of it! They respect him for it. So, I give him credit.

BILL

Hum. Be a sorry day in hell when I give John Fallis credit.
        [BILL produces a flask and pours the SHERIFF another
        drink. They look up at the moon.]

SHERIFF

Beautiful, ain't it? They call that the "Hare Moon." After the rabbits and flowers of spring. 'Say it's full of magic and new beginnings.

        [John FALLIS appears from the shadows. A striking man
        in his thirties. Handsomely dressed in suit and tie, well
        groomed. Hair parted, mustache.]

FALLIS

Evening, Sheriff. Bill.

SHERIFF

Speaking of the devil! What brings you up here to these parts, John Fallis?

FALLIS

Oh, just a sorry day in hell, I guess. Came to talk to Bill. If I could have a minute?

SHERIFF

Well, I . . . Bill, I . . . I guess I can wait . . . a minute for John Fallis. I'll be inside.
        [He exits where there is music and dancing]

BILL

We were just talking about you.

417

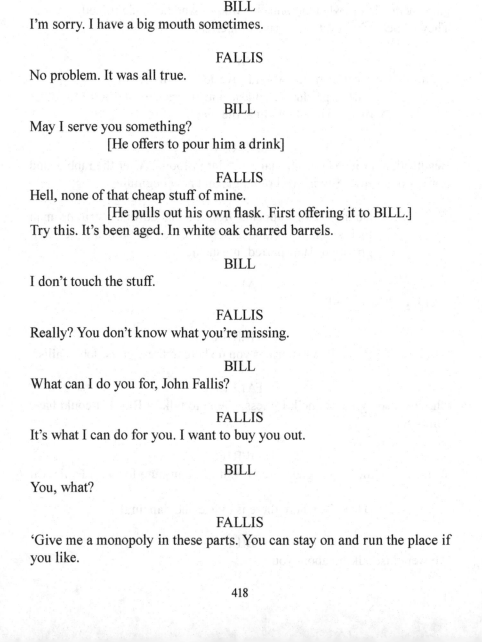

FALLIS

Yeah, I heard.

BILL

How much did you hear?

FALLIS

Enough.

BILL

I'm sorry. I have a big mouth sometimes.

FALLIS

No problem. It was all true.

BILL

May I serve you something?
[He offers to pour him a drink]

FALLIS

Hell, none of that cheap stuff of mine.
[He pulls out his own flask. First offering it to BILL.]
Try this. It's been aged. In white oak charred barrels.

BILL

I don't touch the stuff.

FALLIS

Really? You don't know what you're missing.

BILL

What can I do you for, John Fallis?

FALLIS

It's what I can do for you. I want to buy you out.

BILL

You, what?

FALLIS

'Give me a monopoly in these parts. You can stay on and run the place if
you like.

418

BILL

Thank you, but I like things as they are.

FALLIS

And what's that? You get a few customers off this road? I have people coming from all over the state. Hell, from all over the country! Craw is on the map. You need a bigger vision.

BILL

'Been a stage coach stop up here for a hundred years. Vision is pretty good: can't beat the view of Benson Valley. The Creek. We can look down and keep an eye on folks like you from up here! And no flooding. If it does, we'll have to build an ark.

FALLIS

[FALLIS pulls out a piece of paper, writes a figure.]

What do you think about this offer?

BILL

Very generous.

FALLIS

I want to see you slow down and settle down, Bill. Has there never been a special someone?

BILL

There was someone, once. But love didn't come directly.

FALLIS

Sometimes it doesn't. Sometimes it shines another way. Be smart and accept my offer. Do you really want to be fighting drunks off the place the rest of your life?

BILL

You mean Charlie? Charlie's not a bad guy. Just a mean drunk.

FALLIS

He's been like a brother to you. He has a beautiful wife. Prettiest gal up here on the Knob.

BILL

I hadn't noticed—

FALLIS

Something wrong with a man if he hasn't noticed Hallie Cook. 'Shame she fell for Charlie's good looks and European ways. Sporting a black eye last time I saw her. Or was it a broken arm? 'Got three little girls; they call you "uncle." You're good with those girls. I hear you been teaching the oldest how to shoot?

BILL

Charlie bought her a rifle--just hasn't had time to work with her. Hallie won't touch a gun. Her daughter, now, she's a regular little Annie Oakley! Sharp shooter. Got a good eye.

FALLIS

You had him painting the place. Looks good. Some people just got to stay away from drink. I had no problem when he worked for me.

BILL

He worked for you?

FALLIS

One of my best workers. Helped me build back the house and store.

BILL

That's right. After the police burned you down. You took out most of the police force that day. .

FALLIS

I did. They were beating my son to death. You'd do the same. And our little baby died.

BILL

I didn't know.

FALLIS

A man has to do what he has to do to protect his family.
        [ALENA appears in the bushes. He smiles and waves to her.
        SHERIFF steps onto the porch and she ducks away.]

420

I think little Annie Oakley is keeping her eye on us. Bill, don't give me an answer now. Just sleep on it. I'll be checking back with you. There's no hurry. I got to get back. Good night.

BILL

John . . . thank you. And thank you for being good to my friend, Charlie.

FALLIS

'Evening, Sheriff.

SHERIFF

'Evening, John Fallis. Stay out of trouble.

FALLIS

Now, you know I live for trouble, Sheriff.
    [The two men smile and laugh. FALLIS exits down the steps.]

BILL
    [ALENA approaches from the bushes again.]
Excuse me, Sheriff . . .
    [BILL goes down the steps out into the garden and finds
    ALENA, but he is not out of earshot from FALLIS or the
    SHERIFF]
Sweety, what's wrong?

ALENA
    [She grabs BILL around the legs and begins weeping]
Daddy. He got shot.

BILL

Someone shot Charlie?

ALENA

He's dead. Daddy's dead——

BILL

When?
    [ALENA can only nod her head. BILL kneels down to her
    level.]

ALENA

Tonight. He came home and . . .

BILL

Let's go get your Mama—

ALENA

We put him in the wagon and she took him to town.

BILL

What was she thinking?

ALENA

Mama said to go get you. That you would know what to do.

SHERIFF

Where was she taking him?

        [ALENA, hearing the SHERIFF, starts to hide. BILL
        stops her.]

BILL

It's okay. He's our friend.

ALENA

She went to the police.

BILL

To turn herself in, I'll bet.

SHERIFF

I better get down there.

BILL

I'll go with you--I've got to see Hallie—

SHERIFF

I . . . don't know that that's a good idea.

BILL

What do you mean?

SHERIFF

There's talk in this town about the two of you. Don't stir it up.

BILL

Talk? About Hallie and me? Who the hell––

SHERIFF

Doesn't matter who. They wouldn't matter anyways. If he's shot and dead, you don't need to stir it up right now.

BILL

Charlie is my friend. So, I care about his family. I care about him––

SHERIFF

I know. I know. That's why you better go get his kids. If they've been left alone, they must be scared to death. Why don't you bring them back over here for the night. I'll check on her in town.

BILL

Hallie's never touched a gun. She hates them. Everybody knows that.

SHERIFF

It's going to be all right. You go get her girls. She'll be safe tonight.

[BILL can only nod. SHERIFF exits. To ALENA]

BILL

Let's go get your sisters. You can steer my wagon.
        [He lets her crawl up onto his back and the two exit into the
        night.

        [Hours later. The moon is bright in the sky. Customers have
        gone home, the Inn is quiet. HALLIE, still wearing her
        kitchen blood-stained apron, approaches the steps of the Inn,
        her youthfulness faded by the early hardships of life. BILL
        comes out from the screen door]
Hallie . . .

HALLIE

I'm alright.

423

BILL

They let you go?

HALLIE

Someone paid bail.

BILL

Thank God. Who was it, do you know?

HALLIE

John Fallis, they said. He sent me home with groceries from his store.
Eggs, milk . . .

BILL

Fallis?

HALLIE

Charlie's dead. I just came for the girls.
> [She messes with the stain on her apron, from an earlier
> attempt to wash it but unsuccessfully.]
Oh, Bill, there was so much blood—
> [BILL goes to her but she stops him.]
No. It's not right.

BILL

I'll get you a clean apron. The girls are sleeping inside. You need to stay
here with them for the night. I've given them the good room. The sheets
are clean.

HALLIE

> [Exhausted, she falls into a sitting position on the steps,
> holding to its post. She looks to him with gratitude, then up
> at the moon. He sits opposite her.]
Look at that moon looking down on Benson creek. As if nothing has
happened. As if it ain't seen a thing. So peaceful. It's blind or a liar!
> [She pauses]
I loved Charlie . . .

BILL

I know you did.

424

HALLIE

But it was hard. So damn hard. Love shouldn't be hard.

[She weeps. BILL wants to comfort her but also wants to respect her wishes. She falls into his arms.]

BILL

Sometimes love doesn't come directly. Even in the dark, the sun finds a way to shine—like that moon.

HALLIE

[Laughing away the sentiments, she pulls away, wiping her tears on the apron.]
How do you know such nonsense?
[But she is too tired to listen. She stands and exits up the stairs. After she is gone:]

BILL

I've seen it reflect in your eyes.

ALENA

[ALENA appears from the bushes again.]
Daddy hurt so bad.

BILL

Yes, he did. He hurt real bad. But he's at peace now.

ALENA

Our old horse hurt so bad. Daddy had to shoot it.

BILL

It was the loving thing to do. To "put it down."

HALLIE

[From inside the screen door:]
Alena, you leave Uncle Bill alone, now. He's got to lock up. Come inside with your sisters.

[ALENA looks hard at BILL. He finds a message in her eyes. Although nothing is said, he hears her clearly and nods. She goes inside. HALLIE is putting on an a clean apron.]

HALLIE

Thank you, Bill, for having us here. I'll pay you back.

BILL

No, you won't either.

HALLIE

Well, we'll work that out later.

BILL

Hallie?

HALLIE

Yes, Bill?

BILL

Tell me the truth. Who really shot him?

HALLIE

I told them—

BILL

I know what you told them. But it's just you and me now.

HALLIE

And the moon. They say it's a magic moon this time of year. Full of enchantments and things.

> [The apron tied; she smooths her hands on its pressed surface.
> She pauses, then turns away]

I shot him.

> [She exits inside the house. BILL looks up at the moon that
> has shown over Benson Valley through the night and how it
> strikes the creek below and makes it sparkle.]

CURTAIN

Postscript

Figure 23
William Franklin Vest 1891-1928

Sundown Inn

Built a mile up from the Kentucky River off the Bald Knob Road, the Sundown Inn had been a stage coach stop as far back as the early nineteenth century. My grandfather, William Vest, bought it and ran a General Store and tavern there during Prohibition.

Most of the knowledge I have of the Sundown Inn came from Bernice Moore who was nearing 100 years old but would sit with me on the porch of the old building and share her remembrances. Her mind was as clear as a bell, as they say, and her genetics gave her a much younger appearance. "I know. Everyone always tells me that," she would say. "I've looked like I was in my 50s since I was fifty years old. I get no sympathy." It was true.

My dad, Russell Sr., worked all his life as head of the Dry House at the Frankfort Distillery that has become Buffalo Trace. It made bourbon and had special permission to do so for medicinal purposes during Prohibition. Mom always said that they made "foreign foods." The reputation of the Sundown Inn and the rumors of her mother's first marriage to an alcoholic Italian immigrant put a curse on her as far as any alcoholic beverages were concerned. She threatened us all with our lives that if we ever took a drop of whiskey; she

Figure 24
William Vest, Hallie Vest, Myrtle Vest

427

would "cut us out of her will!" So it was, that when she referred to her father's Inn, it was always a fine establishment, "a store where they had square dancing on weekends." I mentioned this to Mrs. Moore. "Are you kidding?!" she exclaimed. "It was a tavern! A wild place! They were getting drunk and having fights!"

When grandfather died in 1928, Mom was only four years old. She adored him. He was buried on the farm. Mom and her sisters and brother lived in "the big house," the old Inn, until after they had all finished high school and married. Or gone into military service which was my uncle Bill's fate. Grandmother, Hallie Cooke Vest, sold off much of the land, and the Inn, and moved across the street to "the little house" that her husband, Bill Vest, had built for them just before he died. She even sold the land where he had been buried—his grave a fenced in oasis amidst a cow field belonging to strangers. Times must have been hard for her. She worked until her death as a superintendent of Union Underwear. She drove a little car and drank one beer every evening with dinner. Once "the beauty of Bald Knob," she was tough and strange, a force not to be tampered with. I remember being switched by her for touching the blue gazing ball in her garden. But when she was dying of cancer, her bed moved to the living room, and the weather too hot to close the front door, I sang on the porch swing and she heard me through the screen door. Mom and her sisters were taking turns caring for her, and one of them said, "Tell Rusty to be quiet." "No," Grandmother told them. "I like to hear him." He's God the Whole World in His Hands. By that time, the old Inn up across the new highway was in disrepair, was rented to two families: a wire fence separating the front porch. The old road that had come down the hill and passed by it, was abandoned, having been bypassed by Highway 421 that took grandfather's white barn.

The death certificate of my Grandmother's first husband read that he had been shot in the chest by Grandmother. It set on the judge's desk for a while and finally was stamped with discharge. While Grandmother lay dying, the good intentioned pastor came to call and, to help her clear her conscience before she left this earthly burden, begged her to tell him who "really" had shot her first husband. "I did," was her only answer, and she turned her face to the wall.

The murder of Grandmother's first husband was a scandal that people only whispered about. My aunts avoided talking about it. Mother leaked bits and pieces about the incident although she had not been born at the time. I remember Mom saying once, "You can't imagine what it was like having people whisper behind your back all the time that your mother was a murderess." And yet, Grandmother had not committed the crime, not even from self-defense. The judge dismissed the case, having pity on the poor young mother of three children.

John Fallis

Born April 13, 1879, John Fallis was a young child when his parents brought him to Frankfort. His nephew claimed that John's mother was a prostitute who employed her daughters. He carried a temper and a knife, was whipped by his parents, and sang in the Salvation Army choir. His love for singing and attending church became a consistent part of his growing up. Although he

Figure 25
John Fallis 1879--1929

could be a violent man, he was the Robin Hood of the poor and kind and generous to struggling African Americans who had served as or had come from enslaved families prior to the Civil War.[59] The only land they could afford, was land near the Kentucky River where it flooded and became known as "the Bottom" or "Crawfish Bottom."[60]

At age 13, John was working at the Kentucky River Mills, hemp factory. Moved to Louisville, he ran away back to Frankfort and was sent by his mother to The Louisville House of Refuge orphanage and reformatory school. For seventeen years he worked at the O.F.C. Distillery (Old Fire Copper whiskey) in Frankfort.[61] In 1898, he entered the military to fight with the Second Kentucky Infantry in the Spanish-American War, he was decorated and honorably discharged at age 19. Two years later he married

---

[59] Doughlas A. Boyd, *Crawfish Bottom, Recovering a Lost Kentucky Community,* (Lexington, KY: The University Press of Kentucky, 2011), pp. 148-9, 159-60.
[60] Ibid, p. 15.
[61] Richard Taylor, *The Great Crossing, A Historic Journey to Buffalo Trace Distillery,* (Frankfort, KY: Buffalo Trace Distillery, 2002), p. 71.

Anne Thompson Craine, whom he had met and fallen in love with while singing at the Salvation Army.[62]

John ran a grocery store in the Craw, distilling whiskey in the back. Many times, he was convicted of bootlegging. John and Anne made their home at 701 Wilkinson Street and together had five children that survived infancy.[63]

On December 1912, there was a dynamite explosion, and the town thought John Fallis dead. But he appeared four days later about the time his wife was to collect on his life insurance. It is thought that he faked his death after a quarrel with his wife.[64]

When John found his son Carlos Fallis being beaten by policemen for peeking into a carnival tent, he retaliated. Unfortunately, he shot four policemen, two bystanders, and his own son. June 5, 1921. His house and grocery were burned to the ground, and his infant son died. He was indicted by the Franklin County Grand Jury, the verdict of the trial was six months in jail and a $250. fine for shooting one of the policemen, and later an acquittal for the shooting of another.[65]

In 1927, he filed for divorce from Anne but it was never granted. John lived with Anna Mae Blackwell until his death on August 18, 1929 when he was shot by Everett Rigsby in Craw during a card game. His funeral was held on August 20, at the Frankfort Cemetery where he was buried.[66] He died a year after William Vest.

---

[62] Ron Rhody, *Concerning the Matter of the King of Craw*, (Raleigh, North Carolina: Outer Banks Publishing Group, 2016), p. 269

[63] Boyd, *Crawfish Bottom*, 151, 156.

[64] Ibid., pp. 160-166.

[65] *Frankfort State Journal*, "Four Policemen, His Son and Two Citizens are Shot by John Fallis," June 16, 1921; Boyd, *Crawfish Bottom*, pp. 167-172.

[66] Boyd, *Crawfish Bottom*, p. 153, pp. 174-179; *Frankfort State Journal*, "John Fallis Killed," August 18, 1929.

Buffalo Trace Distillery

Figure 26
Buffalo Trace Distillery, Frankfort, Kentucky

Buffalo Trace Distillery is built on the site of "the great buffalo road" one of the most important buffalo trails in the Ohio River Valley that crossed the Kentucky River.[67] That road served the first white settlement of Franklin County known as Lee's Town named after Hancock Lee.

John Fallis, "King of Craw," worked at the distillery in Frankfort that would become Buffalo Trace. He started at 16 years of age and worked until he was 33, from 1895 until 1912, the year my dad Russell Sr. was born. My Dad would work there almost fifty years. He is kneeling front row, fourth from the left.

The distillery was purchased by the Sazerac Company in 1992, and Buffalo Trace bourbon introduced in 1999. As it continued running during Prohibition for

Figure 27
The George T. Stagg Company Safety Committee, March 24, 1939

---

[67] Richard Taylor, *The Great Crossing, A Historic Journey to Buffalo Trace Distillery,* (Frankfort, KY: Buffalo Trace Distillery, 2002), p 4.

431

medicinal purposes, it is thought to be the oldest continuously operating distillery in the United States.

Hancock Lee and his brother Willis Lee started distilling on the site from early as 1775, in what became Lee's Town. Harrison Blanton built its first distillery in 1812. Edmund H. Taylor purchased it in 1870, and gave it the name Old Fire Copper Distillery, and it later sold to George T. Stagg. Today, Buffalo Trace's famous bourbons include: George T. Stagg, Elmer T. Lee Single Barrel, Blanton's Single Barrel, W. L. Weller, Old Charter, Eagle Rare, Blanton's, and Pappy Van Winkles Family Reserve.

Figure 28
Old Taylor House. Oldest residential building in Franklin County, built 1790s by Commodore Richard Taylor. Playwright.

I remember Dad taking me to see the oldest residential home of Lees Town and Franklin County that was on the river side of the Distillery. It had been built in the 1790s by Commodore Richard Taylor, with the second floor added in the 1800s. At the time of our visit, I was a teenager and the house was a complete ruin, a site I was sure would be demolished. Dad brought a settee home from the house that I upholstered. In 2015, the Old Taylor House was restored.

Bibliography

Boyd, Doughlas A. *Crawfish Bottom, Recovering a Lost Kentucky Community.* Lexington, KY: The University Press of Kentucky, 2011.

Frankfort State Journal. "Four Policemen, His Son and Two Citizens are Shot by John Fallis." Frankfort, Kentucky. June 16, 1921.

Hatter, Russell and Nicky Hughes. *Historic Images of Frankfort.* Frankfort, Kentucky: Frankfort Heritage Press, 2004.

Hatter, Russell and Nicky Hughes. *Historic Images of Frankfort, Volume II.* Frankfort, Kentucky: Frankfort Heritage Press, 2005.

Moore, Bernice Gaines. [Mrs. Orville Venton Moore]. May 16, 1916--May 18, 2016. Private conversations with the playwright, 2015, at The Sundown Inn, Bald Knob, Frankfort, Kentucky.

Perkins, Elizabeth and Sprague, Stuart. *Frankfort A Pictorial History.* Virginia Beach, Virginia: Donning Company/Publishers, 1980.

Rhody, Ron. *Concerning the Matter of the King of Craw.* Raleigh, North Carolina: Outer Banks Publishing Group, 2016.

Taylor, Richard. *The Great Crossing, A Historic Journey to Buffalo Trace Distillery.* Frankfort, KY: Buffalo Trace Distillery, 2002.

About the Author

Richard Cavendish is the registered pen name with Dramatists Guild of America for The Rev. Dr. Russell Richard Reichenbach Cavendish. "Rusty," as he has been known, restored the "i" in his family name after they had dropped it during World War One to appear less German. Cavendish was added to his name in 2023 after the death of his father Dr. John Claude Cavendish in 2021.

Richard is a native of Frankfort, Kentucky. He graduated from Transylvania University with a Bachelor of Arts degree majoring in Drama and Religion and completed the Master of Divinity and the Doctor of Ministry degrees from Lexington Theological Seminary. He attended Mansfield College of Oxford, England. He retired from ministry in 2012, to write historical dramas. Dr. Reichenbach Cavendish has restored The Old Parsonage of Andrew Tribble built in 1794, located in Richmond to be used for community events. His play *Botherum* was chosen Best Ten-Minute Play 2017 with Kentucky Theater Association's Roots of the Bluegrass Play Writing Competition, and his plays *Night Music of the River* 2016, *The Botanic Garden* 2018, *Beatin' the Dark Home* 2019, and *Day of Releasement* 2021 were winning finalists. His full-length play, *The Minister's Daughter*, won first place with Kentucky Theater Association's Roots of the Bluegrass Play Writing Competition 2022.

Index

439

Printed in the United States
by Baker & Taylor Publisher Services

Printed in the United States
by Baker & Taylor Publisher Services